TAX POLICY
AND THE ECONOMY 7

edited by **James M. Poterba**

National Bureau of Economic Research
The MIT Press, Cambridge, Massachusetts

Send orders and business correspondence to:
The MIT Press
55 Hayward Street
Cambridge, MA 02142

In the United Kingdom, continental Europe, and the Middle East and Africa, send orders and business correspondence to:
The MIT Press Ltd.
14 Bloomsbury Square
London, WC1A 2LP
ENGLAND

ISSN: 0892-8649
ISBN: hardcover 0-262-16135-4
        paperback 0-262-66081-4

Because this volume is a record of conference proceedings, it has been exempted from the rules governing critical review of manuscripts by the Board of Directors of the National Bureau (resolution adopted 8 June 1948, as revised 21 November 1949 and 20 April 1968).

CONTENTS

INTRODUCTION

James M. Poterba
MIT and NBER

The November 1992 presidential election ended twelve years of divided government in Washington, and raised the possibility of important new initiatives on many dimensions, including tax policy. The new political climate raises new opportunities and challenges for researchers and policy advisors in the tax policy field. There is active discussion of many potential tax reforms, including incremental investment tax credits and changes in the structure of federal income tax rates. The coming debate on the distributional and efficiency effects of such proposals will inevitably draw heavily on economic analyses by both academics and policy makers.

To encourage interaction between these groups, for the last seven years the NBER has sponsored an annual Tax Policy and the Economy Conference in Washington, D.C. The conference facilitates communication between academics engaged in tax policy research, and those in industry and government who are directly involved in the tax policy-making process. The conference is devoted to the presentation of new research findings of relevance for tax policy.

The five papers in this volume represent a cross section of some of the best applied research that bears on tax policy deliberations. Each paper provides new data, and new insights, on questions of ongoing national importance. In several cases, the research papers were motivated by suggestions or questions at previous Tax Policy and the Economy meetings.

The first paper, Bronwyn Hall's study of "R&D Tax Policy During the Eighties: Success or Failure?" suggests that tax incentives have important effects on corporate R&D spending. This paper begins by summarizing how the various tax reforms of the 1980s affected the after-tax price of R&D investment. Hall then uses a large panel data set on individual firm R&D spending, as well as new estimates of the firm-level tax incentive for such spending, to explore how changes in the after-tax cost of R&D projects affects corporate investment. The empirical findings suggest that a 1 percent reduction in the cost of R&D raises firm outlays by about 1 percent in the first two years after the policy takes effect. The spending change would be even larger in the longer run, and there is some evidence that spending became more sensitive to tax incentives in the late 1980s. These results suggest that the R&D tax credit and other tax incentive policies have a large positive effect on corporate R&D spending.

Leslie Papke's paper on "What Do We Know About Enterprise Zones?" provides important evidence on the likely impact of current proposals for a set of federal enterprise zones. Papke describes what the traditional theory of tax incidence implies about the gains and losses from a system of enterprise zones, and she then describes several types of prior empirical evidence on the effect of such zones. After a review of both British experience with enterprise zones in the early 1980s, and U.S. state experience, the paper reports new findings on the employment and economic growth effects of enterprise zones in Indiana. The study finds a weak reduction in unemployment rates in the Indiana enterprise zones but no evidence of an increase in per capita income for enterprise zone residents. Because enterprise zones reduce tax revenue, the results imply that these zones are a relatively expensive way to improve the economic circumstances of enterprise zone residents.

The third paper, by B. Douglas Bernheim and John Scholz, explores several issues relating to "Private Saving and Public Policy." The paper evaluates the adequacy of individual saving for retirement by constructing an elaborate simulation model for household wealth accumulation and consumption. This model shows that many households do not save enough to avoid substantial reductions in their standard of living after they retire. By contrasting the simulation results with actual patterns of wealth accumulation, the authors conclude that more-educated households prepare better for their retirement, and respond more to saving incentives, than less-educated households. These findings suggest that a program like the current system of IRAs, which targets incentives for relatively low-income households but provides a small saving incentive for high-income groups, may not increase saving by as much as several alternative policies. Bernheim and Scholz sketch one such policy that provides both a "floor" and a "ceiling" on the amount of saving households at different income levels must do before they can avail themselves of targeted saving incentives.

Patricia Anderson and Bruce Meyer's paper, "The Unemployment Insurance Payroll Tax and Interindustry and Interfirm Subsidies," reports new evidence on the pattern of cross-subsidy effects that result from the current system of unemployment insurance finance. The authors use previously unexploited data on firm unemployment compensation contributions and benefit claims to measure the level and persistence of cross-subsidies. The findings suggest that the unemployment insurance system generates chronic subsidies to some industries. The authors conclude by calculating the "deadweight loss," or reduction in economic efficiency, associated with these cross-subsidies.

The final paper, by Daniel Feenberg and me, examines "Income Inequality and the Incomes of Very High-Income Taxpayers." This study explores the changing share of adjusted gross income (AGI) reported by taxpayers in the top one-half of 1 percent of the income distribution. The income share of this group increased during the 1980s and rose particularly rapidly in the years 1986–1988. The rise in income inequality appears both for AGI and for most income components, and in particular is not attributable to high capital gains realizations in the years surrounding the Tax Reform Act of 1986. The paper concludes that at least part of the increase in income concentration in the post-1986 period was due to reductions in marginal tax rates, which raised the incentive for high-income households to report current taxable income rather than engage in tax avoidance activities.

There is an important symbiosis between policy making and scholarship in the tax policy field. NBER researchers, and academic researchers more generally, often find research topics in the ongoing debates that take place in Washington and state capitals. In turn, many of the estimates of behavioral elasticities, and the vocabulary that guides policy debates, are derived from academic research. The papers in this year's *Tax Policy and the Economy* volume suggest that this interaction is healthy and ongoing.

ACKNOWLEDGMENTS

Many individuals played a key role in planning and organizing the *Tax Policy and the Economy* meeting. Martin Feldstein, president of the NBER, and Geoffrey Carliner, executive director, have been active supporters of this annual conference for the last seven years. Deborah Mankiw, the NBER's director of Corporate and Foundation Relations, and Amy Curran helped throughout the conference planning process. Candace Morrissey managed the daunting task of ensuring that the five conference papers were prepared on time and in a format that was acceptable for publication. Several members of the NBER Conference Department, Conference Director Kirsten Davis, Lauren Lariviere, and Robert Shannon, oversaw the logistics of our Washington conference with extraordinary efficiency.

I am also grateful to each of the conference paper authors for striving to communicate their important research findings to a largely nonacademic audience. I appreciate their efforts and willingness to participate in this very important opportunity for interchange between academics and policy makers.

R&D TAX POLICY DURING THE 1980s: SUCCESS OR FAILURE?

Bronwyn H. Hall
University of California at Berkeley, NBER, and the Hoover
Institution, Stanford University

EXECUTIVE SUMMARY

R&D tax policy in the United States during the nineteen-eighties is evaluated, with particular emphasis placed on quantifying the impact of the R&D tax credit on the R&D investment of manufacturing firms. Using publicly available data on R&D spending at the firm level, I estimate an average tax price elasticity for R&D spending which is in the neighborhood of unity in the short run. Although the effective credit rate is small (less than five percent until 1990), this relatively strong price response means that the amount of additional R&D spending thus induced was greater than the cost in foregone tax revenue. The recent evolution of features of the U.S. corporate tax system which affect R&D is also reviewed and my results are compared with those of previous researchers.

This paper was prepared for the National Bureau of Economic Research Tax Policy Conference, Washington, D.C., November 17, 1992. I am extremely grateful to Jim Poterba for his advice during the writing of this paper, particularly for his careful comments on the first draft. I have also benefited from discussions with Jeffrey Bernstein, Zvi Griliches, Jim Hines, Ken Judd, Drew Lyons, Ariel Pakes, and Tom Barthold. Thanks also go to Clint Cummins for timely help with the GMM estimation. Naturally I retain full responsibility for remaining inadequacies. Support from the National Science Foundation, the Cox Econometrics Laboratory of the University of California at Berkeley, the National Bureau of Economic Research, and the Hoover Institution is gratefully acknowledged. I also thank MERIT at the Rijksuniversiteit Limburg for their hospitality while this revision was being prepared.

The conclusion is that the R&D tax credit seems to have had the intended effect, although it took several years for firms to fully adjust. I also argue that although the high correlation over time of R&D spending at the firm level makes it difficult to estimate long run effects precisely, the same high correlation makes it probable that these effects are large.

I. INTRODUCTION

For at least the past twenty or thirty years, the tax policy of the U.S. government toward Research and Development (R&D) spending by private industrial firms has been designed to subsidize these expenditures at a rate that has varied over time. There are several features of the tax code that contribute to this policy: first, most R&D expenditures can be expensed as they are incurred,[1] which implies a faster write-off than the economic depreciation of the capital created by these expenditures.[2] Second, since the Economic Recovery Tax Act of 1981, a Research and Experimentation tax credit has been available to firms that increase their expenditures beyond some base level. Third, and somewhat more obscurely, Hines (1992) has shown that to the extent that R&D can be directed toward sales in foreign countries, there is an implicit subsidy to this activity arising from the interaction of the U.S. tax system with that of most foreign countries.

How large are these subsidies in practice, and do they have the desired effect of promoting socially valuable R&D spending? Are they worth the lost tax revenue? Various authors have attempted answers to these questions, sparked by the new tax credits of the early 1980s; most have concluded that the tax credit, at least, has had a relatively minor effect on the R&D spending of U.S. corporations, at least until about 1985.[3] Eisner, Albert, and Sullivan (1984) state, "We have as yet been

[1] Since 1954, under section 174 of the Internal Revenue code, a taxpayer may elect either to deduct or to amortize over sixty months or more the amount of research and experimental expenditures incurred in connection with its trade or business (U.S. Congress Committee on Finance Report, 1986). In practice most firms expense R&D. The definition of R&D in this part of the regulations is not spelled out in the code but has been interpreted by the Treasury to mean "research and development costs in the experimental or laboratory sense."

[2] See Griliches (1979), Pakes and Schankerman (1984), and Hall (1990b) for evidence on the private economic depreciation rate of R&D.

[3] See Eisner, Albert, and Sullivan (1984), Mansfield (1986), Altshuler (1988), and the GAO Report (1989) for studies of the impact of the Research and Experimentation Credit on R&D spending in the early 1980s. All of these studies use data only from the first half of the 1980s, and none of them evaluate the effects of the tinkering with the credit that occurred later in the period. Eisner, Albert and Sullivan (1984) study 592 firms from 1980 to 1982,

unable to detect reliable evidence of a positive impact of the credit on total R&D expenditures." Altshuler (1988) finds that the average ex-ante marginal credit rate is 1.3 percent in 1981 (2.3 percent when weighted by qualified research expenditures) and concludes that with asymmetric taxation and credit carryforwards, "the incentive effects of the credit are reduced even further leading us (*sic*) to question the logic of retaining the credit in its current form." A General Accounting Office study (1989) combines estimates of the effective credit rate (3–5 percent) with an assumed R&D price elasticity of −0.2 to −0.5 to conclude that the credit induced somewhere in the range of $0.2–0.5 billion of research spending per year from 1981 through 1985, which is about 1 percent of total private industrial R&D spending.

In spite of this evidence, the President, some members of Congress, and many high-technology industrial organizations continue to press for a permanent Research and Experimentation (R&E) tax credit, which suggests that the question of its effect is worth reexamination using the almost ten years of history now available to us. There are several other reasons why this topic is worth further study now: the first is that the tax credit was changed in significant ways since the previous work was done, particularly in 1990, when the computation of the base level of R&D was completely altered; this change raised the effective credit rate and, thus, should have increased the response of firms.

However, a more important reason for undertaking the study reported here is the opportunity to study the price responsiveness of R&D, which the data now provide us. The results reported earlier (Altshuler, 1988; Eisner, Albert, and Sullivan, 1984; and the 1989 GAO study) did not estimate a behavioral response of R&D to tax price changes, but merely inferred changes based on price elasticities measured using aggregate data or, in some cases, panel data sets. The best estimates of the price elasticity of R&D capital at the firm level are probably those of Bernstein and Nadiri (1988), which are based on a sample of thirty-five firms in four two-digit industries for eight years from 1959 to 1966. But because the firms effectively all face the same "price" of R&D, identifica-

---

which account for about 80 percent of private industrial R&D during the period; they make use of Compustat data and a privately conducted McGraw-Hill survey as well as OTA tabulations of R&D tax credit returns for 1981. Altshuler uses 5042 nonfinancial public corporations with assets greater than $10 million (1982 dollars) from 1977 to 1984, again covering around 80 percent of R&D. The actual data here come from the Treasury Department's Corporate Tax Model, which samples corporate tax returns annually. The GAO study uses 800 nonfinancial corporations from roughly the same source for 1981–1985; the firms in their sample are considerably larger on average than Altshuler's (assets greater than $250 million [1982 dollars]), but they cover only a slightly smaller amount of total R&D expenditure.

tion of the price elasticity comes from eight years of price data and the functional form of the model. Given this, it is reassuring that they obtain essentially the same number for the long-run price elasticity in all four industries, -0.5.

Other estimates are those of Mansfield (1986), who cites -0.35 as an R&D price elasticity, apparently obtaining the estimate from Mohnen, Nadiri, and Prucha (1986)[4], and Baily and Lawrence (1987, 1992), who obtain estimates on the order of -1.0, using aggregate and industry level data and a dummy for the tax credit. Given the fact that the only measurable variation in the cost of performing R&D is over time, it is extremely difficult to convince oneself of the reliability of estimates based solely on cost. Thus, the advantage of the R&E tax credit and the many variations in its history is the cross-sectional variability that it provides us as researchers in the key price variable, creating a natural experiment in which we can measure the response of R&D investment to changes in its cost. Among the prior studies of the price elasticity of R&D described, only those by Baily and Lawrence[5] attempt to take advantage of this variability; although their results are not without interest, their approach is the somewhat crude one of including a dummy variable for the credit years in an equation computed at the aggregate two-digit industry level. Thus, it seems worth reexamining the R&E tax credit question with firm level data, both to improve on earlier price elasticity estimates, and to evaluate the tax credit itself, particularly for the second half of the 1980s.

[4] Although Mansfield refers to this as an R&D spending elasticity, the Mohnen, Nadiri, and Prucha estimate is in fact an R&D capital elasticity, as was the Bernstein and Nadiri (1988) estimate. The two will coincide in the long run if R&D spending is a constant fraction of R&D capital and the firms are in a long run steady state; this is unlikely to be a realistic description of this sample. In the short run, the R&D spending elasticity will be quite a bit higher than the R&D capital elasticity, about five times as high for a typical firm in this sample. This means that the Bernstein and Nadiri and Mohnen, Nadiri, and Prucha estimates must be converted to about -2 before they can be compared with my estimates or those of Hines (1992) or Baily and Lawrence (1987, 1992). I am grateful to Jeffrey Bernstein for pointing this out to me.

[5] After this paper was written, I became aware of an unpublished study by Berger (1992) that uses individual firm-level data and the dummy variable technique of Baily and Lawrence to evaluate the R&D tax credit. Although the sample selection problem in this study is severe (it is restricted to the 263 firms in my sample who have R&D spending and other data continuously from 1975 to 1989), it does find results similar to mine. From the Berger estimates of the differences in mean R&D intensity for firms who can and cannot use the credit and my computation of effective credit rates during the period, it is possible to compute an average implied price elasticity: the estimates range from -1.0 to -1.5 throughout the 1981–1989 period, which is entirely consistent with my results. Berger, like me, finds that the R&E tax credit was cost-effective, in the sense that it induced more R&D spending than the lost tax revenue.

The present paper addresses itself to this problem. It begins with a brief description of R&D tax policy during the recent past, emphasizing the details of the R&E tax credit. This is followed by the description of a simple investment model that provides a framework for analyzing the response of firms to the tax credit. Tables and a figure showing the effective credit rates, their dispersion, and estimated revenue cost of the credit during the 1980s are then presented. Finally, I use a newly updated database of publicly traded manufacturing firms from Compustat to estimate the tax price responsiveness of R&D investment spending during the 1980s and answer the questions posed earlier.

Why should government have an R&D tax policy, and how should we judge its effectiveness? Beginning with Arrow (1962), a large number of authors have argued that industrial R&D exhibits a classic public goods problem, in that it is both nonrivalrous and not completely excludable (except to the extent that trade secrets, patents, lead time, and other methods of appropriability are successful). Empirical studies (summarized in Griliches, 1991) have confirmed this, finding social rates of return to R&D in both industry and agriculture that are far in excess of measured private rates of return.[6] If true, this result implies that private R&D investment has positive externalities, and an insufficient amount will be performed given competitive markets.[7] The classical public finance solution to such a problem is a subsidy to the activity that generates the positive externality, a subsidy designed to raise the private rate of return to the activity to the social level.[8] This is clearly the primary justification for the form of R&D tax policy in the United States.

But what would be the *optimal* subsidy to this activity, and how would we measure it? In principle, we would like to subsidize the price of R&D

[6] Other researchers (e.g., Dasgupta and Stiglitz, 1980) have argued from economic theory that the patent system or other appropriability mechanisms may lead to overinvestment in R&D in some cases, but the empirical evidence cited by Griliches is overwhelmingly in favor of the underinvestment hypothesis.

[7] Note that even if markets are imperfectly competitive (as they almost surely are for R&D-intensive firms, because of the high fixed-cost component in their production function), the fact that measured social and private rates of return differ is sufficient to conclude that the socially optimal level of R&D is not being performed.

[8] Of course, other solutions to the problem also exist, but again, the measured divergence in rates of return suggests that they are imperfect. These methods also typically have the defect of making the industries affected even more imperfectly competitive than they already are. The most obvious is the patent system, which attempts to increase the appropriability of technological innovations. Another method is to allow joint ventures in R&D in order to internalize the externality *a la* Coase. Either of these solutions clearly creates a monopoly in a particular product to the extent that they are successful, so that they involve the usual uncertain trade-off between the output restrictions caused by monopoly power and more efficient production of innovations.

in such a way as to make the private rate of return equal to the social rate of return at the socially optimal level of R&D spending. This is shown in stylized fashion in Figure 1, where the two curves that slope downward to the right represent the private and social marginal products of R&D investment, respectively. The upward-sloping curve is the required rate of return to R&D investment, which is assumed to increase in the level of R&D performed because of the heterogeneity of projects available and risk considerations. Note that the simplifying assumption that the cost of capital signaled by the investment community is a good reflection of society's willingness to pay has been made in locating the social optimum on this curve.

The problems with actually implementing a tax subsidy to move firms from R_C to R_S are several: first, the gap between social and private rates of return will vary by industry because of the difference in appropriability conditions (see Levin et al. (1989) for survey results by industry). Second, how do we measure the gap at the optimal level of R? If we knew the social optimum and the price elasticity of R&D expenditure, we could calculate how much reduction in price would be necessary to elicit the appropriate increase in quantity. But it is much more likely that we have some idea of the rate of return gap at the current quasi-competitive outcome (C), from which we will have to derive the subsidy required to

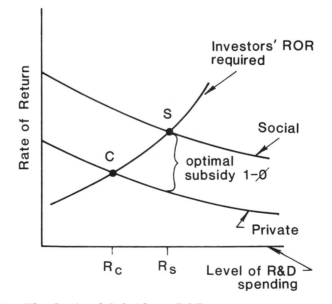

FIGURE 1. *The Optimal Subsidy to R&D.*

get to *S*. Because even this is quite difficult, most analysts have fallen back on a kind of cost benefit analysis: how does the R&D induced by a tax subsidy compare with the tax revenue cost of the subsidy? After presenting estimates of the induced R&D, I will attempt to answer at least this simpler question.

II. A BRIEF HISTORY OF THE R&D TAX CREDIT

The R&E tax credit as it has been implemented during the 1980s is a good example of how even a simple public policy idea that has bipartisan support can emerge from Congress both greatly complicated and weakened in its effects. In the case of the tax credit, the major problems are twofold: first, the need for tax revenue caused it to be greatly diluted in an attempt to focus the effects on the marginal R&D dollar, and second, indecision and lack of agreement on the part of legislators has led to repeated tinkering with and temporary extension of the credit from year to year, rather than a permanent credit that would last at least as long as the typical planning horizon for R&D investment.

A brief summary of the history of R&D tax policy in the United States during the 1980s follows. This policy has had three ingredients: (1) the expensing rules for Research and Development in general (section 174), which have remained essentially unchanged from earlier periods; (2) the R&E tax credit; and (3) the foreign source income allocation rules for R&D, which were changed repeatedly during the 1980s. The first of these policies can be summarized briefly as allowing the expensing of most R&D expenditures against corporate income for tax purposes. The reduction of the corporate tax rate during the 1980s had a substantial impact on the cost of an R&D dollar, because it reduced the benefit of expensing (*relative* to other types of capital investment) by the fall in the tax rate (a reduction of 0.12 for firms with taxable income, possibly more if they face the alternative minimum tax of 20 percent). Note that if a firm undertaking R&D investment faces the same corporate tax rate in all periods, the corporate tax rate is irrelevant to that investment, because the firm spends after-tax dollars on the investment and receives after-tax dollars as income. However, if the tax rate is changing for one reason or another, or the firm is moving in and out of taxable status, the changes in rate will begin to affect the cost of R&D capital faced by the firm (Fullerton and Lyon, 1988; Hall, 1991). For this reason, I have explicitly incorporated a changing corporate tax rate in the model and estimation presented later in the paper.

The R&E tax credit was introduced in the Economic Recovery Tax Act of 1981; it was originally scheduled to be effective from July 1, 1981, to

December 31, 1985. The credit was renewed for two years (January 1, 1986, to December 31, 1988) in a somewhat reduced form by the Tax Reform Act of 1986, and extended for one year through 1989 by the Technical and Miscellaneous Revenue Act of 1988. The Omnibus Budget Reconciliation Act of 1989 effectively extended the credit through 1990, and The Omnibus Budget Reconciliation Act of 1990 did the same for 1991. The Tax Extension Act of 1991 extended the credit through June 30, 1992. Most of these pieces of legislation also made changes to the terms of the credit.[9]

In all cases, the R&E tax credit is computed by taking qualified R&D expenditures that exceed a certain base level, multiplying by the statutory credit rate, and deducting this amount from corporate income taxes. There is a three-year carryback and fifteen-year carryforward in the case of no taxable income in the current year. After 1989, the credit also reduces the R&D expenditure available for deduction from current income under the old section 174 rules. A summary of the changes in the credit rate, qualified expenditure rules, base levels, and corporate income tax rates during the 1980s is shown in Table 1.[10]

In the next section of the paper, I present estimates of the average effective marginal rates of tax credit for U.S. manufacturing firms. These estimates make it clear that although the statutory rate has been between 25 and 20 percent for much of the history of the R&E tax credit, the actual rate has hovered around 4 percent, and only in the last two years does it rise above 5 percent. As previous researchers have pointed out, the primary source of this shortfall is the rolling base level of R&D,

---

[9] From the perspective of a researcher on this topic, one of the most important changes occurred in 1986, when the Tax Reform Act rolled the R&D tax credit into the General Business Credit and subjected it to the General Business Credit limitations. This both makes it more difficult to calculate the effective credit rate from public data, and simultaneously removed the R&D tax credit as a separate line item in the *Statistics on Income*. It is still shown in one of the tables for the whole corporate sector, but we no longer have the industrial detail that was available through 1985.

[10] Another feature of the Tax Reform Act of 1986 that affected R&D incentives was the strengthening of the alternative minimum tax (AMT) system for corporations. If a firm is subject to AMT, it cannot claim the R&D tax credit in the current year, but must carry it forward (for up to fifteen years) until it is subject to regular corporate tax. Also, the rate of taxation under AMT is 20% rather than the statutory corporate rate of 34%. As Lyon (1991) has discussed, this means that firms that are *temporarily* subject to the AMT will face tax incentives that are slightly tilted away from investment in intangibles toward tangibles, relative to what they would face under ordinary corporate taxation. In practice, only a small number of large manufacturing firms in 1988 filed AMT returns, accounting for only 3 percent of the total tax bill paid by manufacturing firms (*Statistics on Income*, 1988), so this is unlikely to be important. However, the reduction in the implicit subsidy to R&D that the AMT creates is likely to be more important in recession years, when corporate profits are down. This may account for some of the reduced nominal R&D spending that we observe in 1990 and 1991. Unfortunately, the data that would allow us to assess this likelihood are not yet available from the IRS.

TABLE 1.
History of R&D Tax Treatment 1981–1991.

Period	Credit Rate	Corporate Tax Rate	Definition of Base	Qualified Expenditures	Sect. 174 Deduction?	Foreign Allocation Rules
Jul 1981 to Dec 1985	0.25	0.46 (0.48 in 1981)	Max of previous 3-year average or 50% of current year	Excluded: Res. done outside U.S.; Humanities & Social Sciences; Research funded by others.	None	100% deduction against domestic income
Jan 1986 to Dec 1986	0.20	0.34	same	Narrowed def. to "technological" research. Exclude leasing.	None	same
Jan 1987 to Dec 1987	0.20	0.34	same	same	None	50% deduction against domestic income 50% allocation
Jan 1988 to Apr 1988	0.20	0.34	same	same	None	64% deduction against domestic income 36% allocation
May 1988 to Dec 1988	0.20	0.34	same	same	None	30% deduction against domestic income 70% allocation
Jan 1989 to Dec 1989	0.20	0.34	same	same	Subtract 50% of credit	64% deduction against domestic income 36% allocation
Jan 1990 to Dec 1991	0.20	0.34	1984-88 R&D to sales ratio times current sales (max ratio of .16); .03 for startups	same	Subtract 100% of credit	same

which was a feature of the credit until 1990. The fact that increasing R&D spending in the current year raises the base in each of the three subsequent years means that for a firm that is always paying taxes, the effective tax credit would be zero except for the presence of discounting. A second feature that weakens the credit is the ceiling on incremental R&D, which is equal to the current year spending. Coupled with the effect of a large increase on the base in future years, this feature of the code produces large *negative* credit rates for rapidly growing firms.

The consequences of the third feature of R&D tax policy (foreign source income allocation rules) for the R&D performance of U.S. multinationals have been well discussed by Hines (1992) and will be covered only briefly here. Basically, the problem is one of allocation of fixed costs across income sources. U.S. tax policy is to tax firms on worldwide income, but to allow credits against that tax for taxes paid to foreign governments (Dept. of Treasury, 1983; Hines, 1992). These credits are limited by the U.S. tax, which would be due on the foreign source income. Thus, the allocation of income, and therefore costs, across jurisdictions matters to firms with excess foreign tax credits. If they already have foreign tax credits they cannot use, allocating more R&D to foreign source income does not reduce their tax liability[11] and will only increase their taxable U.S. income. This is somewhat mitigated by the fact that they are allowed to carry back and carry forward these excess credits.

In 1977, Treasury regulation section 1.861–8 specified the rules by which R&D expenditure should be allocated between foreign and domestic source income: these rules specify that all government mandated R&D (R&D for safety purposes, etc.) plus 30 percent of the remainder can be exclusively allocated to U.S. sales. The 70 percent remaining must be apportioned between domestic and foreign sales using either sales or income as the method of apportionment. The allocations must be done on the basis of product lines (two-digit level). Because of concern on the part of the president and Congress that this method of allocation disadvantages U.S. corporations competing internationally, regulation 1.861–8 was suspended by Section 223(b) of the Economic Recovery Tax Act of 1981; ERTA allowed all R&D expenditure to be allocated against income earned within the United States. The allocation rules have been reviewed and revised continuously since then; a summary of the changes is shown in the last column of Table 1.

Hines (1992) discusses the implication of these allocation rules for the

---

[11] This is because most foreign governments do not allow the expensing of R&D performed in the United States, and, therefore, the R&D allocated to foreign source income does not reduce the foreign tax liability (Hines, 1992; U.S. Dept. of Treasury, 1983).

incentives that multinational firms face to undertake R&D directed at domestic and foreign markets. As a general matter, he finds that the allocation rules tend to make R&D directed toward increasing domestic sales a relatively more expensive input than other ordinary inputs, but that R&D directed toward increasing foreign sales (but conducted in the United States) is substantially less expensive for firms with excess foreign tax credits. This latter fact is due to the relatively light royalty rates that foreign governments impose on royalties (which are the income that results from use of the R&D) paid to the United States. He studies 116 multinational corporations between 1987 and 1989, and finds that only 21 are in a deficit foreign tax credit situation. The average tax price for R&D directed toward domestic sales is 5 percent higher than that for other (noncapital) inputs, and the average tax price for R&D directed toward foreign sales is 15 percent lower, for an overall wedge of 20 percent.

Because of a lack of information on foreign and domestic income and sales, I will not be able to incorporate the features of the tax law that pertain to multinationals in the tax prices that I compute for R&D in the work reported here. Because the firms affected are probably about 10 percent of my sample, I expect that this will not make an enormous difference to the regression estimates, although it will definitely increase the error in the computed tax prices. However, because the tax situation of a multinational in several lines of business and in several countries facing different tax rates is so complex, these errors are unlikely to be systematically correlated with the tax prices I compute, which are based on worldwide R&D spending and taxable income. Under the assumption that this is the case, the estimates here will be valid, although it would be interesting in future work to combine my approach with Hines in order to obtain more precise estimates.

III. FRAMEWORK FOR ANALYSIS

In this section of the paper, I present the simple investment model that will be used to estimate the tax price responsiveness of R&D spending. Assume that a profit-maximizing firm earns revenues every period from its stock of R&D capital, which is the depreciated sum of past R&D investments. The treatment here is parallel to the usual treatment of physical capital; all other input factors are omitted in order to simplify the analysis, because the essential ideas can be seen without the added complication. With no adjustment costs, the firm's problem is

$$\underset{\{R_t\}}{\text{Max}} \sum_{t=0}^{\infty} (1 + r)^{-t}[(1 - \tau)\, S(G_t) - \theta_t\, R_t] \qquad r > 0 \qquad (1)$$

subject to

$$G_t = (1 - \delta)G_{t-1} + R_t, \tag{2}$$

where $S(.)$ is the sales (revenue) function, and θ_t is the tax price of R&D (if R&D is expensed as incurred, for example, θ_t will be $1 - \tau$ where τ is the corporate tax rate). With $S' > 0$ and $S'' < 0$, it is easy to show that the profit- and (value-)maximizing choice of $\{R_t\}$ is given by the Euler equation:

$$(1 - \tau)S'(t) = \theta_t - \frac{(1 - \delta)}{(1 + r)} \theta_{t+1}. \tag{3}$$

Therefore (if one assumes θ_t is equal to $(1 - \tau)$ for the moment), the firm invests so that its marginal revenue product (MRP) each period is equal to the depreciation on the capital stock plus the interest rate discounted to the present $[(\delta + r)/(1 + r)]$.[12] Clearly, a tax subsidy of the form $1 - \theta_t$ will reduce the required MRP and increase the level of R&D spending if $S'' < 0$. This type of subsidy is equivalent to shifting the required rate of return curve in Figure 1 outward by θ_t. Once again, if we knew R_S and the slope of the MRP curve, we could easily calculate the optimal θ_t.[13]

However, there are of course many reasons to think that this analysis is oversimplified: in order of tractability, three important considerations are (1) adjustment costs in R&D; (2) the fact that the required rate of return curve that firms face may be neither smoothly upward sloping nor roughly equal across firms because of liquidity constraints and the complexity of the corporate tax system; and, finally, (3) general equilibrium effects. The first two are considered here.

Many researchers (Bernstein and Nadiri, 1986; Hall, Griliches, and Hausman, 1986; Hall and Hayashi, 1988; Himmelberg and Petersen, 1990) have documented the apparently high adjustment costs that a firm investing in R&D faces. The principal evidence for this is the low variance of R&D expenditures within a firm relative to ordinary investment spending, or low responsiveness of R&D demand to changes in prices.

---

[12] Note that the result for this simple case with constant tax rates does indeed show that the corporate tax rate is irrelevant for R&D spending, even though the returns to R&D are spread over the future. This does *not* mean that R&D is not subsidized relative to investment, only that the subsidy affects investment rather than R&D.

[13] The model presented here is a simplification which is not valid when θ_t depends on future R&D spending (as it will in the case of the tax credit in place from 1981 to 1989). The correct model has a function of R_t, R_{t+1}, . . . in place of $\theta_t R_t$ as the cost of R&D. The appendix presents this more complex model and shows that equations (3) or (5), which will be used for estimation, remain unchanged when the correct model is used to derive them.

The phenomenon is frequently confirmed by those in industry; the fact that R&D budgets are at least 50 percent composed of the salaries of professional scientists and engineers (and that much of the "knowledge" capital of the firm is embodied in these workers) and the long-term nature of many projects would lead to this conclusion. If adjustment costs for R&D investment are indeed high, this fact has important consequences for the conduct of tax policy, particularly in an environment where uncertainty about the future plays an important role. For example, frequent tinkering with the tax system can be expected to diminish greatly the incentive effects of a tax subsidy to R&D, because firms facing both uncertainty about future tax policy and fluctuating tax prices will be reluctant to invest in the presence of high adjustment costs.

To make this concrete, I complicate the previous model by adding external costs of adjustment to R&D investment that are proportional to the intensity of such investment, and are minimized when R&D is exactly replacement investment; the firm's problem is now

$$\operatorname*{Max}_{\{R_t\}} \sum_{t=0}^{\infty} (1 + r)^{-t} \left\{ (1 - \tau)[S(G_t) - \Phi(R_t, G_t)] - \theta_t R_t \right\}. \tag{4}$$

The solution to this problem is the same Euler equation as before, but with a set of terms that describe the difference in adjustment costs between this period and the next:

$$(1 - \tau) \left\{ S'(t) - \Phi_G(t) \right\}$$
$$= \left\{ \theta_t + (1 - \tau)\Phi_R(t) \right\} - \frac{(1 - \delta)}{(1 + r)} \left\{ \theta_{t+1} + (1 - \tau)\Phi_R(t + 1) \right\}. \tag{5}$$

The after-tax marginal revenue product of R&D in period t (which now includes the marginal reduction in adjustment costs as a result of increased capital) has to cover not only the interest and depreciation on the R&D capital, but also the increase in after-tax adjustment costs caused by having made the investment this period rather than next.

A few computations will illustrate why firm behavior is sensitive to the exact form of the subsidy. Assume $r = .10$, $\delta = 0.15$, and $\tau = 0.34$. With no adjustment costs and no additional tax subsidy ($\theta_t = 1 - \tau$), they imply a required pretax marginal revenue product for R&D of about 23 percent. Now assume that marginal adjustment costs $\Phi_R = 1.5$, which is consistent with the results reported later in this paper. The required pretax marginal revenue product for R&D capital is now 58 percent. Unless many such high-return projects can be found, the optimal strategy may be to keep adjustment costs low by deferring investment until a later period.

Although it is not possible to do a complete analysis using the Euler equation without knowing the future path of R&D investment for the firm, it is fairly easy to convince oneself that any wedge in adjustment costs between periods caused by differing investment rates induced by a short-term or temporary tax subsidy to R&D would swamp the direct effect of the subsidy on the required rate of return in this model and with adjustment costs of this magnitude. In other words, the typical manufacturing firm has an enormous incentive to smooth the acquisition of R&D capital, and this greatly inhibits the effectiveness of *temporary* tax instruments.

The preceding analysis is not intended to be conclusive, because there still exists considerable doubt in the literature as to the form and magnitude of the adjustment cost function in this case. However, it does highlight the importance of exploring the question of the responsiveness of R&D to changes in price, particularly in light of the conflicting results in the literature.[14] At the same time, I would suggest that the qualitative implications of the previous estimates of R&D factor demand will remain true even as we improve the modeling of adjustment costs: short-term tax instruments are unlikely to be the cost-effective weapon for increasing R&D investment.

Figure 1 shows a smooth, upward-sloping supply curve for R&D investment funds, representing the changing rate of return required by investors as a firm invests more and more dollars in R&D. This is unlikely to be an accurate description of a world with asymmetric information and taxes. Many economists (Auerbach, 1984; Fazzari, Hubbard, and Petersen, 1988; Poterba and Summers, 1985) have made the point that this supply curve may have kinks at the individual firm level. In a recent series of papers (Hall, 1991, 1992), I have applied this idea to R&D investment and found evidence both that R&D investment is simultaneous with the choice of financial structure (and that highly levered structures are not favored by R&D firms) and that liquidity itself, as measured by cash flow, is as important a determinant of R&D investment as of ordinary investment.

Using a more complex version of the model sketched earlier, which contains three sources of finance (debt, new equity, and retained earnings), corporate and individual taxes, a lemons premium for new equity,

---

[14] As discussed earlier, Hines (1992) finds a price elasticity of about unity for R&D spending, but previous estimates (e.g., Bernstein and Nadiri 1988 or Mansfield 1986) have found numbers of the order of magnitude of 0.2 to 0.5 for R&D capital. Comparing the two sets of numbers is difficult owing to the heterogeneity of the R&D spending patterns for the firms in the data samples used.

and a cost of debt that is increasing in the capital-debt ratio, one can derive a supply curve for investment funds to an individual firm (Fazzari, Hubbard, and Petersen, 1988; Hall, 1992; Poterba and Summers, 1985). This curve has three regions: one where the cost of funds to the firm is low because the marginal source of finance is retained earnings (and even lower if there is a tax-induced wedge between dividends and capital gains), a region where the cost of funds rise, possibly steeply, as the firm borrows to finance investment, and finally a region where the marginal source of finance is new equity, which is issued at a premium because of the possibility of lemons in this market.

Casual observation and the empirical evidence both suggest that R&D firms are likely to find the central portion of this figure rather inhospitable when thinking about R&D investment, and that they will either be pursuing a policy of "living within their means" or, if their investment opportunities look profitable enough, going to the equity or venture capital markets to finance them. This means that tax credits will translate one-for-one into R&D expenditure if the firm has income tax liabilities but is liquidity constrained. On the other hand, because R&D is expensed for tax purposes, young high-technology firms that are investing heavily in R&D may not have tax liabilities against which to use the credit, which will limit its effect.

The main implication of liquidity-constrained investment for optimal R&D tax policy is that the required rate of return or supply curve of funds for an individual firm may not look at all like the one a social planner would use in choosing the optimal level of R&D investment. For example, suppose that a (fully informed) society's required net rate of return for investment is just the discount rate, which implies a flat supply curve of funds. Then the optimal level of R&D investment is likely to be quite large relative to the competitive level, and from this we can calculate an appropriate subsidy. But some individual firms may face steeply rising rather than flat cost of funds schedules, and the R&D elicited by the subsidy will be substantially less than the amount expected by the social planner when he set the subsidy rate. The conclusion is that it might be important to investigate the heterogeneity of R&D response to changes in tax price across firms in different financing regimes in considering the effects of such a subsidy.

IV. THE DATA SAMPLE AND ESTIMATED CREDIT RATES

The analysis in this paper is performed using a large sample of U.S. manufacturing firms drawn from the 1980–1991 Compustat (Standard and Poor, 1992) files. This sample includes essentially all publicly traded manufacturing firms, accounting for about 85 percent of R&D performed and paid for by industry. The panel that is analyzed here is restricted to R&D-performing firms that have at least four years of continuous data between 1977 and 1991. There are about 1,000 firms per year (the exact number is shown in Table 2), with an incomplete sample in 1991 caused by differences in fiscal years.[15] The sample is much the same as the one that I have analyzed in several previous papers (Hall, 1990a, 1991, 1992), but updated through 1991.

There are two major drawbacks to using this data source for the project at hand: lack of information on the fraction of total R&D spending that is qualified under the R&E tax credit, and lack of detailed information on the tax status of the firm. To solve the former problem, I have relied on estimates obtained from confidential tax data by Altshuler (1988); her estimates were consistent with those of Eisner, Albert, and Sullivan (1984), obtained from the McGraw-Hill R&D survey and NSF. I assume that every additional dollar spend on R&D has the same composition of qualified and unqualified expenditures as the average. Obviously this is an oversimplification: presumably part of the intent of the law was to shift spending toward "technological" directions, and it would be interesting to know to what extent this goal was achieved. Without access to confidential data, however, it is not possible to investigate this question. There is a bit of tantalizing information on this question in the GAO Report (1989): by comparing 219 corporations for which they had both confidential tax data and COMPUSTAT R&D spending data, they were able to conclude that although qualified spending grew only 1.04 times more rapidly than total spending over the 1980–1985 period, there was substantial variation (for these firms) within the period, with qualified spending growing 1.46 times as fast in the 1980–1981 period, but only 0.72 times as fast in 1983–1984.[16]

With respect to tax status, COMPUSTAT contains information on taxable income and loss carryforwards, but no detail on unused business credits; in addition, Altshuler and Auerbach (1990) and others have found the tax data on Compustat not always accurate or consistent with IRS records. Because there is very little I can do about this problem without using confidential tax data, it must be kept in mind that my estimated tax prices for R&D are likely to be mismeasured for some firms because of this.

---

[15] Because of the way Compustat dates firm-years, data for firms that close late in fiscal 91, i.e., in the first few months of 1992, are not yet available).

[16] U.S. Government, Report GAO/GGD-89-114, pp. 77–78.

TABLE 2.
U.S. Manufacturing Firms 1980–1991.

Year	Number of Firms	R&D Deflator (1982 Dollars)	Total R&D Spending (B 1982 Dollars)	Share of NSF R&D (Percent)	R&D to Sales (Percent)	Average Growth Rate of R&D (Percent)
1980	1006	0.890	30.30	87.2	1.99	9.13
1981	994	0.957	32.13	85.5	2.05	10.29
1982	991	1.000	33.96	83.5	2.34	10.62
1983	1015	1.036	36.17	82.8	2.55	8.55
1984	1012	1.085	40.29	82.8	2.88	12.28
1985	985	1.134	40.92	80.0	3.03	6.33
1986	978	1.150	43.01	80.9	3.40	5.97
1987	974	1.156	45.33	81.8	3.36	7.94
1988	944	1.196	47.83	84.3	3.27	6.36
1989	893	1.241	50.03	88.3	3.37	4.21
1990	859	1.295	51.14	86.8	3.34	2.93
1991	735	1.343	51.04	89.2	3.62	0.96

The R&D deflator is a weighted average of labor costs and the implicit price deflator in the nonfinancial corporate sector and is described in Hall (1990a).

The NSF R&D numbers are the total R&D expenditure by industry, from Science Indicators 1987, updated by growth rates in the *New York Times* (1992).

The R&D to Sales average is a sales-weighted average, which is the same as the ratio of total R&D during the period to total sales by R&D performing firms.

However, all studies in this area face a more serious measurement problem when using tax prices computed *ex post* with a knowledge of the complete history of the firm over the period. What matters for the optimizing problem sketched in the previous section is the tax price that is expected to prevail when the investment decisions are undertaken. Because of the history of the R&E tax credit legislation, and general uncertainty about taxable income, there is no reason to think that the price expected by the firm is the one that is computed using information from later years, such as future tax status. To solve this problem, I make the usual rational expectations assumption, and compute the expected price faced by the firm as the regression of the realized price on variables known to the firm at time $t - 1$. The instruments used include the past tax status of the firm, and its sales and R&D growth rates. This list of variables should not only be good predictors of the *expected* tax price, but they should also help with ordinary measurement error.

Table 2 shows some of the characteristics of my sample, and highlights the trends in industrial R&D spending during the 1980s. Although the 1991 numbers need to be interpreted with caution because of the incompleteness of the sample for this year, it is possible to draw some simple conclusions from these numbers. The National Science Board has recently issued a report documenting stagnation or decline in industrial R&D during the latter half of this period (National Science Board, 1992). While Table 2 lends some support of their view, it also alters the interpretation slightly. Table 2 shows that real R&D spending, measured either in total, as a weighted R&D to sales ratio, or at the firm level, was rising at about 10 percent per year during the 1980 through 1984 period. From 1985 through 1990, although total spending continued to rise at a much slower rate, and weighted R&D to sales ratios increased somewhat, average firm R&D growth rates were still over 6 percent per year, declining only in 1989 and 1990. The explanation for this inconsistency appears to lie in the fact that the manufacturing sector was shrinking during the period, both in number of firms and in output, so that although R&D stagnated during this period, it did not do so as much as sales, and many smaller firms were increasing their R&D spending substantially, especially before 1990.

By itself and ignoring all other macroeconomic effects, Table 2 seems to suggest success for the first few years of the R&E tax credit, followed by diminishing returns and then complete failure of the improved credit of 1990. As we will see, in addition to ignoring such factors as recession during the latter half of the period, this interpretation fails to take account of the other features of the corporate tax system that were changing at the same time, which had the effect of increasing the *relative* tax price of R&D from 1986 onward. The regression results reported later show that the cross-sectional responsiveness of R&D to differences in tax prices was unabated throughout the period, although there was certainly an unexplained decline in R&D spending for these firms in 1990 and 1991.

Before turning to the regression results, I present some basic facts on the computation of the R&E tax credit in Table 3. As alluded to earlier, R&D tax policy for domestic firms consists of two parts: the expensing of R&D reduces the cost by the corporate tax rate if a firm has taxable income (discounted if there are loss carryforwards) and the subsidy from the credit (multiplied by the share of R&D expenditures which qualify for the credit). These two pieces are shown in the equation for the tax price of R&D:

$$\theta_t = p_t^R (1 - T_t(1 + r)^{-J_t}\tau - \eta_t \text{ERC}_t). \tag{6}$$

p_t^R is the "price" of R&D investment absent taxes, T_t is a dummy that indicates whether a firm has taxable income in the current year (not necessarily whether it actually pays taxes), J_t is the number of years

TABLE 3.
The R&E Tax Credit in Practice.

Year	Average Effective Credit (Percent)	Wtd. Av. Effective Credit (Percent)	Average Tax Price of R&D	Deflated Tax Price of R&D	Revenue Cost (Millions Dollars) This Paper	GAO Estimate	Actual
1980	0.0	0.0	1.000	1.000	0.0	0.0	0.0
1981	3.04	3.45	0.963	0.940	738.	800.	NA
1982	5.05	3.80	0.941	0.905	1025.	1200.	859.2
1983	3.64	5.02	0.958	0.917	1400.	1500.	1277.5
1984	4.60	4.98	0.947	0.909	1953.	1800.	1589.1
1985	5.01	5.38	0.942	0.912	1793.	1700.	1628.0
1986	3.11	3.60	0.970	0.927	1208.	—	1292.0
1987	2.66	3.61	0.975	0.908	1183.	—	1053.3
1988	3.50	4.25	0.967	0.895	1429.	—	1276.9
1989	2.19	3.39	0.980	0.903	1272.	—	NA
1990	7.69	10.52	0.928	0.857	857.	—	NA
1991	7.49	11.17	0.930	0.859	922.	—	NA

See text for calculations of the effective R&E tax credit and the relative tax price of R&D. The column labelled "Wtd." shows the average credit weighted by R&D spending in each firm. The deflated tax price is the tax price multiplied by R&D deflator relative to the GNP deflator (1980 = 1).

The last three columns show the revenue cost of the credit, first estimated from Compustat and inflated by the coverage ratio for the NSF survey shown in Table 2, then from the GAO Report (1989), which is based on *Statistics on Income* data on about 800 large corporations, and finally the actual reported totals from the *Statistics on Income* for the entire corporate sector. NA means the number is not available.

before any loss carryforwards will be exhausted (usually equal to zero), τ_t is the corporate tax rate, η_t is the share of qualified R&D expenditure, and ERC_t is the effective rate of R&E tax credit. This quantity is computed using the following general formula:[17]

$$
\mathrm{ERC}_t = \rho_t\Bigg((1 + r)^{-s}Z_t - (1/3)\bigg\{(1 + r)^{-(1 + J_t + 1)}(Z_{t+1} > 0.5)
$$
$$
+ (1 + r)^{-(2 + J_{t+2})}(Z_{t+2} > 0.5) + (1 + r)^{-(3 + J_{t+3})}(Z_{t+3} > 0.5)\bigg\}\Bigg) \tag{7}
$$

$$
\begin{aligned}
&\phantom{\mathrm{ERC}_t = \rho_t(1}\text{for } t = 81 \text{ to } 89 \\
\mathrm{ERC}_t &= \mathrm{ERC}_t\,(1 - 0.5\tau_t) \qquad \text{for } t = 89 \\
\mathrm{ERC}_t &= \rho_t(1 + r)^{-s}(1 - \tau_t)\,Z_t \qquad \text{for } t = 90, 91,
\end{aligned}
$$

[17] The computation shown here is essentially that in the GAO report (1989) suitably modified to take account of changes in the tax law since 1985. The second term in equation (7) is multiplied by one-half rather than one-third in 1981, because of the special startup rules during the first two years of the credit.

where ρ_t is the statutory credit rate and Z_t is zero, one half, or one, depending on whether R&D spending during the year is below the base level, more than twice the base level, or between one and two times the base level. If the firm can carry back the credit, s is the (negative) number of years it will do so, with a maximum of three. If it must carry forward the credit, s is positive. The terms in brackets represent the effects on the future R&D base of increasing expenditures at the margin this year.

The first two columns of Table 3 give the effective marginal tax credit faced by the average firm in this sample, unweighted and weighted by the actual R&D spending of the firms. The effective credit is somewhat higher than that reported by Altshuler (1988) for 1981 through 1984, because my sample includes only R&D-performing firms, and is consistent with the GAO study for 1981 through 1983. It is clear from the table that firms with more R&D also face a slightly higher credit rate on average (because presumably they are more likely to be above the base expenditure level). Column 3 of Table 3 shows the relative tax price of R&D (the tax price divided by one minus the corporate tax rate actually faced by the firm on earnings); this ratio is unity when there was no R&D credit. Column 4 shows the average of the relative price of R&D actually used in the regressions later; this is the tax price multiplied by the ratio of the R&D deflator to the GNP deflator. It falls more than the tax price during the 1980s because the R&D deflator did not rise as fast as the GNP deflator, because of the large share of labor costs in the former.

From the perspective of the government, there is a cost associated with tax subsidies, in spite of the economic theorist's confidence that nondistortionary lump sum taxation will be used to finance them. In the real world, distributional considerations and the complexities of the existing tax system may preclude that simple solution. The framers for the R&E tax credit legislation clearly were attempting to minimize its revenue cost by focusing on the incentives to increase R&D at the margin: in the simple world of Figure 1, rather than giving $(1 - \theta)R_S$ to the firm, they attempted to set the subsidy at $(1 - \theta)(R_S - R_C)$ by allowing firms to use a credit only on qualified research expenditures above a base determined by the firm's prior history of research spending. It is this feature of the credit that, although admirable in intent, has led to the weak incentive effects observed and controversy over its continuance.

The last three columns of Table 3 give some idea of the revenue cost associated with the R&E tax credit. This was computed by calculating the tax credit that actually would have been claimed in any given year by each of these firms, assuming that I have identified those with taxable income correctly, adding up the numbers, and then inflating them to population totals using the share of NSF R&D expenditures shown in Table 2. For comparison, the GAO (1989) estimates are shown for the period for which they are available. Although they are not identical, it is reassuring that the numbers computed here are not wildly different from estimates computed using actual tax returns. I also show the actual numbers reported by the IRS for the whole corporate sector in *Statistics on Income*; these are generally somewhat lower than both my numbers and the GAO numbers, which may reflect the results of auditing returns, or errors induced by fiscal year timing.

To give an idea of the dispersion in the rates faced by different firms as well as the sources of this heterogeneity, Table 4 shows the fraction of firms whose effective credit rate is *negative*, the share of R&D in firms with negative marginal credit rates, the fraction of firms with R&D below the base amount, and the fraction above twice the base. The share of firms facing a negative credit rate drops to zero and the number of firms

TABLE 4.
The Heterogeneity of the R&E Tax Credit.

Year	Percent of Firms with Negative Effective Credit	Share of R&D in Firms with Negative Credit	Percent of Firms below Base R&D	Percent of Firms above 2*Base	Percent of Firms with Taxable Income
1977	—	—	20.5	9.9	93.6
1978	—	—	16.9	9.8	94.1
1979	—	—	16.2	10.9	93.1
1980	—	—	13.1	13.2	89.8
1981	17.9	6.4	19.3	5.3	90.1
1982	19.2	13.5	20.2	9.9	80.7
1983	24.2	8.9	23.9	12.7	82.5
1984	21.7	13.3	20.9	13.6	83.7
1985	21.0	8.4	21.5	12.0	80.5
1986	24.4	10.3	26.5	9.4	81.2
1987	26.7	11.2	29.8	10.0	85.1
1988	22.4	10.2	28.3	9.2	85.8
1989	30.6	11.3	25.4	8.5	83.8
1990	0.0	0.0	38.2	8.3	83.5
1991	0.0	0.0	40.1	7.6	78.9

Firms with a negative effective credit are those whose marginal R&E tax credit rate as computed by equation (7) is less than zero. The second column shows the total share of R&D spending which is in such firms.

The share of firms below and above base R&D for the years 1977 through 1980 is a hypothetical computation which assumes that the base is the average of the last three years of spending.

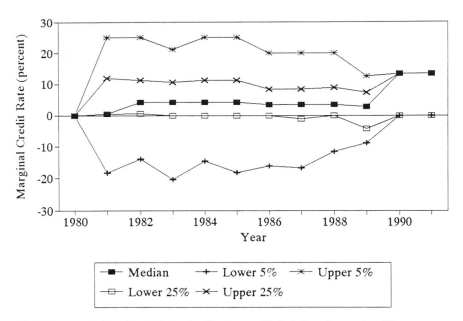

FIGURE 2. *Effective R&D Credit Rate: U.S. Manufacturing Firms 1981–1991.*

below the base level increases when the new formula for the base is introduced in 1990. The dispersion in effective credit rates is also shown in Figure 2, where the median, interquartile range, and 5 and 95 percent bounds of the effective credit rate are plotted against time. For the early years, the dispersion is extremely large; it falls slightly in 1986 when the corporate tax rate and statutory credit rate were reduced, and again in 1989 when the offset to section 174 deductions is introduced. After the Budget Act of 1989, there are basically two rates: 13.2 percent (= (1 − .34)*.20) for firms above the base who have taxable income, and zero for firms which are below the base or do not have taxable income.[18]

The interaction between the R&E tax credit or accelerated depreciation and the tax status of firms has not gone unnoticed by previous researchers in this area, but there is no consensus on the importance of the effect. Eisner, Albert, and Sullivan (1984) seem to have been the first to make the point that the effective rate of tax credit can be substantially less than

[18] In the last few years, I am unable to look ahead to when the firm will have taxable income against which to use the credit, so I am forced to assume that all firms become taxable in 1992 in order to perform the computations. This overestimates the average credit slightly.

the statutory rate, and possibly even negative for firms *currently* in an excess tax credit position but not expecting to be in future years.[19] They find that 15 percent of their sample cannot use the credit in 1981, and 35 percent in 1982, which suggests a considerable weakening of the desired effect. On the other hand, the GAO (1989) study claims that the actual average effective tax credit rises only from 5.2 percent to 5.9 percent in 1982 (the year with the *largest* effect) if one makes the counterfactual assumption that companies receive refunds for credit amounts that they cannot use immediately. The explanation for these results appears to lie in the intertemporal behavior of tax status, as reported by Altshuler (1988): she finds that during the early 1980s, only 3 percent of firms on average transit from nontaxable state to a taxable state. It is these firms that experience the most negative incentives from the tax credit, but they are so few in number that it is not surprising that they have minimal effect on the computation of average behavior. The majority of tax-exhausted firms one year remain tax-exhausted in the future, and these firms experience neither an incentive nor a disincentive effect from the tax credit.

V. ESTIMATION RESULTS

Estimating investment demand equations at the firm level is difficult and prone to fragile results; there is also a large literature on the subject that is not discussed extensively here because of space considerations. In earlier work (Hall, 1991, 1992), I have investigated the modeling and specification of the R&D investment equation. The estimates reported here rely heavily on insights and specification testing that was performed in the course of that work. The approach used is to assume a Cobb-Douglas form for the production function (with a coefficient γ for R&D capital G_t) and an adjustment cost function of the form

$$\Phi(R_t, G_t) = \frac{\phi}{2} \left\{ \frac{R_t}{G_t} \right\} R_t. \tag{8}$$

In the appendix, these assumptions are combined with equation (5) to obtain a Euler equation for investment, which can be written as follows:

---

[19] This seemingly bizarre result occurs because qualified research spending done in the current year raises the base above which the increment is calculated in future years, thus lowering the amount that is eligible for the credit in the future year. The firm gets no credit in the current year and can carry the credit forward for only three years, while it may find that future credits have been reduced because of the increased spending.

$$\left(\frac{R_t + 1}{G_t + 1} \right) = \frac{(1 + r)}{(1 - \delta)} \left\{ \left(\frac{R_t}{G_t} \right) - \frac{1}{2} \left(\frac{R_t}{G_t} \right)^2 + \phi^{-1} \left\{ \frac{\theta_t}{(1 - \tau_t)} - \gamma \frac{S_t}{G_t} \right\} \right\}$$ (9)

$$- \phi^{-1} \frac{\theta_t + 1}{(1 - \tau_{t+1})}$$

This equation specifies that the current rate of investment depends on the lagged rate through the adjustment cost terms, and is related negatively to the lagged marginal product of capital (because the firm will have invested last period if the marginal product was high) and negatively to the discounted increase in the price of R&D.

Estimating an equation like equation (9) requires the use of instrumental variables for several reasons: all of the right-hand-side variables (even the actual tax price faced) are under control of the firm at the same time

TABLE 5a.

The Response of R&D to the Tax Price, U.S. Manufacturing 1980–1991
GMM Estimates.

Independent Variable	1980–1991	1980–1985	1986–1991	First Diff. 1980–1991
Sales-R&D Capital Ratio Lagged	.0001(.0001)	.0001(.0001)	.0002(.0001)	.0009(.0014)
R&D Investment Rate Lagged	.988 (.031)	.957 (.047)	.973 (.029)	.656 (.181)
Squared R&D Investment Rate Lagged	−.221 (.034)	−.137 (.052)	−.248 (.033)	−.187 (.149)
Tax Price	−.362 (.042)	−.320 (.063)	−.356 (.053)	−1.21 (.29)
Tax Price$_{-1}$	.250 (.059)	.305 (.098)	.147 (.054)	.374 (.095)
$\chi^2(2)$ for price effects	74.1	38.0	46.2	17.2
Year Dummies	incl.	incl.	incl.	incl.
Std. Err.	.096	.102	.087	.195
Std. Dev. of Dep. Var.	.183	.187	.180	.079
No. of Obs.	9167	4807	4360	9167

The method of estimation is Generalized Method of Moments (GMM) (robust to heteroskedasticity) where the instruments include the right-hand-side variables lagged twice and three times, the growth rates of R&D, sales, and taxes lagged twice, and tax status (whether taxable income and whether actually paying taxes) lagged once and twice.

Standard error estimates are robust to the presence of heteroskedasticity and first order serial correlation.

as it is planning its future R&D expenditure path, so we expect that there will be a relationship between the disturbance to this equation and the right-hand-side variables. In addition, many of the variables are likely to be measured with error. In particular, as discussed earlier, the tax price variable that I have computed is extremely unlikely to be the actual tax price the firm faced, and it is certainly not the price that the firm expected at the time the investment decisions were being made; in fact, as the history of the R&E tax credit legislation shows, firms are unlikely to have been able to forecast the exact tax treatment of R&D more than six months or so in advance. For all these reasons, the estimates of this equation reported in Tables 5(a) and 5(b) use values of the right-hand-side variables lagged twice and three times as well as lagged tax status and lagged growth rates in R&D and sales as instruments.

TABLE 5b.
The Response of R&D to the Tax Price, U.S. Manufacturing 1980–1991, December Fiscal Year Close Only
GMM estimates.

Independent Variable	1980–1991	1980–1985	1986–1991	First Diff. 1980–1991
Sales-R&D Capital Ratio Lagged	−.0002(.0001)	−.0001(.0001)	.0001(.0001)	.0008(.0019)
R&D Investment Rate Lagged	.936 (.037)	.878 (.054)	.968 (.040)	.552 (.288)
Squared R&D Investment Rate Lagged	−.165 (.045)	−.032 (.057)	−.224 (.045)	−.103 (.235)
Tax Price	−.368 (.048)	−.315 (.057)	−.374 (.063)	−.585 (.270)
Tax Price$_{-1}$	.195 (.052)	.222 (.074)	.155 (.060)	.179 (.092)
$\chi^2(2)$ for price effects	39.1	32.6	36.1	4.69
Year Dummies	incl.	incl.	incl.	incl.
Std. Err.	.081	.080	.078	.112
Std. Dev. of Dep. Var.	.162	.159	.166	.083
No. of Obs.	5077	2650	2427	5077

The method of estimation is Generalized Method of Moments (GMM) where the instruments are the right-hand-side variables lagged twice and three times, the growth rates of R&D, sales, and taxes lagged twice, and tax status (whether taxable income and whether actually paying taxes) lagged once and twice.

Standard error estimates are robust to the presence of heteroskedasticity and first order serial correlation.

The model in equation (9) is a rather rigid structural model with which to estimate the behavior of over 1,000 manufacturing firms in many industries: besides the fact that it does not allow for the heterogeneity in such a sample, there is no reason to think that either the functional form or the assumption that R&D can be analyzed independently of other inputs, are close to correct. Thus, it is reassuring to see in Table 5(a) that the signs and magnitudes of the estimated coefficients are not wildly at variance with our priors. The signs and orders of magnitude of all significant coefficients (those on the lagged R&D investment rate and its square, and on the current and lagged tax prices) are correct. It is discouraging, however, that the output-capital does not play a role: the implied γ is about .0004–.0008, which is far below the value of .05 or .10 that might have been expected given price-taking firms with R&D capital shares of roughly that order of magnitude. This is undoubtedly due in part to the unrealistic production model presented here, which is oversimplified to the extent of ignoring all other inputs into the production process. As is usual in R&D investment regressions at the firm level, by far the most significant predictor of R&D investment is past R&D investment: this is just another aspect of the adjustment cost story, but it may also indicate substantial technology-related firm heterogeneity. For example, in a steady-state world with differing depreciation rates for R&D capital across industries, we would expect the lagged R&D investment rate to be a good predictor of the current rate. Lagged R&D investment may also be a fairly good indicator of the marginal revenue product of R&D capital, which would account for the disappointingly low coefficient on the output-capital ratio.

The main result of the estimation reported in Table 5(a) is that the tax price response of R&D is significant and not due to simultaneity of taxable income and R&D. However, when the sample is broken into two periods corresponding to before and after the 1986 Tax Reform Act, the price response is stronger in the latter period than in the former (a joint significance test for the two coefficients that is based on the heteroskedastic-consistent standard errors is shown in the table). It is intriguing that the earlier period shows a somewhat weaker response, which might be expected as firms adjust their R&D spending plans to the new law, and become reassured that it is quasi-permanent.

The last column of Table 5(a) presents estimates based on first differences of the variables; these estimates control for unexplained differences across firms that may be related to the right-hand-side variables and, therefore, bias the coefficient estimates. Although somewhat less precise, these estimates confirm those in the first three columns and in fact show a substantially larger effect of the tax price, controlling for unexplained differences across firms and industries.

TABLE 6.
R&D Response to the Tax Price: Logarithmic Specification, U.S.
Manufacturing 1980–1991
9167 Observations
GMM Estimates.

Independent Variable	Estimates in Levels		Estimates in First Differences		
Log R_{-1}	1.003(.004)	.999(.004)	.431(.071)	.307(.051)	—
Log P	−2.48 (.16)	−1.90 (.14)	−1.95 (.47)	−.83 (.16)	−1.21(.14)
Log P_{-1}	1.39 (.19)	—	.40 (.16)	—	—
Log S_{-1}	−.031(.004)	−.011(.004)	.34 (.09)	.51 (.06)	.74(.05)
Std. Err.	.329	.311	.355	.297	.296
DW stat.	1.95	1.56	2.53	2.27	2.03

R, P, and S are R&D expenditures, the tax price, and sales respectively. All equations and instrument lists contain time dummies. The instruments are the same as for Table 5, in logarithmic form (levels and growth rates).

The method of estimation is Generalized Method of Moments and the standard error estimates are robust to heteroskedasticity and first order serial correlation.

One possible measurement problem with the preceding results arises because the fiscal year closings of firms are spread throughout the year rather than coincidental with the end of the calendar year. This could create difficulties with my measured tax prices because the tax law is generally on a calendar year basis. Therefore, Table 5(b) shows the same estimates as Table 5(a), with the sample constrained to those firms whose fiscal year ends in December. These estimates are similar to those in Table 5(a), so the timing of the tax changes does not seem to be a serious problem for estimation.

There are many reasons to think that the Euler equation approach to estimating investment behavior is not necessarily a good approximation to the behavior of large heterogeneous manufacturing firms.[20] Therefore, Table 6 presents a purely descriptive log-log regression of R&D on tax price to check the results obtained previously using a more robust specification. The results in this table strongly confirm the previous estimates, and in fact strengthen them: in all specifications of the model, the tax price elasticity of R&D is unity or slightly above. Because the original model included a lagged endogenous variable whose estimated coefficient was near unity, moving to first differences does not change

[20] For example, the possible failure of firms to maximize profits dynamically, variations in the form of the production function and adjustment cost function across firms and industries, aggregation over many lines of business within a firm, and failure of the expectational assumptions necessary to justify the equation.

the estimates or standard error of estimate that much, but it does have implications for the sales coefficient. When we look across firms at the level of R&D spending, the lagged R&D coefficient leaves little for any other variables to explain, particularly one like log sales, which is highly collinear with log R&D in the cross section. On the other hand, when we focus on growth rates, lagged sales growth does help to predict R&D growth, even in the presence of lagged R&D growth. Because tests of whether the firm effects are not correlated with the right-hand-side variables in this regression usually reject strongly (Hall, 1991, 1992), I am more inclined to rely on the estimates in the last three columns than in the first two.

From the estimates in Tables 5 and 6, it is possible to compute the predicted effect of changes in the tax credit on R&D investment, but it is important to distinguish between short- and long-term changes in so doing. The implied short-run price elasticity of R&D (based on the first-differenced specifications evaluated at the average R&D investment rate) is $-0.84(.20)$ for column 4 of Table 5(a) and $-1.5(0.3)$ for column 4 of Table 6. This means that a fully anticipated one-time reduction in the tax price of R&D of 5 percent (or an increase in the credit of 5 percent) would increase R&D spending after two years by approximately 13 percent using the estimates in Table 5(a) or 8 percent using the estimates in Table 6.

The long-run estimates based on these coefficients are larger, because of the multiplier implied by the lagged R&D coefficient in either version of the model. Unfortunately, this multiplier also makes the estimates quite imprecise: the long-run price elasticity in Table 5(a) at the mean R&D investment rate of 0.22 is $-2.0(0.8)$, and for Table 6 it is $-2.7(0.8)$. These estimates imply that a permanent R&E tax credit of 0.05 would be followed by permanent increases in R&D spending of anywhere from 10 to 15 percent *holding all else constant;* most of this increase would occur in the first three or four years of the credit. This estimate should be viewed with caution, because it may not be appropriate to extrapolate the relatively fragile linearized R&D investment demand equations to changes of this order of magnitude. Even though the marginal product of R&D capital has not entered the relationship significantly in Tables 5(a) and 5(b), we might still expect diminishing returns to play a role with changes on the order of 15 percent.

VI. DISCUSSION AND CONCLUSION

The GAO study (1989) estimated that the R&E tax credit stimulated between $1 billion and $2.5 billion dollars additional spending on research at a cost in foregone revenue of approximately $7 billion dollars during the 1981–1985 period. Baily and Lawrence (1992) obtained much higher estimates using aggregate data, averaging about $2.8 billion (1982 dollars) per year from 1982 to 1989. The present study shows that the earlier GAO estimates and other studies cited may have understated the benefits of the tax credit, and that the Baily and Lawrence estimates may be closer to the truth. I estimate that the additional spending stimulated in the short run was about $2 billion (1982 dollars) per year, while the foregone tax revenue was about $1 billion (1982 dollars) per year.[21] However, it needs to be kept firmly in mind that my tax data estimates are not likely to be as good as those constructed using IRS data, and that it might be worthwhile to update earlier studies that made use of these confidential data. Still, the numbers reported here do suggest that the credit is now having an impact, after a somewhat slow beginning.

If we accept the evidence that the R&E tax credit has increased the publicly reported R&D spending of U.S. manufacturing firms, there remains the question of whether this R&D spending truly reflects increased spending of the sort envisioned by Congress (research and experimentation in the laboratory or technological sense), or merely a relabeling of related expenses as research, and an increase in such expenses as new-product-related market research, etc. Answering this question is beyond the scope of either this study or the data now available. However, there is some evidence on the topic: in the early years of the credit, in particular, the IRS frequently (in more than half the cases) audited the credit claimed, with differing outcomes for the firms. A survey of IRS agents conducted by GAO provides evidence on this question (GAO, 1989). Although firms undoubtedly tried to claim some unqualified expenditures under the credit, the total amounts disallowed remain fairly small. In addition, there has always been an incentive to relabel investment expenses as R&D in the tax system, and this type of relabeling is already in the base level of R&D from which the incremental effect is calculated. For both these reasons, it seems likely that a large share of the reported increase in R&D in response to the tax credit is real, rather than spurious.

The main contribution of this paper is to confirm that the R&D spending of a firm does respond to financial incentives on the margin, al-

---

[21] These estimates are obtained by simulation at the individual firm level and then adding up the numbers, so that they reflect the heterogeneity inherent in the data. Previous studies have relied on estimates evaluated at the aggregate level, which may not give a completely accurate picture in the presence of significant nonlinearities. Because of the redesign of the credit in 1990 and 1991, for these years the R&D spending induced by the tax credit appears to be even higher, on the order of 5 billion per year. This number is almost too large to be credible (it is about 10 percent of R&D spending), and deserves further investigation as more data become available.

though the response is greatly dampened by the long-run nature of such investment. Together with the initial defects in the credit design, the high adjustment costs of R&D and learning by firms are probably the reason that the response appears to have been slightly larger in the latter half of the 1980s. In addition, two points about R&D tax policy and tax policy in general that have emerged here should be underlined: first, it may not be possible to achieve a long-term investment strategy with a short-term tax policy. Second, tax instruments cannot be viewed in isolation; it is important to look at the whole corporate tax system as it impinges on the activity in question when evaluating its effects. In the case of R&D, the interaction of the foreign tax credit, the R&E tax credit, and the AMT deserve further study, and can conceivably lead to quite perverse investment incentives. Of course, combining both these bits of wisdom into action may be an impossible task!

REFERENCES

Altshuler, Rosanne (1988). "A Dynamic Analysis of the Research and Experimentation Credit." *National Tax Journal* 41, 453–466.

———, and Alan J. Auerbach (1990). "The Significance of Tax Law Asymmetries: An Empirical Investigation." *Quarterly Journal of Economics* 105, 63–86.

Arrow, Kenneth J. (1962). "Economic Welfare and the Allocation of Resources to Invention." In *The Rate and Direction of Inventive Activity*. Richard Nelson, ed. Princeton, NJ: Princeton University Press.

Auerbach, Alan J. (1984). "Taxes, Firm Financial Policy, and the Cost of Capital: An Empirical Analysis." *Journal of Public Economics* 23, 27–57.

Baily, Martin Neil, and Robert Z. Lawrence. (1987). "Tax Policies for Innovation and Competitiveness." Washington, DC: Study commissioned by the Council on Research and Technology. Photocopied.

———, and ——— (1992). "Tax Incentives for R&D: What Do the Data Tell Us?" Washington, DC: Study commissioned by the Council on Research and Technology. Photocopied.

Berger, Philip G. (1992). "Explicit and Implicit Tax Effects of the R&D Tax Credit." Wharton School, University of Pennsylvania. Photocopied.

Bernstein, Jeffrey L., and M. Ishaq Nadiri (1986). "Financing and Investment in Plant and Equipment and Research and Development." In *Prices, Competition, and Equilibrium*. M. H. Pesaran and R. E. Quandt, eds., 233–248. Oxford: Philip Allan; Totowa, NJ: Barnes and Noble.

———, and ——— (1988). "Rates of Return on Physical and R&D Capital and Structure of Production Process: Cross Section and Time Series Evidence." National Bureau of Economic Research Working Paper No. 2570.

———, and ——— (1989). "Research and Development and Intra-industry Spillovers: An Empirical Application of Dynamic Duality." *Review of Economic Studies* 56, 249–269.

Carlson, George (1981). "Tax Policy toward Research and Development." U.S. Dept. of Treasury, Office of Tax Analysis Paper No. 45.

Collins, Eileen L. (ed.) 1982. "Tax Policy and Investment in Innovation (A Colloquium)." National Science Foundation, PRA Report 83-1.

———— (1983). "An Early Assessment of Three R&D Tax Incentives Provided by the Economic Recovery Tax Act of 1981." National Science Foundation, PRA Report 83-7 (April 1983).

Dasgupta, Partha, and Joseph Stiglitz (1980). "Uncertainty, Industrial Structure, and the Speed of R&D." *Bell Journal of Economics* 11, 1–28.

Eisner, Robert, Steven H. Albert, and Martin A. Sullivan (1984). "The New Incremental Tax Credit for R&D: Incentive or Disincentive?" *National Tax Journal* 37, 171–183.

Fazzari, Steven M., R. Glenn Hubbard, and Bruce C. Petersen (1988). "Financing Constraints and Corporate Investment." *Brookings papers on Economic Activity* 1988, 1, 271–283.

Fullerton, Don, and Andrew B. Lyon (1988). "Tax Neutrality and Intangible Capital." In *Tax Policy and the Economy.* Lawrence H. Summers, ed., vol. 2, pp. 63–88.

Griliches, Zvi (1979). "Issues in Assessing the Contribution of R&D to Productivity Growth." *Bell Journal of Economics* 10, 92–116.

———— (1991). "The Search for R&D Spillovers." National Bureau of Economic Research Working Paper No. 3768.

Hall, Bronwyn H. (1990a). "The Manufacturing Sector Master File: 1959–1987." National Bureau of Economic Research Working Paper No. 3366.

———— (1990b). "The Value of Intangible Corporate Assets: An Empirical Study of Tobin's Q." University of California at Berkeley and the National Bureau of Economic Research. Photocopied.

———— (1991). "Firm-Level Investment with Liquidity Constraints: What Can the Euler Equations Tell Us?" University of California at Berkeley and the National Bureau of Economic Research. Photocopied.

———— (1992). "Investment and R&D at the Firm Level: Does the Source of Financing Matter?" National Bureau of Economic Research Working Paper No. 4096.

————, Zvi Griliches, and Jerry A. Hausman (1986). "Patents and R&D: Is There a Lag?" *International Economic Review* 27, 265–283.

————, and Fumio Hayashi (1988). "Research and Development as an Investment." National Bureau of Economic Research Working Paper No. 2973.

Himmelberg, Charles P., and Bruce C. Petersen (1990). "R&D and Internal Finance: A Panel Study of Small Firms in High-Tech Industries." Federal Reserve Bank of Chicago. Photocopied.

Hines, James R. (1992). "On the Sensitivity of R&D to Delicate Tax Changes: The Case of U.S. Multinationals." In *International Taxation.* Alberto Giovannini, R. Glenn Hubbard, and Joel Slemrod, eds. Chicago: Chicago University Press (forthcoming).

Lach, Shaul, and Mark Schankerman (1989). "Dynamics of R&D Investment in the Scientific Sector." *Journal of Political Economy* 91, 880–904.

Levin, Richard C., Alvin Klevorick, Richard Nelson, and Sidney G. Winter (1989). *Brookings Papers on Economic Activity (Micro):* ————.

Lyon, Andrew B. (1991). *Economic Effects of the Corporate Alternative Minimum Tax.* Monograph Series on Tax and Environmental Policies and U.S. Economic Growth. Washington, D.C.: American Council for Capital Formation Center for Policy Research.

Mansfield, Edwin (1986). "The R&D Tax Credit and Other Technology Policy Issues." *American Economic Review* 76, 190–194.

National Science Board. 1991. *Science and Engineering Indicators*. Washington, DC: Superintendent of Documents.

Pakes, Ariel, and Mark Schankerman (1984). "The Rate of Obsolescence of Patents, Research Gestation Lags, and the Private Rate of Return to Research Resources." In *R&D, Patents, and Productivity*. Zvi Griliches, ed. Chicago: University of Chicago Press.

Poterba, James, and Lawrence H. Summers (1985). "The Economic Effects of Dividend Taxation." In *Recent Advances in Corporate Finance*. Edward I. Altman and Marti G. Subrahmanyam, eds. Homewood, Ill: Richard D. Irwin.

Roberts, Russell D. (1987). "Financing Public Goods." *Journal of Political Economy* 95, 420–437.

Standard and Poor (1992). Compustat Industrial and OTC Annual and Research Files. New York.

U.S. Congress (1986). *Tax Reform Act of 1986*, Report of the Committee on Finance, U.S. Senate, No. 99–313.

———— (1991). *Factors Affecting the International Competitiveness of the United States."* Staff Report of the Joint Committee on Taxation. Washington, DC: U.S. Government Printing Office.

———— (1992). *Description and Analysis of Tax Provisions Expiring in 1992*. Staff Report of the Joint Committee on Taxation. Washington, DC: U.S. Government Printing Office.

U.S. Government, General Accounting Office (1989). *The Research Tax Credit Has Stimulated Some Additional Research Spending*. Washington, DC: Report GAO/GGD-89-114.

U.S. Government, Department of the Treasury (1983). *The Impact of the Section 861-8 Regulation on U.S. Research and Development*. Washington, DC (June 1983).

U.S. Government, Internal Revenue Service (1988). *Statistics on Income Corporation Source Book*. Washington, DC: Publication No. 1053.

APPENDIX: THE R&D INVESTMENT EQUATION UNDER UNCERTAINTY

Equation (9) in the body of the paper is used to estimate the demand for R&D investment given the tax price of R&D. This equation actually describes an equilibrium relationship between R&D performed in different periods as a function of changing tax prices, a relationship that holds conditionally on information available to the firm at the time it chooses its R&D policy. Thus, the appropriate method of estimation is instrumental variable (where the instruments are drawn from the information set of the firm at time t) rather than ordinary least squares. The problem of the firm is inherently subject to uncertainty about its own future demand and costs, and about future tax policy, but the model presented in the paper has abstracted from this uncertainty in order to simplify the presentation. This appendix describes the derivation of equation (9) from an expected dynamic profit maximization problem at the firm level.

The firm's problem is to choose an R&D policy to maximize the following expression:

$$E_t \sum_{s=0}^{\infty} (1 + r)^{-s} \Big\{ (1 - \tau)[S(G_{t+s}) - \Phi(R_{t+s}, G_{t+s})]$$

$$- h(R_{t+s}, R_{t+s-1}, R_{t+s-2}, R_{t+s-3}) \Big\}$$

subject to the capital accumulation constraint given in equation (2) of the paper. The function $h(.)$ represents the total after-tax cost of R&D performed this year; this cost is a function of R&D spending during the last three years because of the effect of the base R&D level on the tax credit which will be earned this year. The information set at time t includes the current capital stock G_t, the tax rate τ, the depreciation rate for R&D capital δ, the interest rate r, as well as all the past history of the firm, but not the tax parameters of the current R&D cost function h. When $h(.)$ is linear in R_t (the normal situation without the R&D tax credit) and under suitable convexity and concavity assumptions on $S(\cdot)$ and $\Phi(\cdot,\cdot)$, a solution to this model will exist.[1] With the R&D tax credit, however, h has a complex step function form:

$$
\begin{aligned}
h(R_t, R_{t-1}, R_{t-2}, R_{t-3}) &= (1 - \tau)R_t - \eta_t \rho_t(R_t - B_t) && \text{if } B_t < R_t < 2B_t \\
&= (1 - \tau)R_t && \text{if } R_t < B_t \\
&= (1 - \tau)R_t - \eta_t \rho_t(R_t/2) && \text{if } R_t > 2B_t
\end{aligned}
$$

where $B_t = (R_{t-1} + R_{t-2} + R_{t-3})/3$ is the base level of R&D expenditure.[2] η_t is the fraction of qualified expenditures and ρ_t is the statutory credit rate. Although it is not possible to solve the model completely in this case, the

---

[1] The alert reader will observe that some of the estimates in the paper imply an optimal R&D policy that may not satisfy the assumptions needed to guarantee that the problem does not blow up at infinity. Either the discount rate r must be large enough to prevent that from happening, or the optimal R&D trajectory must exhibit something less than pure random walk behavior in practice. The first differenced estimates suggest that this is indeed the case once we control for permanent unobserved differences across firms, but of course these estimates require that we give up any notion of a representative firm in our modeling.

[2] The exposition here is for the R&D tax credit which was in place for the 1982–1988 period. A similar analysis, suitably modified for changes in the tax code, applies for 1981 and 1989–1991.

Euler equation for optimal R&D investment is a slightly modified equation (5):

$$E_t \left\{ \frac{1-\delta}{1+r} [\frac{\theta_{t+1}}{1-\tau} + \Phi_R(t+1)] - [\frac{\theta_t}{(1-\tau)} + \Phi_R(t)] - \Phi_G(t) + S'(t) \right\} = 0$$

$\Phi_R(t)$ and $\Phi_G(t)$ denote the partials of the adjustment cost function with respect to R_t and G_t in an obvious notation. θ_t is the marginal cost of R&D investment at time t, including its effects on the future cost of R&D spending through the computation of the base:

$$\theta_t = \sum_{s=0}^{3} (1+r)^{-s} h_{s+1} (R_{t+s}, R_{t+s+1}, R_{t+s+2}, R_{t+s+3})$$

h_{s+1} denotes the partial derivative of the cost function $h(.)$ with respect to argument $(s+1)$. Equations (6) and (7) in the paper give the exact form of θ_t, derived from the expression for h given above.

To obtain the estimating equation actually used for the estimates in Tables 5a and 5b, I write the adjustment cost function as in equation (8) and the sales function as

$$S(G_t) = A\, G_t^{\gamma} \qquad 0 < \gamma < 1$$

where A contains all other inputs; if S is a Cobb-Douglas function of these inputs, and they are all variable (can be freely adjusted to optimal levels given G_t), then there is no loss of generality in suppressing the other inputs. Even if the firm is not a price-taker, so that sales are not directly proportional to output, this equation will remain appropriate if the demand function is constant elasticity.

The set of assumptions that justify the use of this equation are not realistic, but provide a simple first-order approximation to the problem in order to make it tractable. The most obvious weakness is the failure to treat ordinary investment in parallel with R&D, because it is both subject to adjustment costs and interacts with the output of research (Bernstein and Nadiri 1988, Hall and Hayashi 1988, Lach and Schankerman 1989); a full tax treatment of investment is beyond the scope of the present paper and is left to future work (and the past work of others).

Cobb-Douglas production together with equations (8) and the Euler equation given above yield the following version of equation (9):

$$E_t \left\{ \frac{1-\delta}{1+r} [\frac{\theta_{t+1}}{1-\tau} + \phi \frac{R_{t+1}}{G_{t+1}}] - [\frac{\phi_t}{(1-\tau)} + \phi \frac{R_t}{G_t}] + \frac{\phi}{2} (\frac{R_t}{G_t})^2 - \gamma \frac{S_t}{G_t} \right\} = 0$$

Because τ, r, and δ are known at time t, this equation can be written in the form actually estimated. Note that the appropriate instruments for expectational reasons are things that the firm knows at the beginning of period t, including those that will help predict the tax prices at t and $t + 1$. I have chosen a more restrictive set of instruments dated lag 2 and earlier because of the measurement error issues, but the law of iterated expectations means that my estimates will also be consistent.

WHAT DO WE KNOW ABOUT ENTERPRISE ZONES?

Leslie E. Papke
Michigan State University

EXECUTIVE SUMMARY

In the last decade, most states have targeted certain depressed areas for revitalization by providing a combination of labor and capital tax incentives to firms operating in an "enterprise zone" (EZ). Britain is also completing a federal program that designated zones for a ten-year period. These zone experiments can add to our understanding of the influence of tax policy on business investment, and provide insights into the design and implementation of federal programs with similar objectives. This paper summarizes the theory and empirical evidence on the operational success of these EZ programs.

Economic theory predicts that the effect of tax incentives on zone wages and employment will depend on the elasticity of supply of factors to the zone and on the elasticity of demand for zone output. For plausible parameter values, a labor subsidy or an equal-cost subsidy to zone capital and zone resident labor will raise zone wages. A capital subsidy alone may actually reduce zone wages. Employment effects are likely to be small if labor is inelastically supplied.

The British national EZ program was intended to promote new economic activity in vacant areas with little or no industry and few residents. Studies of this program found that between 50 and 80 percent of zone businesses were relocations, at an annual cost per job of approximately $15,000.

EZ programs at the state level, by contrast, have an explicit commu-

This paper was prepared for the NBER Conference on Tax Policy and the Economy in Washington, D.C., November 17, 1992. I thank Charley Ballard, Dan Hamermesh, Harry Holzer, Jim Papke, Jim Poterba, and Jeff Wooldridge for helpful comments.

nity revitalization focus and areas with relatively high unemployment and poverty rates are targeted. Estimates of the average cost per zone job in the United States range from $4,564 to $13,000 annually, and about $31,113 per zone resident job.

While there is much survey evidence on the states' experiences, relatively few studies have been able to address the question, how did zones perform relative to what would have been their performance in the absence of zone designation? Evidence on this issue is summarized for the state of Indiana, where the zone program appears to have increased inventory investment and reduced unemployment claims. But new evidence based on the 1990 Census of Population indicates that the economic well-being of zone residents in Indiana has not appreciably improved.

Enterprise zone programs are geographically targeted tax, expenditure, and regulatory inducements that have been part of subnational economic development strategy since the early 1980s. At least count, thirty-seven states and the District of Columbia have established some form of EZ initiative. While they differ in specifics, all the programs provide tax preferences to capital and/or labor and other development incentives in an attempt to induce investment expansion or location, and to enhance employment opportunities for residents in depressed areas.[1]

EZs have appeared in federal legislation on several occasions over the last decade, but there is currently no federal EZ program. The concept returned to national prominence most recently following the civil disturbances in Los Angeles in April and May 1992. The U.S. House of Representatives and Senate of the 103rd Congress adopted H.R. 11. It contained a pilot program to establish fifty EZs over a five-year period.[2] The tax incentives included a 50 percent reduction in capital gains taxes for profits from interests held in a zone for at least five years (the current maximum rate is 28 percent), a $20,000 immediate expense deduction for newly purchased capital equipment, a 15 percent credit on wages paid to zone residents with a cap of $3,000 per worker annually, and an annual deduction of up to $25,000 for purchases of stock in businesses investing in EZs, up to $250,000 for each person. President Bush vetoed the legislation on November 4, 1992.

EZs have been criticized on the grounds that they will be ineffective and inefficient in stimulating new economic activity. This criticism is part of a longstanding debate on the effects of intersite tax differentials on the

---

[1] Most EZs are designated in urban areas, but occasionally rural areas are selected. Federal legislation included rural areas as well. See Erickson and Friedman (1990).

[2] See Lavation and Miller (1992) and the Joint Committee on Taxation (1992) for a discussion of proposals in 1992.

location of capital investment. If any tax-induced investment only represents relocation from another state, then tax competition is a zero-sum game for the country as a whole. In addition, the preferential treatment of certain types of investment or employment within EZs may induce decisions that would be uneconomic in the absence of the tax incentives.

The concern with net capital investment may be less relevant for EZs because redistribution even within the state may be an end in itself.[3] If investment is relocated from local labor markets with low unemployment to local labor markets with higher unemployment, the incentives may generate efficiency gains for the economy as underutilized resources are tapped. Efficiency gains may also result if reductions in unemployment produce positive externalities such as reductions in social unrest.

It is also possible that, in addition to encouraging existing businesses to locate in particular geographic areas, the incentives may induce the creation of new businesses that would not otherwise have been started. Such new businesses could produce taxable profits and incomes that would reduce the revenue cost of the incentives.

The empirical evidence on the effect of differential state taxes on the location of industrial activity is mixed. Surveys of firm location have found that firms choose sites on the basis of primary locational factors (proximity to markets, labor costs, infrastructure, and utility costs), while tax cost differentials are influential at the margin when these other factors are similar at alternative sites. EZ tax incentives may have a greater influence across localities within a state than across states in a federal EZ program.

Recent econometric analyses have emphasized the importance of controlling for interstate differences in public service provision when one is estimating the effects of tax differentials. While low-tax jurisdictions directly reduce business costs, high-tax jurisdictions may have highly skilled workers and a high quality of public services, both of which indirectly reduce the costs of doing business. Using firm-level data, Bartik (1985) and L. Papke (1991a) find statistically significant elasticities of industrial activity with respect to state and local taxes.[4] These

---

[3] EZ investment may give individuals employment experience that enhances their long-run employability. Thus, even a relatively short-run economic development program may have long-run effects (see Bartik, 1991).

[4] Bartik finds an elasticity of -0.2 to -0.3 of new branch plants with respect to state corporate tax rates. L. Papke examines start-up firms in five manufacturing industries, and estimates elasticities with respect to combined federal, state, and local tax rates of -1.59 (furniture), -5.62 (communication equipment), and -15.7 (womens' outerwear). Additional examples on both sides of the issue include Carlton (1979), L. Papke (1987), and Bartik (1991). Carroll and Wasylenko (1990) review seventeen recent studies.

estimates suggest that EZ incentives might well generate new capital investment.

The experience and appraisal of EZs are the subject of this paper. The next section outlines a conceptual framework for analyzing the effects of an EZ program inside and outside zone boundaries. I present estimates of the percentage change in zone wages under several incentive scenarios. In section II, I discuss some methodological issues involved in measuring the success of an EZ program. The British EZ experiment is described in section III, and section IV surveys the state EZ programs in the United States. Section V focuses on the EZ program in Indiana. It is one of the oldest state programs and has been evaluated with a variety of types of data. New evidence is presented on the well-being of Indiana zone residents using 1980 and 1990 Census data. I briefly discuss the difficult issue of program cost effectiveness in section VI and conclude in section 7 with observations about a proposed federal program and some unresolved issues.

I. CONCEPTUAL FRAMEWORK

This section presents a theoretical framework for analyzing the effects of EZ incentives on zone wages and employment. First, the effects of EZ incentives on wages and employment inside the zone are analyzed in a partial equilibrium model. Estimates of changes in wages and employment for different EZ wage and capital subsidy packages are presented, and the major findings are summarized. Second, while zone tax incentives are confined to zone firms and the factors they employ, the effects of the program may not be. The section concludes with a general overview of the implication of an EZ program for aggregate national employment and investment.

In brief, if zones are small relative to the rest of the economy, economic theory predicts that the effect on zone wages and employment will depend on the elasticity of supply of factors to the zone, and on the elasticity of demand for zone output. For plausible parameter values, a labor subsidy or an equal-cost subsidy to both zone capital and zone resident labor will raise zone wages. A capital subsidy alone may actually reduce zone wages. Employment effects are likely to be small if labor is inelastically supplied.

If zones are relatively large, and spillovers into the rest of the economy are considered, the effects are more difficult to predict. The net employment effects for the nation of a federal EZ program depend on parameters in both the zone and nonzone sectors of the economy: the relative size of the two sectors, the elasticity of substitution of factors in the two sectors, the elasticity of substitution of the zone and nonzone products in consumption, and the aggregate elasticities of supply of factors of production. The greater the number of areas designated EZs, the smaller the effects on zone wages. If capital is relatively fixed in the aggregate, as many empirical studies suggest, the net effect will be to relocate productive facilities inside the zone.

A. An Overview of the Model

The typical EZ program offers tax incentives that reduce the costs of businesses located in the zone. These benefits may include subsidies to capital or labor, or both, or a benefit related to total costs (an equal proportional subsidy for capital and labor). All these subsidies would tend to increase zone production—existing zone firms increase production, and new firms begin production in the zone. "New" zone firms may be start-up companies, but they may also be existing firms that relocate or expand into the zone. This output effect encourages firms to employ more of both labor and capital in the zone.

If only one of the factors is subsidized, or if one is tax-favored, a substitution effect accompanies the output effect. For example, a subsidy to labor alone lowers costs and increases output. This would increase the use of both capital and labor. In addition, the firm substitutes the subsidized labor for capital in its production process. In the case of a labor subsidy, this substitution effect reinforces the output effect and encourages increases in employment.

In the case of a capital subsidy, capital becomes relatively less expensive, and firms substitute away from labor and toward capital. While the output effect of a capital subsidy encourages firms to hire more of both labor and capital, the substitution effect causes firms to substitute capital for labor. A subsidy to capital promotes employment only through the output effect and may actually reduce employment if the substitution effect dominates.

The relative magnitudes of the output and substitution effects depend on the elasticity of demand for the product and the ease with which labor can be substituted for capital in the production process. In addition, the effect of either subsidy on wages and employment depends on the labor supply response. The relatively small labor supply elasticity that is suggested by most empirical evidence means that either subsidy would have a larger impact on zone wages than on zone employment.

B. Effects Inside the Zone

A partial equilibrium model of zone production (detailed in Appendix 1) is used to illustrate the effects of different EZ tax incentives on zone wages and employment.[5] Zone firms produce output with the labor of people living inside the zone (zone resident labor), with the labor of people who commute from outside the zone (nonzone resident labor), and capital. The model allows for two types of labor because many EZ programs restrict labor subsidies to zone residents. The two types of labor may have different supply elasticities. Capital is free to flow into the zone in response to the incentives (i.e., in infinitely elastic supply).[6]

The numerical estimates depend on the output (or product demand), substitution, and labor supply responses. If zone products are close substitutes for products produced outside of the zone, then the elasticity of demand for zone products will be relatively large. This would be typical of manufacturing products. However, surveys of zone firms suggest that much zone production is for a local market (trade and services, e.g.), and heterogeneous enough to have a rather small elasticity of demand.[7]

In Indiana, for example, 74 percent of total receipts of firms participating in the program is derived from sources inside the zone. The 1990 Census data for Indiana indicate that while 36 percent of zone workers are employed in manufacturing, 60 percent are employed in a service industry. Consequently, smaller demand elasticities may be typical of most zone businesses; calculations are presented for a range of elasticities.

For a cost-minimizing firm, the factor substitution elasticity is the percentage change in the ratio of capital to labor divided by the percentage change in the ratio of rate of return on capital to the wage rate. A high substitution elasticity indicates that it is relatively easy to substitute one input for the other. The common Cobb–Douglas assumption of unitary factor substitution elasticity is used in these calculations, as suggested by long-run estimates.[8]

---

[5] The "spatial mismatch" literature provides an alternative approach to modeling EZs. But this literature focuses on the movement of people and firms to the suburbs as the cause of employment problems for those who continue to live in the inner cities, especially blacks (see Holzer, 1991); it may be less relevant to small EZs within a larger metropolitan area.

[6] Capital will flow into the zone until the rate of return, net of the subsidy, returns to its original level.

[7] These smaller trade and service firms are often the specific target of zone incentives. See, for example, the statement of Fred T. Goldberg, Jr., assistant secretary (Tax Policy), Department of the Treasury (1992). The emphasis on small firm job creation is based on Birch's (1981) much-popularized finding that small businesses were the source of most new job opportunities. Subsequent research indicates that the true proportion of jobs generated by smaller firms is close to their actual share of the workforce (Armington and Odle, 1982; Brown, Hamilton, and Medoff, 1990).

[8] See Ballard, Fullerton, Shoven, and Whalley (1985) for a discussion of the range of estimates.

A high labor supply elasticity means that the number of people willing to work rises substantially with a small increase in the wage rate. Empirical evidence suggests that overall labor supply response is small.[9] However, the labor of disadvantaged or unskilled workers may be more elastically supplied, so again a range of labor supply elasticities is included.[10]

Some EZ programs distinguish between types of employees. Zone labor subsidies might apply, for example, to any worker employed in the zone, or the subsidy may apply only to the wages of zone residents. Both types of labor subsidies are included in the model in Appendix 2.

I illustrate three types of zone incentive packages below: a subsidy to zone wages, a subsidy to zone capital, and an equal-cost subsidy to zone labor and zone capital. The major findings are summarized here:

- A subsidy to all labor employed in the zone always increases zone wages (and employment). The effect on the wage is larger, the larger is the elasticity of demand (in absolute value), and the smaller is the elasticity of labor supply. If labor supply is completely inelastic, a 1 percent increase in the wage subsidy raises the wage by 1 percent regardless of the product demand elasticity. A labor subsidy targeted to zone residents increases zone wages by more than a general labor subsidy.
- A capital subsidy reduces zone wages at low elasticities of product demand and low labor supply elasticities. Even for products with relatively elastic demand, the increase in the zone wage is much smaller from a 10 percent capital subsidy than with a 10 percent labor subsidy.
- Most EZ programs involve a subsidy to both capital and labor. An equal-cost subsidy to all labor and capital employed in the zone will also reduce zone wages if the demand for the zone product is completely inelastic.[11] At higher product demand elasticities, an equal-cost subsidy to both factors increases zone wages by from 0.33 to 1.54 percent. When zone residents are targeted, that is, only their wages are subsidized, an equal-cost subsidy has a substantially larger effect.[12] The estimated increase in zone wages ranges from 2.5 to 5.2 percent.
- The changes in the price of capital and labor outside the zone will be

[9] See Hamermesh (1993) and Killingsworth (1983).

[10] Juhn, Murphy, and Topel (1991) estimate a labor supply elasticity of 0.4 for men in the lowest decile of the wage distribution.

[11] Wage income is assumed to be three times the size of capital income, so the rate of wage subsidy is one-third that of the capital subsidy. An equal cost subsidy is, for example, a 1 percent subsidy on capital and a 0.33 percent subsidy to labor. See Appendix 1 for details.

[12] An equal cost subsidy when capital's share is 0.25 and zone-resident labor share is 0.05 is a 1 percent capital subsidy and a 5 percent labor subsidy.

small. However, the total effect on nonzone capital or labor returns will not be.[13] For example, Bradford (1978) illustrates that a subsidy to capital in a small jurisdiction raises the gross (and net) return to capital outside of the zone only marginally. But this small increase accrues to all capital in the rest of the economy. Thus, the total effect of the EZ policy on the return to capital is the product of the change in the return to capital (which is small) times the total amount of affected capital (which is large). The total effect on capital income will be of the same order of magnitude as the sum of EZ subsidies provided.

C. *General Equilibrium Effects*

The previous partial equilibrium discussion does not allow for feedback effects from nonzone production and nonzone factors of production. If zones are small relative to the rest of the economy, as in state programs and proposed federal legislation, then the feedback effects will be negligible. Gravelle (1992) illustrates that as zones become larger, however, general equilibrium effects should be considered.[14]

The net employment effects will depend on the relative size of the zone and nonzone sectors, the elasticity of substitution of factors in the two sectors, the elasticity of substitution of the zone and nonzone products in consumption, and the aggregate elasticities of supply of factors of production.[15] Gravelle (1992) illustrates the importance of the size of the zone in a general equilibrium analysis of a capital subsidy. The major conclusions follow:

- As the number of zones (or fraction of initial output eligible for zone incentives) becomes larger, the impact of the subsidy on zone wages and employment becomes smaller. In the limit, if the entire country is designated a zone, a capital subsidy has no effect on zone wages. When the capital subsidy does increase wages, each additional zone reduces the benefits to existing zones in direct proportion.
- Nonzone wages and employment will be affected by a zone subsidy to

[13] Partial equilibrium analysis assumes that zones are small relative to the rest of the economy. Capital is completely elastically supplied to the zone with no or little change in the price of capital. Table A-1 illustrates that the change in nonzone wages is small.

[14] While in the partial equilibrium case, capital is elastically supplied to the zone; in this static general equilibrium framework, capital is fixed in the aggregate. Gravelle cites several empirical studies that fail to find a statistically significant savings response to changes in the after-tax return to capital. See Ballard (1993) for a review of the evidence.

[15] Gravelle (1992) simplifies the analysis by assuming certain parameter values for these elasticities. In McLure's (1970) general equilibrium analysis of the locational effects of tax policy, he substitutes parameters of interjurisdictional mobility for the traditional Harberger assumptions that both factors are completely mobile.

capital. Whatever the percentage increase in zone wages and employment, wages and employment outside of the zone will fall by an equal percentage. Aggregate employment in the country will be unaffected.
- The same general outcome would occur with a general equilibrium model of a labor subsidy. The more areas that are designated zones, the smaller the effects on zone wages and employment. With very mobile labor, the result would be to relocate production locations, with little effect on relative incomes. The primary effect would be inefficiency in the location of investment.

II. HOW IS ZONE SUCCESS MEASURED?

Zone evaluation depends primarily on two factors—program goals and the nature of the available data. Often, the legislation is unclear about whether the goal of the zone program is to increase net employment or investment. Some have argued that these areas are in such economic distress that maintaining the existing levels of employment and investment are desirable EZ goals. The studies reviewed here typically assume that the intent of the legislation is to create new jobs in the zone, not merely relocate jobs from outside of the zone. These jobs may be full-time, part-time, or of limited duration, because the legislation typically does not specify the type of duration of job it is intended to create.

In practice, zone success is frequently measured by the amount of investment undertaken after the designation, the increase in the number of firms in the zone, and the change in zone employment. Cost-effectiveness is measured by direct spending and foregone revenue per job created (or, if the goal of the program is zone resident employment, cost per zone resident job).

Determining which jobs were relocated from outside of the zone presents a practical difficulty. This problem could be addressed with more detailed data (tracking employer identification numbers, e.g.). The key methodological issue is how to separate the effects of zone designation from jobs and investment that arise from other factors—for example, general upturns in the economy or in the area surrounding the zone. Alternatively, which of the measured changes in jobs and investment are attributable solely to the zone program?

Survey or case study methodologies provide useful information on zone participation, but they cannot definitively answer this question. Firm managers' estimates of net job creation or investment are subjective, and even candid managers may have difficulty attributing a certain number of new jobs to zone incentives alone. Surveys of zone administrators are even more problematic, because the responses may be self-serving.

Positive survey results alone are not enough to declare a program a success, because the difference between a success (net job creator) and a failure (relocated jobs) may reflect differences in the relative candor of the respondents.

Econometric analysis is better suited to performing the "but for the zone" experiment. If the zone sites were randomly selected, the effect of the program could be measured by comparing the performance of the experimental and control groups. Actual EZ designation, of course, is based on economic performance, so the data are nonexperimental. This sample selection problem can be addressed with a variety of techniques.[16]

But econometric analyses of zone success face a practical difficulty. Conventional economic data are not available by zone because most zone boundaries are drawn solely for the purposes of the program. In most states, zones do not coincide with census tracts or taxing jurisdictions. As a result, zone areas cannot be pinpointed in standard data collections. While econometric analysis can address the sample selection problem, it must contend with a geographic mismatch problem.

In the next few sections, I present survey and econometric evidence on zone success in Britain and in the states. The British national program was intended to generate new industrial activity in areas with little or no industry and few residents. State EZ programs, by contrast, typically designate zones in areas with relatively high unemployment rates where the residents meet some predetermined poverty threshold. Thus, state EZs have an explicit community revitalization focus.

III. THE BRITISH EXPERIENCE

In 1981, two years into the Thatcher government, the United Kingdom designated eleven areas as EZs, expanding to twenty-four in total in 1983.[17] The zones were small relative to U.S. zones, ranging in size from 100 to 900 acres, and consisting of vacant, unoccupied, or deteriorating industrial land within an economically declining community. In contrast to the state zones in the United States, British zone boundaries excluded both existing business and residential areas. The U.K. program focused almost exclusively on industrial development—community development was not a specific goal of the program.

The U.K. program included a four-part, ten-year incentive package:

---

[16] See L. Papke (1991b) for a discussion of alternative estimation techniques.

[17] Hall (1977) reportedly introduced the original notion of geographic areas free of normal government regulatory policies and import duties ("freeports") in a 1977 address to the Royal Town Planning Institute.

- an exemption from local property taxes on industrial and commercial property,
- a 100 percent allowance (deduction) from corporation and income taxes for capital expenditures on industrial and commercial buildings,
- an exemption of sales of undeveloped lands from the Development Land Tax, and
- reductions in administrative requirements such as planning permission and government statistical reporting for a ten-year period.

The British program also included public ownership of facilities. Significant public-sector involvement was a characteristic of a number of zones even before designation, such as direct land ownership or nationalized corporate ownership of property or buildings. For example, in the zone in Swansea, 450 acres of derelict land were reclaimed and new infrastructure provided before designation.[18] In Swansea alone, public ownership of vacant land rose from 47 percent in 1981 to 89 percent in 1986, and public investment over this period, excluding the EZ incentives of rates relief and capital allowance, totalled £16 million.

The British experience has been evaluated in a number of studies, which include government-funded monitoring reports (Roger Tym and Partners, 1984) and private evaluations of specific zones.[19] Most are detailed firm level surveys and personal interviews with entrepreneurs both inside and outside the zone. While different researchers employed different measures of zone success, there is remarkable agreement across studies that the British zone program has failed in its goal of generating *new* industrial activity.

The Tym report covers the initial eleven zones. There was a substantial increase in industrial activity in the zone—by 1987, over 4,300 firms were operating in the zones. However, the Tym report indicates that the primary effect of the zone was intrametropolitan relocation—86 percent of firms relocating in the zone were from the same county, and their managers reported that they considered moving to the zone prior to the EZ program.

The survey found no differences between employment generation, investment activities, or production of companies in zones versus outside the zones. The (surprisingly candid) managers of zone firms responded via the survey that only about 25 percent of new jobs in the zone were attributed to zone designation.

[18] See Bromley and Morgan (1985) and Bromley and Rees (1988) for details of the Swansea enterprise zone.

[19] See B. Rubin and Richards (1993) for a detailed comparison of British and several U.S. state EZ programs.

Other studies of individual U.K. zones report similar findings.[20] Summarizing, it appears that between 50 and 70 percent of zone firms represented relocations. Zone firm managers reported that the property tax incentive (exemption) was the only significant incentive provided by the zone program, and frequently ranked this factor third in importance after site characteristics and market access.

While the British EZ program had no explicit labor subsidy, there were effects on zone employment. About 13,000 out of 63,300 zone jobs were thought to represent net new employment.[21] None of the studies includes a figure for disadvantaged workers.

Schwarz and Volgy (1988) estimate that the cost per new job between 1981 and 1986 for the original eleven zones was approximately £45,000, or $67,000. A follow-up government-sponsored study to the Tym report considers job creation in the local economy surrounding all twenty-four of the U.K. zones and estimates the cost at £23,000 per new job.[22] This estimate includes jobs created in the local economy as well as inside the zone. Using this figure, Rubin and Richards (1992) calculate the cost of a new zone job to be £50,000 or $75,000, or between $13,400 and $15,000 on an annual basis. The government study continues to find that over 70 percent of jobs created in the zone were relocations from outside of the zone.

The shift of firms into zones did have an effect on land prices. Erickson and Syms (1985) identify a boundary effect on the local property market from zone designation. They find that a moderate increase in the price of zone industrial land accompanied the slight increase in business development activity in the two zones they examine. Thus, capitalization of zone incentives into zone land prices came at the expense of property bordering the zone where land values declined.

Citing the uniformity of evidence indicating that relocations were the source of activity in the zones, the British government decided to phase out the EZ program. The tax incentives for the initial zones expired in 1991, and the last two zones designated will expire in 1999.

IV. STATE ENTERPRISE ZONES

While there is no operational federal EZ program, thirty-seven states have enacted EZ programs as part of their economic development policies. They differ widely in purpose, coverage, and incentive provisions.

---

[20] See Shutt (1984), Barnes and Preston (1985), Thomas and Bromley (1987), Talbot (1988), and Schwarz and Volgy (1988).

[21] Great Britain Department of the Environment (1986).

[22] PA Cambridge Economics (1987).

For example, Michigan has only one zone, while Louisiana has over 800. Most programs offer a combination of capital investment and employment incentives with generally more resources allocated to investment than employment incentives. Investment incentives include the exemption of business-related purchases from state sales and use taxes, investment tax credits, or corporate income or unemployment tax rebates. Labor subsidies include employer tax credits for all new hires, or zone resident new hires, employee income tax credits, or job training tax credits. Some states also assist firms financially with investment funds or industrial development bonds.

Unlike in the United Kingdom, the criteria for eligibility in the states depend upon zone population characteristics. These include comparative unemployment rates, population levels and trends, poverty status, median incomes, and percentage of welfare recipients.

Typical U.S. zone characteristics are reported in a comprehensive survey by Erickson and Friedman (1990, 1991a, 1991b). Most zones experience negative population growth prior to designation and have unemployment rates well above the state and national averages. Unemployment in the adjacent communities at the time of zone designation is also generally above these averages. Median family income in the zones surveyed in 1979 was less than 60 percent of the comparable national figure, and the average proportion of families in poverty was over three times the national mean and 70 percent higher than that in the general community. Minority residents comprise 45 percent of the typical EZ population, about double the proportion in the larger community and nearly three times the national average.

Zones are relatively small in area and population size. The sample mean resident population is approximately 14,500, but the median is 4,500 persons. The median zone size is 1.8 square miles, and 75 percent of the zones contain less than 5.6 square miles, although the mean is 25.6. Zones generally have different land-use patterns than their surrounding communities. The average share of industrial land (18.1 percent) is over twice as large as in the host community, and the share of commercial land (15.3 percent) is about 70 percent higher than in their host communities.

A survey of businesses located in EZs by the Department of Housing and Urban Development found that only 9.1 percent had relocated from outside the zone.[23] An additional 7.5 percent of the business surveyed were branches of nonzone firms, 26.4 percent were new businesses, 2.2 percent were businesses that reportedly had been kept from closing, and

---

[23] See Erickson, Friedman, and McCluskey (1989).

54.8 percent of zone investments represented expansion of existing zone businesses. The study was not able to determine, with the exception of the firms that would have closed, whether zone investments would have occurred in the absence of zone subsidies.

State EZ programs have been evaluated and compared in a number of studies. As in the United Kingdom, most studies analyze survey responses of managers of zone firms. Program specifics and findings vary widely—Appendix 1 lists evaluations of individual state programs and multiple-state comparisons. The scope and quality of these evaluations vary.

Rather than examining the diverse survey data from a large number of programs, the remainder of this paper focuses on a program for which there is both detailed longitudinal survey evidence and econometric analysis of conventional data. Like many state programs, the Indiana EZ program includes both subsidies to capital and labor. It has been in operation since 1984—long enough to generate several years of post-EZ data. Several of the survey studies mentioned earlier have concluded that Indiana's program is one of the most successful.[24]

V. THE INDIANA ENTERPRISE ZONE PROGRAM

Initially, areas in six Indiana central cities were designated as EZs in 1984; subsequently, others were added to bring the current total to fifteen. Each zone has a ten-year duration, subject to renewal. Firms participating in the program have been required to report credits claimed, employment and wage figures, origin of receipts and the like, to the Indiana Enterprise Zone Board beginning in 1986.

To qualify for consideration and possible designation, the area must have an unemployment rate at least 1.5 times the average statewide unemployment rate, and a resident household poverty rate at least 25 percent above the U.S. poverty level. Its resident population must be between 2,000 and 8,000 persons and its geographic area between 0.75 and three square miles, all with a continuous boundary. While there is no explicit statement of its goals in the original legislation, presumably the intention of Indiana's program is to increase employment, investment, and the economic well-being of zone residents. The employment tax credits provided are similar to those in other states, but the capital incentives are unusual, as explained below. The tax incentives included in the Indiana EZ program are the following:

---

[24] See Wilder and B. Rubin (1988) and Sheldon and Elling (1989).

- A tax credit against local property tax liability equal to 100 percent of the property tax imposed on all inventories located in the zone.
- A total exemption from the corporate gross income (receipts) tax of all incremental income (receipts) derived from sources within the zone after the designation base year; however, if the sale giving rise to the incremental income is outside of the zone, it is ineligible for the exemption.[25]
- A tax credit of 5 percent of interest income received from loans to zone businesses and residents for residential or business real property improvement. (Existing loans qualify for the credit, as well as new loans, and lenders claiming the credit need not be located in the zone.)
- A tax credit for employers hiring zone residents equal to 10 percent of wages with a ceiling of $1,500 per qualified employee.
- Zone residents are allowed an income tax deduction equal to one-half of their qualified adjusted gross income with a ceiling of $7,500.[26]

Indiana's employment tax credits are typical of other EZ programs. The labor incentives are targeted at zone residents. The property tax credit will be valuable to both profitable and unprofitable (i.e., non-taxpaying) firms alike. However, because the dollar amounts of both the tax credit for firms and the deduction for employees are capped and not indexed for inflation, these incentives have lost about 20 percent of their value since adoption.[27]

Like other zone programs, the value of the tax preferences is tilted heavily toward capital investment. Indiana's most valuable investment incentive from a tax savings standpoint, the inventory tax credit, is an unusual mechanism for increasing investment. First, most states do not include inventories in the base of the business tangible personal property tax.[28] Eight states do not tax any tangible personal property, and

[25] Indiana's gross income or receipts tax is a tax on instate receipts. Corporations pay the greater of this tax and the corporate net income tax (where profits are allocated to the state based on the conventional three-factor formula). Typically, a small firm will pay the gross income tax because no deductions are taken in computing tax liability. Eligibility for the exemption requires that the enterprise be legally organized as a corporation; sole proprietorships, partnerships, and Subchapter S corporations do not qualify because they are not liable for the gross income tax.

[26] A sixth incentive provides an income tax credit of up to 30 percent to individual investors for the purchase of stock in start-up or expanding zone businesses. There are no data indicating that this incentive has ever been used.

[27] This deterioration in value may explain, in part, the low participation rate in the employment subsidy. Although 2,779 zone residents were employed by 949 registered zone businesses in 1988, only seventy-seven firms (less than 3 percent) claimed wage credits for employing qualified zone residents. See J. Papke (1990).

[28] Unlike machinery and equipment, inventories are not depreciable.

another twenty-five states specifically exempt inventories. Like Indiana, neighboring Ohio and Kentucky also tax inventories.

Second, zone programs in other states typically provide incentives for investment in machinery or equipment rather than inventories. U.S. inventories are sharply procyclical, and it is not clear what a large stock of site-specific inventories represents. Further, the stock of inventories held (whether inputs, good in process, or finished goods) will vary with the production process of the firm. The value of the credit will also vary by type of firm.[29] J. Papke and I (1992) calculate, for example, that the inventory tax credit raises net profit rates (after-tax rates of return) by from 1 to 7 percent, depending on the local property tax rate and industry type.

Third, the inventory tax credit applies to the total stock of inventories in each tax year, not just to incremental values.[30] The 1988 total direct budgetary cost (revenue foregone) of the Indiana EZ tax preferences amounted to $13.6 million, of which 84 percent was attributable to the inventory property tax credit.

At a minimum, the inventory tax credit enhances the cash flow for firms that hold inventories. It will also increase profits (decrease losses) of zone firms and may compensate them for the noncapitalized profit-reducing characteristics of their EZ location (e.g., crime). Because the price of holding inventories falls, a zone firm will find it profitable to hold a higher level of inventories than if it were a nonzone firm. This may increase economic activity in the zone and stimulate investment in machinery and equipment that would not have occurred in the absence of the program (particularly if production for inventories takes place in the zone).

The characteristics of Indiana's zone firms and their employees have been detailed in five consecutive years of registration data. These characteristics are briefly described in the following.

A. An Overview of Zone Participants

The number and characteristics of participating firms have not changed much over the life of the program.[31] The number of participating firms averaged about 1,000 each year. Retailers constitute the largest single

[29] For example, instrument manufacturers and retailers hold about 25 percent of total capital in inventories, compared to only 5 percent for manufacturers of petroleum products and providers of business services. These fractions are calculated from the Internal Revenue Service's *Source Book of Statistics of Income,* 1988.

[30] In 1991, the Indiana House Ways and Means Committee voted to eliminate the inventory tax credit. See Carlson, (1991).

[31] J. Papke (1990) summarizes the first three years of data. The registration data from 1989 and 1990 are presented in preliminary form by Rowings, Powers, and Sigalow (1992).

group, accounting for about one-third of all participants. Business and professional service enterprises ranked second (about 30 percent), followed by manufacturers (about 19 percent) and wholesale distributors (13 percent). Eighty percent of firms are organized as corporations (36 percent of those as S-corporations). About two-thirds of the participants have fewer than twenty employees.

Firms reported 2,897 new jobs created in 1988, with 14.7 percent of those jobs going to zone residents. The preliminary 1990 data indicate that zone residents comprised 4.1 percent of total zone employment, and 19 percent of all new zone jobs. On average, the zone residents were paid about half as much as the other employees (between $7,000 and $8,000). The average tax saving per participating firm was $13,933 in 1988. The average tax preference increases with the size of the business. For example, the tax savings for the smallest firm (fewer than eleven employees) averaged $4,106, while the largest firms (over 100 employees) claimed $98,493 on average. Manufacturing firms accounted for over 50 percent of the total tax saving.

B. The Employment and Investment Effects of Zone Designation

This section summarizes an econometric analysis of the investment and employment effects of the Indiana EZ program. Sample selection issues are discussed. This section also illustrates the types of equations that can be estimated to isolate the effects caused by an EZ program alone.

L. Papke (1991b) analyzes the effects of the Indiana EZ program on investment and unemployment. I include several specifications designed to separate the effects of zone designation from other influences. I examine two types of capital investment—inventories, which are targeted by the investment incentives, and investment in machinery and equipment, which would likely coincide with increased economic development. The investment data are derived from the tax records of the taxing districts surrounding the zone.[32]

Labor market effects of zone designation are estimated with data on annual unemployment claims. Because one unemployment office typically serves an entire city, the geographical mismatch problem discussed in section III is more severe for the unemployment claims data. But the data will reflect any spillover effects from the zone into the community's labor market.

As discussed in section II, the question of EZ effectiveness could be

---

[32] A taxing district is a geographic area within which property is taxed by the same taxing unit and is taxed at the same total rate. It is generally smaller in area than a township and is approximately the same size as an EZ.

easily addressed if the programs were administered as traditional experiments. But the data are nonexperimental because actual EZ designation is based on economic performance. Nevertheless, if one controls for sample selection, the data can be used to address the counterfactual question, how did zones perform relative to what their performance would have been in the absence of zone designation?

The correct estimation technique for an experiment is determined by the assumptions about the nature of the data. If zones are selected randomly, the effects of the program are consistently estimated by a cross-section comparison of means between the control and experimental groups. No time-series variation is necessary. Alternatively, if data are available only for the experimental group, but are available both before and after the experiment, then means can be compared across time. In this case, consistent estimation does not require random selection, but it does assume that all changes across time are attributable solely to the experiment—there are no external influences.

With panel data on zones before and after designation, as well as nonzone jurisdictions, aggregate time effects can control for external influences over time. Because EZs are selected on the basis of depressed economic conditions, specifications that allow for different types of sample selection should be estimated. In particular, the specifications should allow for EZ designation to be correlated with unobservables affecting economic performance.

The three specifications include jurisdiction fixed effects. Fixed effects take account of permanent differences across zones that are likely to influence designation. For example, zones may vary with respect to industrial composition and characteristics of the labor force. In a second specification, in addition to the fixed effects, selection is allowed to depend on jurisdiction-specific growth rates. This allows for zones to grow at different rates and allows program designation to depend on these growth rates.[33] The third specification allows designation to be based on lagged values of the dependent variable as well as the zone-specific time invariant unobservables (fixed effects). For example, this allows zone designation to depend on the level of employment or investment in the previous period.

The most basic model is given by equation (1):

$$\log y_{it} = \alpha_i + \beta_t + \delta EZ_{it} + u_{it}. \tag{1}$$

---

[33] For example, M. Rubin (1992) claims that the New Jersey program targets fast growing areas in preference to slow-growing ones. Slow-growing areas might be targeted in other states.

EZ_{it} equals 1 if jurisdiction i is a zone in year t, and 0 otherwise. The variable y_{it} is either the annual level of inventories, machinery and equipment, or unemployment claims. The coefficient on the EZ dummy, when multiplied by 100, measures the percentage change in inventories, for example, caused by zone designation. This specification includes a linear time trend β_t, and the α_is control for unobservables that are time-invariant over the sample period and may be correlated with zone designation.

The second specification, the random growth rates model given by

$$\log y_{it} = \alpha_i + \beta_{1i}t + \beta_{2t} + \delta EZ_{it} + u_{it}, \tag{2}$$

allows zone selection to be based not only on the level of activity α_i, but on the growth rates β_{1i} as well. This generalization is desirable if, for example, fast- or slow-growing areas are more likely to be selected. This second model is more general than the first in that aggregate time effects, β_{2t}, replace the linear time trend.

Specifications (1) and (2) control for varying degrees of sample selection, but they impose the restriction that zone designation has the same effect in each year after designation. That is, EZ designation causes a permanent shift in the level of activity in the zone, relative to its nonzone state. This may be too restrictive if the influences of the incentives change over time. This restriction is relaxed in

$$\log y_{it} = \alpha_i + \beta_t + \delta_1 EZYR1_{it} + \delta_2 EZYR2_{it} + \ldots + \delta_5 EZYR5_{it} + u_{it}. \tag{3}$$

This is an extension of equation (1) that allows the effect of zone designation to vary over its life. The EZ dummy is replaced by a series of dummy variables for each year of zone designation; for example, $EZYR2_{it}$ takes on the value 1 if jurisdiction i has been a zone for two years in year t, and 0 otherwise.

The third specification, equation (4), accounts for the possibility that designation is based on the lagged value of the dependent variable before designation:

$$\log y_{it} = \alpha_i + \beta_{2t} + \rho \log y_{i,t-1} + \delta EZ_{it} + u_{it}. \tag{4}$$

The estimated effects are similar across specifications.[34] They indicate that the Indiana EZ program has permanently increased the value of inventories by about 8 percent in the zones relative to what it would have been without the program. However, the value of machinery and equipment is reduced by about 13 percent. The latter could be a transi-

---

[34] See L. Papke (1991b) for a discussion of estimation techniques for these specifications.

tory one-time adjustment, but the imprecision of the estimates make it difficult to determine. Evaluated at the means of the sample, this is equivalent to about a $5 million drop in the value of depreciable personal property, and a $3.2 million increase in the value of the inventories.[35]

Zone designation appears also to have a positive impact on the local labor market. Unemployment claims decline by about 19 percent following designation, although this finding is more in question because of the geographic mismatch. At the mean of unemployment claims, this is about 1,500 fewer claims per year. The evidence for a permanent effect on unemployment claims is stronger than that for capital.

To summarize, it appears that the Indiana zone program has had a positive effect on employment and inventories. A decline in unemployment claims in the surrounding community, however, does not necessarily imply an increase in the employment or the economic well-being of zone residents. What has happened to the income of zone residents? New evidence on their economic status based on the 1990 Census is presented in the following.

C. The Economic Well-being of Zone Residents

The 1980 and 1990 census years bracket the operation of the Indiana EZ program, which, as indicated earlier, began in 1984. This section compares the economic status of zone residents before the zone program began to a point six years after zone designation. These differences are compared to changes over the same period of time for nonzone residents in Indiana.

The decennial Census of Population and Housing contains data on population, labor force, and housing characteristics at different geographic levels. These levels include, in decreasing order of size, state, county, minor civil division or township, place, census tract, block group, and block.

Some housing characteristics and 100 percent population counts are available by census block.[36] Other economic data (such as income and labor force characteristics) are available by block group. A geographic block group consists of a cluster of blocks within a census tract (or block numbering area for areas without census tracts) that generally contain between 250 and 550 housing units. The Bureau of the Census Summary

---

[35] Anecdotal evidence presented at a hearing of the Indiana Legislative Tax Incentive Study Committee in June 1992 indicated that some of the new zone firms are liquor stores and gun shop warehouses that hold comparatively large inventories.

[36] Census blocks are small areas bounded on all sides by visible features such as streets, roads, streams, and railroad tracks, and by invisible boundaries such as city, town, township, and county limits, property limits, and imaginary extensions of roads.

TABLE 1.
Average Indiana Zone Characteristics.

	1990 Census	Change from 1980 to 1990
Total population	11,021.67	−2,303.77
Workers 16 years and over	7,942.78	−1,545.11
Households	4,202.33	−673.56
Per capita income	$5,234.53	−$124.38
Percent white	59.50	−2.44
Percent black	36.22	0.93
Percent unemployed	7.98	−1.32
Percent unemployed men	9.30	−2.16
Percent unemployed women	6.89	−0.6
Percent out of the labor force	38.70	−2.94
Percent men out of labor force	29.58	0.77
Percent women out of labor force	46.33	−6.14
Percent who work in place of residence	68.61	3.93

Source: Author's calculations from the Census of Population and Housing, 1980, 1990: Summary Tape File 3 (Indiana).
Note: Zone characteristics are constructed by aggregating over block group data. Per capita income is from the prior year and reported in 1980 dollars. Racial composition characteristics are a fraction of total population. Labor force characteristics are fractions of workers 16 years and older.

Tape File 3 contains block group level data: 100 percent counts of population, and economic sample data weighted to represent the total population in the block group.

After identifying the census tracts and blocks in each Indiana zone, I identified the block groups that contain these census blocks. In some cases, the block groups may contain blocks that are not designated EZs, but economic data are not available at a finer level of disaggregation.[37]

Table 1 contains a summary of zone resident characteristics from the 1990 census and the change in these characteristics since the 1980 census. The change between the two census years reflects either five or six years of zone tax benefits. Zone characteristics are constructed by aggregating all the block groups within each zone in 1980 and 1990. I then average these data to obtain the zone characteristics provided in Table 1.

Zones lost population over this period. Zones lost about 2,300 people and 674 households on average. Per capital income also fell about 2 percent, to an average of $5,235 (1980 dollars). Most zone residents are white, but the white population fell by about two percentage points to 60 percent on average. Black population increased by one percentage point

---

[37] Population is available by block (Summary tape file 1A) and could be aggregated to obtain exact zone population. Population figures reported here are from block group aggregates, so it will exceed the statutory maximum population for zones.

TABLE 2.
Industrial Composition of Employment of Indiana Zone Residents.

	1980 Census	1990 Census	Change from 1980 to 1990
Percent in agriculture, forestry, fisheries, and mining	0.67	0.79	0.12
Percent in construction	4.14	4.61	0.47
Percent in manufacturing	36.21	29.96	−6.25
Percent in transportation and communication	6.32	6.54	0.22
Percent in wholesale	3.71	3.52	−0.19
Percent in retail	17.00	18.98	1.98
Percent in finance and entertainment	11.80	13.34	1.54
Percent professionals in health, education, and other	16.65	18.86	2.21
Percent in public administration	3.45	3.20	−0.25

Note: See Table 1.

to 36 percent. Zone unemployment fell by 1.3 percent overall to about 8 percent, with most of the drop occurring in the male unemployment rate. In addition, the fraction of people who reported "working in their place of residence" increased by almost 4 percent (where "place" refers to the Census geographic definition).

Table 2 presents the industrial composition of zone resident employment in 1980 and 1990 and the changes between the two censuses. About 30 percent of residents work in manufacturing, down six percentage points from 1980. The proportion working in retail (19 percent), finance and entertainment services (13 percent), and professional, health-, and education-related services (19 percent) each rose about two percentage points over this period.

To determine whether the changes in economic status described in Table 1 were unusual, it is useful to compare the experience of the zones with urban nonzones of comparable size within the state. As a comparison group, I randomly selected block groups within twenty-four other urban Indiana places to compare with the block groups that contain the zones designated in 1984 and 1985. Table 3 presents the difference between zones and nonzones in the changes before and after the zone program. That is, the change in nonzone characteristics between 1980 and 1990 is subtracted from the change in zone characteristics across that same period. Tables 4 and 5 contain the economic characteristics for zone and nonzone block groups from which the Table 3 calculations were made.

TABLE 3.
Difference of Differences: Differences Between Zone Block Changes Between 1980 and 1990 and Nonzone Block Changes Between 1980 and 1990 in Indiana.

	Zone change from 1980 to 1990 minus nonzone change from 1980 to 1990
Total population	−44.58
Workers 16 years and over	−27.75
Households	−25.63
Per capita income	−$172.94
Percent white	−0.16
Percent black	1.29
Percent unemployed	−0.15
Percent unemployed men	−0.11
Percent unemployed women	−0.17
Percent out of the labor force	−1.15
Percent men out of labor force	−2.10
Percent women out of labor force	0.66
Percent who work in place of residence	0.42

Source: See Table 1.
Note: Per capita income is from the prior year and reported in 1980 dollars. Racial composition characteristics are a fraction of total population. Labor force characteristics are fractions of workers 16 years and older.

TABLE 4.
Average Indiana Zone Block Characteristics.

	1990 Census	Change from 1980 to 1990
Total block population	614.23	−124.92
Workers 16 years and over	447.81	−85.68
Households	237.21	−38.61
Per capita income	$5,196.82	−$116.41
Percent white	49.43	0.01
Percent black	41.01	4.89
Percent unemployed	8.52	−0.73
Percent unemployed men	10.54	−1.30
Percent unemployed women	6.86	−0.23
Percent out of the labor force	40.68	−2.73
Percent men out of labor force	31.73	0.56
Percent women out of labor force	48.37	−4.84
Percent who work in place of residence	69.83	6.36

Source: See Table 1.
Note: These data are for block groups that had become part of a zone by 1990. Per capita income is from the prior year and reported in 1980 dollars. Racial composition characteristics are a fraction of total population. Labor force characteristics are fractions of workers 16 years and older.

TABLE 5.
Average Indiana Nonzone Block characteristics.

	1990 Census	Change from 1980 to 1990
Total population	844.13	−80.34
Workers 16 years and over	650.17	−57.93
Households	331.59	−12.98
Per capita income	$7,289.69	$56.53
Percent white	63.58	0.17
Percent black	24.30	3.60
Percent unemployed	5.58	−0.58
Percent unemployed men	6.68	−1.19
Percent unemployed women	4.60	−0.06
Percent out of the labor force	37.47	−1.58
Percent men out of labor force	29.13	2.66
Percent women out of labor force	44.54	−5.50
Percent who work in place of residence	73.78	5.94

Source: See Table 1.
Note: These data are for non-zone block groups. Per capita income is from the prior year and reported in 1980 dollars. Racial composition characteristics are a fraction of total population. Labor force characteristics are fractions of workers 16 years and older.

The difference of differences reported in Table 3 indicate that the population loss was greater for zones, but population also fell in nonzones. On average, block groups in zones lost forty-five more people (twenty-six more households) than did nonzones. Per capita income in zones in 1980 ($5,313) was substantially less than in nonzones ($6,722), and zone per capita income fell over the ten-year period while nonzone per capita income rose to $7,290. Unemployment fell more in zones than nonzones, but the difference is small (0.11 percent). Fewer zone residents work in their place of residence relative to nonzones in 1990 (70 percent vs. 74 percent), but the ratio did increase fractionally more in the zone (0.42 percent).

These zone effects estimated with the census data are much weaker than those estimated econometrically. One interpretation of this finding is that the econometric analysis allowed zone selection to depend on place-specific growth rates. Similar sample selection corrections cannot be made with only two years of census data. For example, if slower-growing sites are selected, and the selection is controlled for, then the zone program has a large measured effect. This selection correction cannot be made with the census numbers, thus accounting for the smaller measured zone effects.

In summary, while the direction of the zone effects from the census data are similar to those from the econometric analysis, the results are much less strong. In spite of the reduction in unemployment rates in the zones, the income numbers suggest that zone residents are not appreciably better off with the Indiana EZ program.

VI. MEASURING THE COST-EFFECTIVENESS OF ENTERPRISE ZONES

This section briefly discusses the limited evidence on EZ cost effectiveness. Estimated costs per job from EZ programs are compared to other federal employment programs. Cost-effectiveness is measured by direct spending and foregone revenue per job created or cost per zone resident job. These measures provide an accounting of the initial level of public investment required per zone job created. But they are not a full cost-benefit accounting of the program, because they do not account for second-round feedback effects (such as zone employee removal from welfare and income tax payments). The difficulty in determining which jobs may be relocations has already been discussed.[38]

Generating jobs in distressed areas entails a variety of costs depending on the type of program. The JOBS program of the late 1960s and early 1970s subsidized the hiring of disadvantaged, unemployed workers. The gross placement cost was $3,200 (in 1969 dollars, or $10,752 in 1990 dollars) per hire.[39] Bendick (1981) states that costs per job ranged from $11,570 ($17,058 in $1990) in the Urban Development Action Grant Program, through $13,000 ($19,110) per job in the Business Loan program of the Economic Development Administration, to $60,000 ($88,200) per job in the local Public Works program of the Economic Development Administration.

Cost per job estimates from zone programs are not that different from these earlier U.S. experiences with job subsidies. Using survey responses for number of new zone jobs, M. Rubin (1992) puts New Jersey's cost per job at between $8,000 and $13,000 annually. J. Papke (1990) calculates that the annual cost of an Indiana zone job was $4,564, and $31,113 per zone resident job. It amounted to over $100,000 per zone resident job in some zones.

[38] There is no accounting for the length of job tenure or type of job. For example, Indiana's EZ program may encourage annual hiring and firing because the employment tax credit is based on annual average hires.

[39] Hamermesh (1978) explains that, while the subsidy was fairly high, few employers took advantage of it.

Calculations of state EZ costs are complicated by the fact that, in some state programs, local governments bear the brunt of the cost. In New Jersey, the state funds the EZ program.[40] But in Indiana the most generous tax incentive is the inventory tax credit against the local property tax. The credit reduces the assessed value of taxable property in the zone and shifts the remaining tax burden onto other local property sources. The cost per zone job varies across zones.[41] From 1986 to 1988, for example, the average cost of the inventory tax credit alone per new job ranged from $526 to $10,238, and from $1,154 to $67,571 for new zone resident jobs.

VII. CONCLUSION

Some have argued that the uneven pattern of economic growth across states and cities is evidence of a market failure and that government subsidies may be appropriate to encourage a more geographically even growth path. EZs can become valuable tools for evaluating the effectiveness of tax incentives as economic development policy, and can add to the longstanding debate on the effects of tax competition on the location of capital investment.

Based on the U.S. state and British experiences, it is possible to speculate about the likely effects of some of the proposed federal EZ initiatives.[42] First, the capital incentives are likely to increase zone investment. It is not possible to predict whether this will be net new investment or relocation of existing businesses—our limited U.S. survey evidence on this issue indicates that start-up firms average about 25 percent of "new" zone businesses. Capital incentives may revitalize economic activity in depressed areas, but it may well be at the expense of neighboring areas. Data from zone programs suggest that the surrounding community is struggling economically as well.

State zone programs do not seem to have improved the economic

[40] The most valuable incentives New Jersey offers include business tax credits for employee hires of public assistance recipients, an exemption from state sales and use taxes on purchases of tangible personal property, and materials and services for construction activities, and a 50 percent rebate on unemployment insurance taxes paid by employers on low-paid employees.

[41] For example, the 1987 assessed value of the exempt inventories in the Elkhart EZ was $4.2 million, or 2.7 percent of the total taxable property values in Concord township. To make up this loss in tax base, $331,000 of taxes were shifted to the remaining nonexempt properties. Without the exemption, the gross tax rate in the district would have been $9.7807 (in dollars per $100 of assessed value); with the exemption, the actual tax rate was $9.8870, an increase of 1.1 percent. See J. A. Papke (1990) for additional estimates of the tax cost shifted to local residents in each zone.

[42] Green (1990) and Steuerle (1992) make recommendations specific to a federal EZ program.

status of zone residents. Proposed federal wage credits may stand a better chance of increasing zone resident income, because the cap is higher than that in most states, and it might also be indexed. Certainly, the chances for improvement are greater when zones are smaller relative to the rest of the economy. It is unlikely that the proposed credit for stock purchases will be influential, because few zone firms issue stock specifically for zone location.

Several unresolved issues remain. If investment in certain geographic areas is inhibited because the perceived riskiness of an area increases the required cost of capital, EZ tax incentives may at least partially offset the high cost of funds. But high costs of capital may not be the problem if investment is discouraged because of infrastructure deficiencies or an unskilled work force.

If the goal of an EZ program is to improve the economic status of zone residents, issues relating to their employability are relevant. There may be few income gains if zone businesses require labor skills not possessed by residents of the area. If the business is attracted to the area to use its low-skilled, low-wage labor, there may be employment growth without income growth. Current residents may even be displaced by economic development.

Direct assistance to business may be the most controversial type of state and local economic development policy. Tax concessions or tax expenditures transfer the discretionary authority for a public program to a nonpublic third party—the firm, in the case of EZs. The employment and investment effects of these tax expenditure policies are still being evaluated.

APPENDIX 1: PARTIAL EQUILIBRIUM ANALYSIS OF ZONE INCENTIVES

Appendix 1 employs a partial equilibrium model to analyze the effects on zone wages of a labor subsidy, a capital subsidy, and an equal-cost subsidy to capital and labor. Labor subsidies that target zone residents are also analyzed.

Production in the zone uses three inputs—capital K, zone resident labor L_Z, and labor from outside of the zone L_N. The package of zone tax incentives may include a subsidy to zone capital τ_K, zone resident labor τ_Z, and/or nonzone labor τ_N expressed as percentages (in decimal) of factor cost.

The production process in the zone is described by

$$Q = F(K, L_Z, L_N). \tag{A-1}$$

The demand function for the zone product is described by

$$Q = f(P). \tag{A-2}$$

The two labor supply equations are

$$L_Z = g_Z(w) \tag{A-3}$$

$$L_N = g_N(w). \tag{A-4}$$

Capital is assumed to be in infinitely elastic supply to the zone, or

$$r = r_0. \tag{A-5}$$

Under the assumptions of perfect competition and profit maximization, the zone economy is summarized by the following equations:

$$\hat{Q} = (1 - a_Z - a_N)\hat{K} + a_Z\hat{L}_Z + a_N\hat{L}_N \tag{A-6}$$
$$\hat{Q} = -e_p\hat{P} \tag{A-7}$$
$$\hat{K} - \hat{L}_Z = \sigma_Z(\hat{w}_Z - d\tau_z + d\tau_K - \hat{r}) \tag{A-8}$$
$$\hat{K} - \hat{L}_N = \sigma_N(\hat{w}_N - d\tau_N + d\tau_K - \hat{r}) \tag{A-9}$$
$$\hat{P} = a_Z(\hat{w}_Z - d\tau_Z) + a_N(\hat{w}_N - d\tau_N) + (1 - a_Z - a_N)(\hat{r} - d\tau_K) \tag{A-10}$$
$$\hat{L}_Z = e_Z\hat{w}_Z \tag{A-11}$$
$$\hat{L}_N = e_N\hat{w}_N \tag{A-12}$$
$$\hat{r} = 0, \tag{A-13}$$

where $\hat{Q}$, $\hat{P}$, $\hat{K}$, $\hat{L}_N$, $\hat{L}_Z$, $\hat{w}_N$, $\hat{w}_Z$, and $\hat{r}$ are the percentage changes in output, price of output, capital, nonzone resident labor and zone resident labor, and their wages, respectively, and the after-tax rate of return on capital. In addition, a_Z is zone labor's share of total income, a_N is the nonzone labor's share of total income, e_Z and e_N are the elasticities of labor supply for the two types of labor, σ_Z and σ_N are the elasticities of substitution between capital and the two types of labor.

This system results in the following two equations, which describe the percentage change in wages for the two types of labor in response to any of the subsidies:

$$\%\Delta w_Z = \frac{c_1b_{22} - c_2b_{12}}{b_{11}b_{22} - b_{12}b_{21}} \tag{A-14}$$

$$\%\Delta w_N = \frac{c_2b_{11} - c_1b_{21}}{b_{11}b_{22} - b_{12}b_{21}}, \tag{A-15}$$

TABLE A-1.
*Subsidizing Zone Resident Labor Only.**

	% Δ zone resident wage e_Z Zone resident labor supply elasticity			% Δ non-zone resident wage e_Z Zone resident labor supply elasticity		
e_P	0.0	0.3	0.5	0.0	0.3	0.5
Panel 1: 1 percent wage subsidy: zone residents only						
0.0	1.0	0.7353	0.6250	0.0	0.0	0.0
0.5	1.0	0.7496	0.6423	0.0	0.0039	0.0057
1.0	1.0	0.7578	0.6524	0.0	0.0064	0.0091
1.5	1.0	0.7632	0.6591	0.0	0.0078	0.0113
Panel 2: 1 percent zone capital subsidy						
0.0	−1.0	−0.7353	−0.6250	−0.2083	−0.2083	−0.2083
0.5	−0.3593	−0.2693	−0.2308	−0.0750	−0.0763	−0.0769
1.0	0.0	0.0	0.0	0.0	0.0	0.0
1.5	0.2299	0.1754	0.1515	0.0478	0.0497	0.0505
Panel 3: Equal-cost subsidy to zone resident labor and capital						
0.0	4.0	2.9412	2.5	−0.2083	−0.2083	−0.2083
0.5	4.6402	3.4785	2.9808	−0.0748	−0.0561	−0.0481
1.0	5.0	3.7890	3.2622	0.0	0.0319	0.0457
1.5	5.2299	3.9912	3.4470	0.0478	0.0891	0.1073

Source: Author's calculations. See Appendix 1 for derivations.
*Percentage change in zone resident wages and nonzone resident wages for various demand and labor supply elasticities under three types of EZ tax incentives

where $b_{11} = e_P a_Z + (1 - a_N)e_Z + a_K \sigma_Z$, $b_{12} = e_P a_N$, $b_{21} = e_P a_Z$, $b_{22} = e_P a_N + (1 - a_Z)e_N + a_K \sigma_N$, $c_1 = (e_P a_Z + a_K \sigma_Z)d\tau_Z + e_P a_N d\tau_N + (e_P a_K - a_K \sigma_Z)d\tau_K$, and $c_2 = e_P a_Z d\tau_Z + (e_P a_N + a_K \sigma_N)d\tau_N + (e_P a_K - a_K \sigma_N)d\tau_K$.

Land is an input to production as well, but excluding land from the model does not significantly alter the calculated wage effects. A stylized fact of income distribution theory is that most of national income is attributable to labor, and the rest is largely a return to capital. Because land is such a small share of total income, its inclusion would not appreciably affect the estimated wage effects.[43]

Calculations are presented for a range of labor supply and demand elasticities in Tables A-1 and A-2. The estimates are in the form of a percentage change in wages for each percentage point change in the

---

[43] As in Britain, EZ subsidies may increase the price of zone land if its supply is fairly inelastic. While the total amount of land in the zone is fixed in supply, the supply of industrial land may not be. Exactly how much the price of land will rise will depend on its elasticity of supply and the substitution elasticities between land and the other inputs.

TABLE A-2.
Percentage Change in Zone Wages for Various Demand and Labor Supply Elasticities Under Three Types of EZ Tax Incentives.

Demand elasticity e_P	Zone labor supply elasticity e_L		
	0.0	*0.3*	*0.5*
Panel 1: 1 percent zone labor subsidy			
0.0	1.0	0.4545	0.3333
0.5	1.0	0.6757	0.5556
1.0	1.0	0.7692	0.6667
1.5	1.0	0.8209	0.7333
Panel 2: 1 percent zone capital subsidy			
0.0	−1.0	−0.4545	−0.3333
0.5	−0.2	−0.1351	−0.1111
1.0	0.0	0.0	0.0
1.5	0.0909	0.0746	0.0667
Panel 3: Equal-cost subsidy to zone labor and capital			
0.0	−2.0	−0.9091	−0.6667
0.5	0.6	0.4054	0.3333
1.0	1.25	0.9615	0.8333
1.5	1.5455	1.2687	1.1333

Source: Author's calculations. See Appendix 1 for derivations.

subsidy. For example, an estimate of 0.4 means that a one percentage point increase in the wage or capital subsidy increases the wage by 0.4 percent. The percentage change in the wage can be converted into a percentage change in employment by multiplying this estimate by the elasticity of labor supply.

Case 1: Homogeneous labor

Consider first a type of EZ program that makes no distinction between employment of zone residents and nonzone residents. A labor subsidy is provided for all zone employment. (This is a special case of the previous model.) Both zone and nonzone residents share a common elasticity of labor supply.[44] The estimates of the percentage change in wages for a one-percentage point increase in the labor subsidy are presented in panel 1 of Table A-2.

A subsidy to zone labor always increases the wage (and employment). The effect on the wage is larger, the larger the elasticity of demand (in

[44] Following Gravelle (1992), a labor share in total output of 0.75 is assumed.

absolute value) and the smaller the elasticity of labor supply. If labor is completely inelastic, a 1 percent increase in the wage subsidy raises the wage by one percent. The increase in the wage is 0.68 percent at a more elastic labor supply elasticity of 0.3, and product demand elasticity of 0.5.

The resulting percentage change in employment is found by multiplying the percentage change in the wage by the labor supply elasticity. For example, a 6.8 percent increase in the wage causes an increase in employment of 2.04 percent if the labor supply elasticity is 0.3.

Panel 2 presents the wage effects of a capital subsidy. A capital subsidy reduces the wage at low elasticities of product demand and labor supply. There is a small positive increase in the wage for products with a relatively elastic demand, ranging from 0.09 percent with inelastic labor supply to 0.07 percent with a 0.5 labor supply elasticity.

Most EZ programs involve a subsidy to both capital and labor. The effect of an equal-cost subsidy to labor and capital is presented in panel 3. Wage income is assumed to be three times the size of capital income, so the rate of wage subsidy is one-third that of the capital subsidy. This combined subsidy will reduce zone wages if the demand for the zone product is completely inelastic. If the product elasticity is fairly high (1.5) and labor is still relatively inelastic (0.3), an equal-cost subsidy to capital and labor (one percent increase in the capital subsidy combined with a one-third percent wage subsidy) increases wages by 1.27 percent.

Case 2: Heterogeneous labor

Often an EZ labor subsidy is provided for the wages of zone residents only (Indiana's program and H.R. 11 are examples). In the previous model, zone resident labor and nonzone resident labor are treated as separate inputs in the production process. Nonzone resident labor is assumed to be highly mobile across zone boundaries. (An elasticity of nonzone labor supply of 1.0 is assumed.)

Zone resident labor's share in total income is assumed to be 0.05, and nonzone resident labor's share is assumed to be 0.70. This accords with survey data from the Indiana program that indicates that zone residents are about 7 percent of total zone employment (provided zone residents are paid the same wage as nonzone residents). If zone residents are paid half as much as nonzone residents (as Indiana survey data also indicate), then these income shares correspond to zone employees comprising 14 percent of total zone employment. Capital's income share remains 0.25.

The effects on the wages of zone residents and nonzone residents of a labor subsidy, capital subsidy, and equal-cost labor and capital subsidy are illustrated in Table A-1. When only zone resident wages are subsidized (panel 1), variation in the elasticity of demand has little effect on the change in the wage. If zone resident labor is inelastically supplied, a 1 percent subsidy to their wages alone increases their wages by 1 percent (and there is no effect on nonzone resident wages). Zone resident wages increase by about 0.75 percent if their elasticity of labor supply is 0.3, and by about 0.65 percent if their labor supply is 0.5. The increase in nonzone resident wages is less than 0.01 percent in all cases. Thus, at lower elasticities of demand, a subsidy to zone-resident wages only is more effective at increasing the wages (and employment) of zone residents than is a subsidy to all labor employed in the zone.

As in the homogeneous labor case, a capital subsidy causes firms to substitute away from both types of labor, and wages to zone residents and nonzone residents alike fall (panel 2). If the product demand is very elastic (1.5), a capital subsidy increases zone resident wages by 0.18 percent (with an elasticity of labor supply of 0.3).

An equal-cost subsidy to zone resident labor and capital has a substantially larger effect on the zone resident wage (panel 3). An equal-cost subsidy corresponds to a 1 percent capital subsidy and a 5 percent labor subsidy. At a zone resident labor supply of 0.3, an equal-cost subsidy increases zone-resident wages by about 3 percent, regardless of the product demand elasticity. If only zone resident wages are subsidized, the EZ incentive can fund a much larger percentage increase in the labor subsidy with a correspondingly larger effect on the zone resident wage.[45]

---

[45] These results assume highly mobile nonzone resident labor (a labor supply elasticity of 1.0). Calculations not reported here illustrate that the equal cost subsidy estimates are not appreciably altered by assuming a completely inelastic supply of nonzone resident labor, or by assuming that zone-resident and nonzone resident labor have an equal share in total output.

APPENDIX 2

Studies of U.S. Enterprise Zones

State	Author
Multiple states	L. Revzan (1983)
	R. Funkhouser and E. Lorenz (1987)
	M. Bendick, Jr., and D. W. Rasmussen (1986)
	M. Brintnall and R. Green (1988)
	M. G. Wilder and B. M. Rubin (1988)
	R. A. Erickson and S. W. Friedman (1990, 1991a, 1991b)
	R. A. Erickson, S. W. Friedman, and R. E. McCluskey (1989)
	S. A. Lavation and E. I. Miller (1992)
	B. M. Rubin and M. G. Wilder (1989)
	A. W. Sheldon and R. C. Elling (1989)
California	E. Litster (1990)
Connecticut	Connecticut Department of Economic Development (1985)
Illinois	E. R. Jones (1985, 1987)
Indiana	J. A. Papke (1988, 1989, 1990)
	J. A. Papke and L. E. Papke (1992)
	L. E. Papke (1991)
Louisiana	A. C. Nelson and R. W. Whelan (1988)
Maryland	U. S. General Accounting Office (1988)
New Jersey	M. Rubin and R. B. Armstrong (1989)
Ohio	S. Staley (1988)

REFERENCES

Armington, C., and M. Odle (1982). "Small Business—How Many Jobs?" *The Brookings Review*, 1, 14–17.

Ballard, C. L. (forthcoming). "Taxation and Saving." In *Taxation Issues in the 1990s*. J. G. Head, ed.

Ballard, C. L., D. Fullerton, J. B. Shoven, and J. Whalley (1985). *A General Equilibrium Model for Tax Policy Evaluation*. NBER, Chicago: University of Chicago Press.

Barnes, I., and J. Preston (1985). "The Scunthorpe Enterprise Zone: An Example of Muddled Interventionism." *Public Administration* 63, 171–181.

Bartik, T. J. (1985). "Business Location Decisions in the United States: Estimates of the Effects of Unionization, Taxes, and Other Characteristics of States." *Journal of Business and Economic Statistics* 3, 14–22.

———— (1991). *Who Benefits from State and Local Economic Development Policies?"* Kalamazoo, MI: W. E. Upjohn Institute for Employment Research.

Bendick, M., Jr. (1981). "Employment, Training, and Economic Development." In *The Reagan Experiment*, 263–265. J. L. Palmer and I. V. Sawhill, eds. Washington, DC: The Urban Institute.

————, and D. W. Rasmussen (1986). "Enterprise Zones and Inner-City Economic Revitalization." In *Reagan and the Cities*, 97–129. G. E. Peterson and C. W. Lewis, eds., Washington DC: The Urban Institute.

Birch, D. L. (1981). "Who Creates Jobs?" *The Public Interest*, 65, 3–14.

Bradford, D. F. (1978). "Factor Prices May be Constant but Factor Returns Are Not." *Economics Letters* 1, 199–203.

Brintnall, M., and R. Green (1988). "Comparing State Enterprise Zone Programs: Variations in Structure and Coverage." *Economic Development Quarterly* 2, 50–68.

Bromley, R. D. F., and R. H. Morgan (1985). "The Effects of Enterprise Zone Policy: Evidence from Swansea." *Regional Studies*, 19, 403–413.

———, and J. C. M. Rees (1988). "The First Five Years of the Swansea Enterprise Zone." *Regional Studies* 22, 263–275.

Brown, C., J. Hamilton, and J. Medoff (1990). *Employers Large and Small*, Cambridge, MA: Harvard University Press.

Carlson, E. (1991), "Impact of Zones for Enterprise is Ambiguous," *Wall Street Journal*, April 1.

Carlton, D. (1979). "Why New Firms Locate Where They Do: An Econometric Model." In *Interregional Movements and Regional Growth*. W. Wheaton, ed. Washington, DC: Urban Institute.

Carroll, R., and M. Wasylenko (1990). "The Shifting Fate of Fiscal Variables and Their Effect on Economic Development." Paper presented at the National Tax Association, Proceedings of the Eighty-second Annual Conference, Columbus, OH.

Connecticut Department of Economic Development (1985). *Enterprise Zones: The Connecticut Experiment*. Hartford, CT.

Erickson, R. A. (1991a). "Enterprise Zones 2: A Comparative Analysis of Zone Performance and State Government Policies." Mimeo, Pennsylvania State University.

——— (1991b). "Comparative Dimensions of State Enterprise Zone Policies." In *Enterprise Zones: New Directions in Economic Development*, 136–154. R. E. Green, ed. Sage Focus Edition. Newbury Park, CA.

———, ———, and R. E. McCluskey (1989). *Enterprise Zones: An Evaluation of State Government Policies*. Report to the U.S. Economic Development Administration, Pennsylvania State University, Center for Regional Analysis.

Erickson, R. A., and S. W. Friedman, (1990). "Enterprise Zones 1: Investment and Job Creation of State Government Programs in the United States of America." *Environment and Planning C: Government and Policy*, vol. 8, 251–267.

———, and P. M. Syms (1985). "The Effects of Enterprise Zones on Local Property Markets." *Regional Studies* 20, 1–14.

Funkhouser, R., and E. Lorenz (1987). "Fiscal and Employment Impacts of Enterprise Zones." *Atlantic Economic Journal* 15, 62–76.

Goldberg, F. T., Jr. (1992). Statement before the Committee on Finance, the U.S. Senate, June 3, p. 3.

Gravelle, J. G. (1992). "Enterprise Zones: The Design of Tax Incentives." CRS Report for Congress 92-476 S, Congressional Research Service, The Library of Congress, June 3.

Great Britain Department of the Environment (1986). "An Evaluation of the Enterprise Zone Experiment." London: Her Majesty's Stationery Office, 1987, p. 86.

Green, R. E. (1990). "Is There a Place in the 1990s for Federally Designated

Enterprise Zones within the Context of State-Administered Enterprise Zone Program Experience?" *Journal of Planning Literature* 5, 39–46.

Hall, P. (1977). "Green Fields and Grey Areas." In *Proceedings of the Royal Town Planning Institute Annual Conference*, 15–17. P. Hall, ed. London: Royal Town Planning Institute.

Hamermesh, D. S. (1978). "Subsidies for Jobs in the Private Sector." In *Creating Jobs: Public Employment Programs and Wage Subsidies.* J. Palmer, ed. Washington, DC: The Brookings Institution.

——— (1993). *Labor Demand.* Princeton, NJ: Princeton University Press.

Holzer, H. J. (1991). "The Spatial Mismatch Hypothesis: What Has the Evidence Shown?" In *Urban Studies*, vol. 28, 105–122.

Jones, E. R. (1985). "Enterprise Zone Programs and Neighborhood Revitalization: The First Two Years." Urbana, IL: Department of Urban and Regional Planning, University of Illinois.

——— (1987). "Enterprise Zones for the Black Community—Promise or Product: A Case Study." *The Western Journal of Black Studies* 11, 1–10.

Joint Committee on Taxation (1992). "Staff Description of Proposals and Issues Relating to Tax Incentives for Enterprise Zones." JCS-12-92, June 2.

Juhn, C., K. M. Murphy, and R. H. Topel (1991). "Why Has the Natural Rate of Unemployment Increased Over Time?" *Brookings Papers on Economic Activity* 2, 75–126.

Killingsworth, M. (1983). *Labor Supply.* Cambridge, UK, Cambridge University Press.

Lavation, S. A., and E. I. Miller (1992). "Enterprise Zones: A Promise Based on Rhetoric." Occasional Paper 1992-1, Center for Social Policy Studies, George Washington University, March.

Litster, E. (1990). "California Enterprise Zones: Assessment of Enterprise Zone Effectiveness and the Resulting Impact on Business Location and Employment." Unpublished Master's thesis, UCLA Department of Urban Planning.

McLure, C. E., Jr. (1970). "Taxation, Substitution, and Industrial Location." *The Journal of Political Economy*, 78, 112–132.

Nelson, A. C., and R. W. Whelan, (1988). "Do Enterprise Zones Make a Difference: Survey Research Results of Louisiana's Rural Enterprise Zones." Paper presented at the 18th Annual Meetings of the Urban Affairs Association, St. Louis, March.

PA Cambridge Economics (1987). *An Evaluation of the Enterprise Zone Experiment.* London: Department of the Environment, HMSO.

Papke, J. A. (1988). *The Indiana Enterprise Zone Experiment: Concepts, Issues, and Impacts.* Center for Tax Policy Studies, Purdue University.

——— (1989). *Monitoring Indiana Enterprise Zones: Analysis and Appraisal—Year Two Report.* Center for Tax Policy Studies, Purdue University.

——— (1990). *The Role of Market Based Public Policy in Economic Development and Urban Revitalization: A Retrospective Analysis and Appraisal of the Indiana Enterprise Zone Program—Year Three Report.* Center for Tax Policy Studies, Purdue University, West Lafayette, IN.

———, and L. E. Papke, (1992). "The Labor Participation, Income, and Investment Effects of Tax Concessions: Empirical Evidence from an Enterprise Zone Experiment." Paper presented at the 48th Congress of the International Institute of Public Finance, Seoul, Korea, August 24–27, Session 6.

Papke, L. E. (1987). "Subnational Taxation and Capital Mobility: Estimates of Tax-Price Elasticities." *National Tax Journal* 40, 191–204.

——— (1991a). "Interstate Business Tax Differentials and New Firm Location: Evidence from Panel Data," *Journal of Public Economics* 45, 47–68.

——— (1991b). "Tax Policy and Urban Development: Evidence from an Enterprise Zone Program." NBER Working Paper Number 3945.

Revzan, L. (1983). "Enterprise Zones: Present Status and Potential Impact." *Government Finance* 12, 31–37.

Roger Tym and Partners (1984). "Monitoring Enterprise Zones: Year Three Report." London: Department of the Environment, HMSO.

Rowings, J., D. Powers, and B. Sigalow (1992). "Background Materials Prepared for the Tax Incentive Study Committee." Legislative Services Agency, State of Indiana, Indianapolis, June 3.

Rubin, B. M., and M. G. Wilder (1989). "Urban Enterprise Zones: Employment Impacts and Fiscal Incentives." *Journal of the American Planning Association*, 55, 418–431.

———, and C. M. Richards (1993). "A Transatlantic Comparison of Enterprise Zone Impacts: The British and American Experience." *Economic Development Quarterly*.

Rubin, M. (1992). Testimony before the Subcommittee on Economic Stabilization of the Committee on Banking, Finance, and Urban Affairs, House of Representatives, February 20, Serial No. 102–99, Government Printing Office, Washington, D.C.

———, and R. B. Armstrong (1989). "The New Jersey Urban Enterprise Zone Program: An Evaluation." Report prepared for the New Jersey Department of Commerce, Trenton, NJ.

Schwarz, J. E., and T. H. Volgy (1988). "Experiments in Employment: A British Cure; Saving Jobs by Decree Can Kill an Industry; Saving Companies by Design Can Rescue an Industry." *Harvard Business Review* 66, 104–112.

Sheldon, A. W., and R. C. Elling, (1989). "Patterns and Determinants of Enterprise Zone Success in Four States." Paper presented at the 1989 Annual Meeting of the Urban Affairs Association, Baltimore, MD, March 15–18.

Shutt, J. (1984). "Tory Enterprise Zones and the Labour Movement." *Capital and Class* 23, 19–44.

Staley, S. (1988). "Differences in Firm Attitudes and the Implications for Inner City Economic Development: A Case Study of Participants in the Dayton, Ohio, Enterprise Zone Program." Paper presented at the Annual Meeting of the Urban Affairs Association, St. Louis, MO, March.

Steuerle, G. (1992). "Enterprise Zones: Efforts that Might Work." In *Tax Notes,* June 15, 1545–1546.

Talbot, J. (1988) "Have Enterprise Zones Encouraged Enterprise? Some Empirical Evidence from Tynside." *Regional Studies* 22, 507–514.

Thomas, C. J., and R. D. F. Bromley (1987). "The Growth and Functioning of an Unplanned Retail Park: The Swansea Enterprise Zone." *Regional Studies* 21, 287–300.

U.S. General Accounting Office (1988). *Enterprise Zones: Lessons from the Maryland Experience.* GAO/PEMD-89-2.

Wilder, M. G., and B. M. Rubin (1988). "Targeted Redevelopment Through Urban Enterprise Zones." *Journal of Urban Affairs* 10, 1–17.

PRIVATE SAVING AND PUBLIC POLICY

B. Douglas Bernheim
Princeton University and NBER

John Karl Scholz
University of Wisconsin-Madison and NBER

EXECUTIVE SUMMARY

The evidence presented in this paper supports the view that many Americans, particularly those without a college education, save too little. Our analysis also indicates that it should be possible to increase total personal saving among lower income households by encouraging the formation and expansion of private pension plans. It is doubtful that favorable tax treatment of capital income would stimulate significant additional saving by this group. Conversely, the expansion of private pensions would probably have little effect on saving by higher income households. However, these households are more likely to increase saving significantly in response to favorable tax treatment of capital income. Currently, eligibility for IRAs is linked to an AGI cap, and pension coverage is more common among higher income households than among low income households. The most effective system for promoting personal saving would have precisely the opposite features. Extending tax incentives for saving to higher income households is problematic. We discuss three competing policy options, IRAs with AGI

This paper was prepared for a conference on "Tax Policy and the Economy," Washington, D.C., November 17, 1992. The second author is grateful to the National Science Foundation, which provided research support through Grant Number SES-9211553. We also gratefully acknowledge the work of Robert Avery and Arthur Kennickell, who developed a clean copy of the 1983–1986 Survey of Consumer Finances, and provided extensive documentation.

caps, the universal IRA, and the Premium Saving Account (PSA). Our analysis reveals that the PSA system is a more cost-effective vehicle for providing saving incentives to all households, particularly those in the top quintile of the income distribution.

I. INTRODUCTION

Since the mid-1980s, low rates of national saving in the United States have generated an enormous amount of concern among both economists and policy makers. Proposals to address these concerns fall into two broad categories. One category consists of policies designed to increase public saving; the other consists of policies that are intended to promote private saving. The first category is synonymous with deficit reduction, while the second includes tax incentives, pension policy, and strategies for discouraging the use of private debt. Some economists argue that deficit reduction is the most reliable and efficacious method of increasing national saving (see, e.g., Summers, 1985), while others maintain that it is essential to restore adequate rates of saving in the private sector (see, e.g., Bernheim, 1991). To evaluate the merits of strategies that target private saving, one must resolve two issues. First, aside from the obvious fact that private saving is one component of national saving, are there reasons to be concerned about the rate of private saving? Second, are there any effective and reliable methods of promoting private saving?

This paper investigates several factual matters bearing on both of these questions. Four central findings emerge from our analysis. First, many households do not save enough to provide themselves with adequate financial security and, as a result, will be forced to accept significantly reduced standards of living during retirement. This phenomenon is especially prevalent when the head of the household lacks a college education. Second, patterns of asset accumulation among those without college education bear little or no resemblance to the patterns that emerge from standard economic theories. In contrast, those with a college education not only save more adequately for retirement, but also generally behave in a way that more closely resembles "textbook" life cycle planning. Third, consistent with this second finding, employer-provided pensions do not appear to displace other personal saving in cases where the head of the household lacks a college education. However, for college-educated households, pensions do appear to crowd out private saving. Fourth, it is likely that high-income households respond more vigorously to tax incentives for saving than do moderate- and low-income households.

These findings have important implications for public policy. To the extent that many households prepare poorly for retirement, there is cause to be concerned about the rate of personal saving per se. Although lower-income households may not respond significantly to tax incentives, it should be possible to stimulate rates of saving among this group by encouraging the creation and expansion of private pension plans. For high-income households, the implications are reversed: although pensions displace other forms of saving, tax incentives for saving are probably efficacious.

Because eligibility for deductible contributions to Individual Retirement Accounts (IRAs) is subject to an adjusted gross earnings (AGI) cap, lower-income households currently receive the most favorable tax incentives for saving. Conversely, households with higher levels of income and education are much more likely to be covered by private pensions. Thus, the current system appears to be designed in a way that minimizes the impact of public policy on personal saving.

Unfortunately, it is difficult to modify the current system in a way that would extend tax incentives to higher-income households without raising a host of new problems. The most common proposals are either to drop the AGI cap on IRAs or to design some new, "universal IRA" system without an AGI cap. The efficacy of these proposals is questionable. For many high-income households, saving for retirement may already exceed the proposed contribution limits; in that case, an IRA does not offer any reward for *incremental* saving. To the extent that IRAs simply generate windfall gains for many wealthy individuals, the system would be perceived as inequitable. Finally, the expansion of IRA eligibility could significantly reduce public saving (increase federal deficits) and thereby defeat the purpose of the proposal.

An alternative method of extending tax incentives for saving to higher-income households is through a system of Premium Savings Accounts (PSAs) (see Bernheim and Scholz, 1992). In brief, a household becomes eligible to contribute to a PSA only when its total saving exceeds a minimum threshold (the floor); beyond that point, incremental saving may be placed into a PSA, up to a cap (the ceiling). These floors and ceilings are tied to AGI: higher-income households must save more before becoming eligible.

If one believes that it is desirable to provide high-income households with tax incentives for saving, does the PSA proposal offer an attractive alternative to universal IRAs? To answer this question, we undertake a comparison of the two proposals. For each proposal, we calculate an index of effectiveness and a measure of windfalls received by higher-income individuals. We also assess the relative budgetary costs of these proposals. Our analysis suggests that, relative to a universal IRA system, the PSA proposal would significantly enhance incentives to save among higher-income households even as it would reduce both budgetary costs and windfalls to the wealthy.

This paper is organized as follows: section II presents evidence on the adequacy of personal saving; section III examines evidence on the effectiveness of pension policy; section IV discusses the impact of tax incentives for saving; and section V concludes.

II. THE ADEQUACY OF PERSONAL SAVING

According to common wisdom, Americans consume too much and save too little. This impression is largely traceable to widely publicized statistics on aggregate personal saving. International comparisons reveal that U.S. households save significantly less than their foreign counterparts. Between 1980 and 1989, Americans saved (net) 7.4% of disposable personal income, compared with 11.4% for OECD Europe and 16.0% for Japan (OECD, 1989). Moreover, since the mid-1980s, the rate of household saving in the United States has been well below its historical average (see Figure 1).

Although these statistics raise legitimate concerns, they do not provide definitive evidence of a problem. As measured, personal saving excludes capital gains. Thus, households could in principle accumulate wealth at a rapid rate even when measured saving is low. Rates of personal saving can also vary across both time and countries for reasons unrelated to the adequacy of saving considered from the perspective of individual households. To understand this second point, consider the following hypothetical example. Envision two countries, A and B, that are identical in all respects, except that the elderly make up a larger fraction of the population in A than in B. Because households tend to accumulate wealth prior to retirement and decumulate wealth thereafter, one would expect to observe a higher rate of aggregate personal saving in country B. Indeed, in an economy with no growth in either population or productivity, dissaving by retirees could completely offset saving by workers: one could in principle observe no personal saving in the aggregate, regardless of how well individual households prepared for retirement. Thus, ultimately, one can only judge the adequacy of personal saving by examining microeconomic data on the behavior of individual households.

Generally, the available evidence suggests that U.S. workers have prepared poorly for retirement. According to Diamond (1977), during the 1960s roughly 40% of married couples and over 50% of unmarried individuals reported that, after retirement, they received no money income

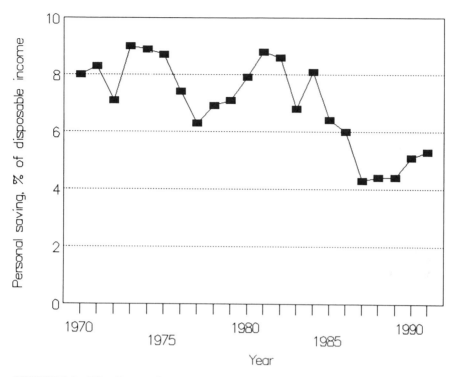

FIGURE 1. *The Rate of Personal Saving, National Income Accounts.*

from assets. At age sixty, nearly 30% of middle-class individuals lacked sufficient wealth to replace two years' worth of income. Similarly, Hammermesh (1984) concluded that, during the 1970s, most elderly individuals failed to accumulate resources sufficient to sustain their accustomed standards of living. Indeed, consumption shortly after retirement exceeded the highest sustainable level of consumption by an average of 14%. Hammermesh found that, within a few years of retirement, most households were forced to reduce their expenditures substantially.[1] Hausman and Paquette (1987) also documented substantial declines in consumption for men who involuntarily retired earlier than expected.

Unfortunately, these microeconomic studies of the adequacy of personal saving are now somewhat dated. In addition, they tend to use fairly arbitrary standards of income or consumption replacement to judge the adequacy of wealth accumulation. In this study, we adopt a

[1] Other economists have reached somewhat more optimistic conclusions. See Kotlikoff, Spivak, and Summers (1982).

different strategy. Using an elaborate model of household decision making, we simulate asset accumulation profiles.[2] We then compare these simulated profiles with actual profiles estimated from more recent household survey data.

The simulation model uses a life cycle planning framework to establish the criteria for household decision making. In this framework, a household's standard of living at any point is taken to be a function of its material consumption per capita, and its overall well-being depends upon both its present and future standards of living. Loosely speaking, the life cycle framework implies that a household should accumulate wealth sufficient to finance a standard of living during retirement that is consistent with its standard of living prior to retirement.

The model takes as inputs certain descriptive data concerning a household, including age, birth cohort, current earnings, pension coverage, education, marital status, and gender (if single). Based on these characteristics, the model imputes an earnings history, a family composition history, and mortality probabilities. The earnings history is extrapolated from cross-sectional age-earnings profiles and is adjusted to reflect the economy's baseline wage growth. Similarly, the family composition history is constructed from estimates of the relationship between household size and various household characteristics. Mortality probabilities are obtained from gender-specific actuarial tables. The model also incorporates important macroeconomic factors, such as interest rates, inflation, economic growth rates, aspects of the federal, state, and local income tax systems, and social security statutes.

The model generates consumption and asset trajectories through an iterative procedure. The first step in this procedure determines the household's asset accumulation plan for the first year of its economic life (taken to be age 26). The choice of a plan is based in part upon forecasts of its future economic prospects.[3] Decisions taken in the initial year determine the level of retirement assets that the household carries into the following year. The second step of the procedure determines the household's asset accumulation plan in its second year of economic life. Because the household may learn more about its economic prospects between the first and the second years, its forecasts may change. Consequently, the household's second-year plan may deviate from the plan that it envisioned in the first year. For example, if during the second year, rates of interest rise unexpectedly, the household may decide to

[2] Development of this model was sponsored by Merrill Lynch & Co., Inc. For a detailed description of the model, see Bernheim (1992b).

[3] Forecasts of macroeconomic variables are calculated using simple econometric models.

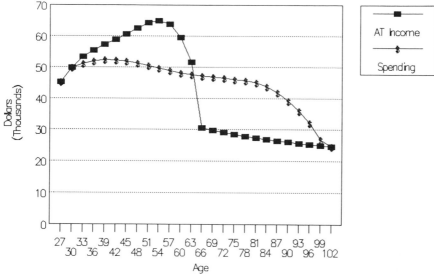

FIGURE 2. *Simulated After-Tax Income and Consumption Trajectories.*

take advantage of this development by saving more than it had planned previously. Financial decisions taken in the second year establish the level of retirement assets carried over into the third year. This procedure is repeated, until the current year is reached. The household's asset accumulation plan for the current year supplies the forecast for future asset and consumption trajectories.[4]

It is important to understand that the model describes the accumulation of assets only for retirement. There are, of course, many reasons to save. Households should prepare for the possibility of illness, layoff, disability, death, and other risks for which they are imperfectly insured. In addition, most households accumulate resources to pay for large expenses such as college tuition or the purchase of an automobile. In the current study, no attempt is made to estimate the extent to which households should save for these other reasons.

Figures 2 and 3 depict the output of an illustrative simulation run. This

---

[4] It should be noted that, in each year, the model treats all forecasts of future prospects as if these prospects were known with certainty. Yet, in each decision year, additional information is acquired, and forecasts are revised. It would be preferable to employ a simulation model that would explicitly recognize uncertainty concerning future conditions and incorporate this uncertainty into consumer decision making. However, this alternative approach poses considerable technical problems. The simplified approach adopted here probably has the effect of understanding the ideal level of asset accumulation, because, in the presence of uncertainty, households would also have a precautionary motive for saving.

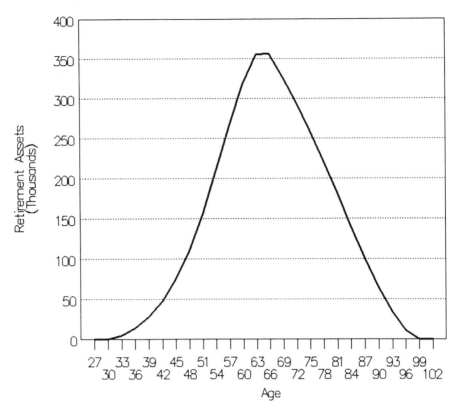

FIGURE 3. *Simulated Wealth Trajectory.*

particular simulation was constructed for a household with the following characteristics: age 27 (as of 1991), some college education, married, current earnings of $60,540, and the primary earner is covered by a private pension. Figure 2 displays, in constant 1991 dollars, this household's trajectory of after-tax earned income (including pensions and social security) and its consumption. Note that after-tax earnings rise steeply early in life. Earnings growth continues at a reduced level until the individual reaches age 55, at which point it begins to fall. After retirement, earned income consists of social security and private pension benefits. Because pensions are less than perfectly indexed for inflation, real benefits decline gradually over time.

As a direct consequence of its rapid earnings growth early in life, the household saves nothing for retirement prior to age 30. In fact, during its 20s, the household would prefer to borrow against future income in order to consume more than its current after-tax income. However, the model does not permit these households to obtain loans because they lack collateral. Between ages 30 and 80, the consumption trajectory is relatively flat. This property reflects the household's preference for a stable standard of living. However, during the 30s and 40s, consumption is somewhat elevated relative to the 60s and 70s. This pattern results from changes in household composition: between the ages of 30 and 50, the typical household incurs significant child-rearing costs. Consumption declines rapidly after age 80 until, at age 101, it matches after-tax retirement benefits. Falling survival probabilities drive this end-of-life decline. Because there is a relatively low probability of reaching age 90, the household would prefer to sacrifice the standard of living that it would receive at age 90 (if it survived that long) in favor of a higher standard of living earlier in life.

Figure 3 depicts the associated trajectory of retirement assets. Assets are accumulated at an increasing rate early in life. They reach a peak at retirement and then steadily decline until they are exhausted at age 100.

Actual asset trajectories are estimated using the 1983 and 1986 waves of the Survey of Consumer Finances (SCF). The Federal Reserve in conjunction with other federal agencies sponsored the SCF, and it is recognized as one of the best available sources for data on household balance sheets.[5]

We restrict attention to married couples for which the husband was fully employed and between the ages of 25 and 64 in 1986. A total of 1,314 households in the SCF sample satisfy these criteria. Our measure of accumulated net worth includes stocks and mutual funds, bonds, checking and savings accounts, IRA and Keogh accounts, money market accounts, certificates of deposit, profit sharing and thrift accounts, the dollar cash value of whole life insurance, and other financial assets, as well as net equity in property (other than primary residences) and business assets, less credit card debt, consumer debt, and other debt.[6] This measure of net worth excludes all assets and liabilities associated with homes and vehicles. This is appropriate because households appear to have a strong aversion to paying living expenses during retirement by reducing home equity (see Venti and Wise, 1989); moreover, it seems likely that few individuals save for retirement by accumulating wealth in the form of vehicles.

We divide the sample into two subgroups, based upon whether or not

[5] See Avery and Elliehausen (1988) and Avery and Kennickell (1988) for a more complete discussion of the SCF.

[6] Accumulated wealth for 1983 is expressed in 1986 dollars using the Consumer Price Index.

the husband completed college. Our sample includes 474 husbands who completed college and 840 husbands who did not complete college. Education is of interest for two reasons. First, it may be related to differences in behavior, either because education enhances an individual's ability to formulate coherent long-range plans, or because those who pursue more education do so precisely because they are more likely to be concerned about the future. Second, education is highly correlated with income. Adjusted for age, the median earnings of households in which the husband is college educated are roughly 57% higher than the median earnings of households in which the husband is not college educated. Because IRA eligibility is subject to an AGI cap, differences in saving behavior across income categories is of particular interest. Although it might seem more natural to divide the sample by income in order to examine these differences, that approach poses the practical difficulty that income varies with age. For example, a household with earnings of $50,000 at age 27 is probably much wealthier over the course of a lifetime than a household with earnings of $55,000 at age 55. For this purpose, one can think of education as a proxy for permanent income.

As a first step in our analysis, we examine changes in wealth between 1983 and 1986. In order to control for differences in resources across households, we focus our discussion on the ratio of the change in wealth to total wage income. We divide out sample into subgroups based upon age (25–29, 30–34, 34–39, 40–44, 45–49, 50–54, 55–59, 60–64). For each of these subgroups, we calculate the median change-in-wealth-to-wages ratio (adjusting for sampling weights). The use of medians rather than means is important, because the distribution of assets is highly skewed. Although mean wealth is quite high for many population subgroups, this fact tells us very little about the adequacy of saving for the typical household within these groups. Rather, it primarily reflects the extreme behavior of a few unrepresentative households. In contrast, median wealth is not influenced by extreme outliers.

We then simulate asset accumulation trajectories for households that are representative of each population subgroup. The household characteristics (wage income, years of education) chosen for these simulations are based on within-subgroup population medians. Two simulations are conducted for each population subgroup: one assumes that the primary earner is covered by a private pension, while the other assumes that the primary earner is not covered by a private pension.

When one is comparing estimated and simulated trajectories, it is important to bear in mind that the simulations focus on preparation for retirement as the sole motive for saving. Unfortunately, when examining the data, one cannot determine whether particular assets were accumulated for retirement or for some other purpose. Aside from excluding residences and vehicles, we make no attempt to discern saving motives. Consequently, the comparison between estimated trajectories and simulated trajectories may provide an overly optimistic picture of the adequacy of retirement saving.

Figure 4 depicts results for the "no-college" sample. "Actual" refers to median change-in-wealth-to-wage ratios based upon the SCF, "Sim/no pen" indicates simulated change-in-wealth-to-wage ratios for a representative household without pension coverage for the primary earner, and "Sim/pen" denotes simulated change-in-wealth-to-wage ratios for a representative household with pension coverage for the primary earner. Note that simulated change-in-wealth-to-wage ratios rise steeply with age. This occurs for two reasons. First, wages increase more rapidly than consumption during most of an individual's working life (refer back to Figure 2). Second, reinvested capital income rises as the household accumulates assets. In contrast, the actual change-in-wealth-to-wage ratios do not vary significantly with age. By the time the household reaches middle age, simulated asset accumulation exceeds actual accumulation by a wide margin. Although actual asset accumulation is higher than the simulated profiles at ages 27 and 32, this result is of little consequence, because the data reflect saving for a variety of purposes aside from retirement. Overall, Figure 4 suggests that, between 1983 and 1986,

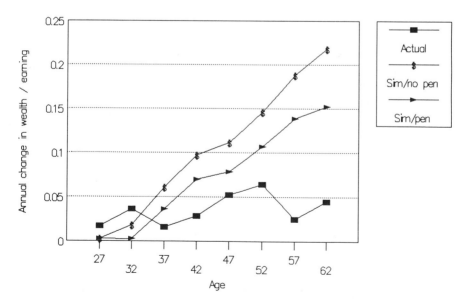

FIGURE 4. *Rates of Asset Accumulation, No College.*

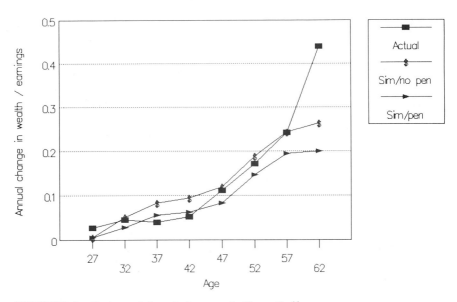

FIGURE 5. *Rates of Asset Accumulation, College.*

households without a college education saved far less than our simulation model predicts.

Figure 5 depicts results for the "college" sample. The contrast between Figures 4 and 5 is remarkable. In cases where the head of household has completed college, both simulated and actual change-in-wealth-to-wage ratios rise steeply with age. Moreover, simulated asset accumulation tracks actual asset accumulation remarkably well. Taken at face value, Figure 5 suggests that college-educated households saved adequately for retirement between 1983 and 1986.

Low rates of asset accumulation do not necessarily imply that households are inadequately prepared for retirement. In principle, a household with high initial assets in 1983 (relative to the simulated trajectory) could save little between 1983 and 1986 and still remain above the simulated asset trajectory in 1986. Conversely, high rates of asset accumulation do not necessarily imply that households are adequately prepared for retirement, because these households may have started out well below the simulated trajectory. To evaluate the adequacy of retirement preparation, one must therefore examine levels of wealth in addition to changes in wealth.

Consequently, as a second step in our analysis, we examine levels of wealth for 1986. We proceed exactly as in the first step, except that we focus on wealth-to-wage ratios, rather than on change-in-wealth-to-wage

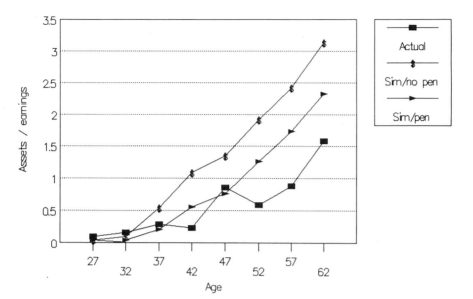

FIGURE 6. *Total Assets, No College.*

ratios. Figures 6 and 7 depict the results. These figures reinforce the lessons drawn from Figures 4 and 5. In particular, actual asset trajectories are far below simulated trajectories for the "no-college" sample, while actual and simulated trajectories track each other rather well for the "college" sample. Indeed, because the majority of college educated workers are covered by private pensions, it appears that actual asset trajectories are actually above simulated trajectories for those with a college education.

Although it is tempting to conclude that inadequate saving is largely confined to those without a college education, this conclusion must be tempered by two considerations. First, as indicated by Figure 1, personal saving declined sharply *after* the 1983–1986 period. Using a sample of relatively young individuals (ages 25–44) surveyed in early 1992, Bernheim (1992a) found much more pervasive evidence of inadequate saving. Second, the model probably understates the amount of wealth that each household ought to accumulate. The most obvious reason for this bias is that the simulations envision retirement planning as the sole motive for saving. In addition, it is quite likely that the model overstates mortality probabilities (because it does not make any allowance for the fact that average life expectancy is projected to increase), understates the importance of health and long-term care costs for the elderly, and fails to consider the effects of mounting economic pressures that may force Congress and employers to scale back existing retirement benefits.

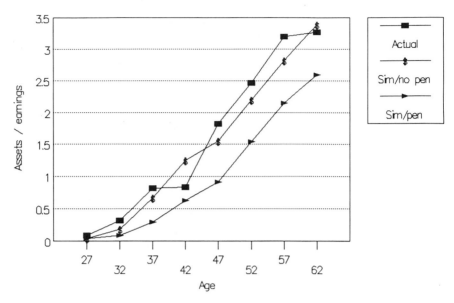

FIGURE 7. *Total Assets, College.*

Before one proceeds to the next section, it is important to discuss a potential criticism of this analysis. Some readers may be inclined to argue that our investigation sheds more light on the nature of tastes than on the adequacy of saving for retirement (see, e.g., Lazear, 1992). After all, any measure of adequacy is subjective. If a household has chosen to save relatively little, who are we to argue? Presumably, the household has its own best interests at heart.

We are not persuaded by this argument. Even in the context of the traditional life cycle hypothesis, individuals may face incentives that lead to inefficiently low levels of saving. For example, as individuals save more, they may lose the benefits from social insurance programs (Hubbard, Skinner, and Zeldes, 1992), risk the loss of eligibility for college scholarships (Feldstein, 1992), or reduce assistance from other members of the extended family (Bernheim and Stark, 1988).[7] These considerations may be particularly important for lower-income individuals.

It is also possible that, for some households, the life cycle hypothesis may not adequately characterize saving behavior. For some economic decisions, one can argue that, through trial and error, an individual

---

[7] Bernheim (1992c) provides a more comprehensive discussion of the factors that could produce an inefficiently low level of saving within the standard life cycle framework.

eventually learns to behave in a way that is consistent with utility maximization. This argument, however, is less persuasive in the context of life cycle saving. Each individual accumulates resources for retirement only once; there is no opportunity to learn from one's mistakes. Moreover, the life cycle saving decision is extraordinarily complex, in that it requires an individual to contemplate labor earnings, investment strategies, macroeconomic trends, and a vast assortment of risks, all over a very long time frame. It would be surprising if the average individual, in isolation, with no practice and little or no training, would act as a perfectly rational, farsighted utility maximizer. Manski (1993) discusses the circumstances in which learning from others can take the place of personal experience. Even with good role models and reference groups, however, it is difficult to imagine that households do not deviate from their optimal life cycle consumption profiles.

In recent years, a number of economists have argued against the view that individuals act as if they maximize an intertemporal utility function, and have instead emphasized the importance of behavioral concepts such as habit, mental accounting, and self-control (see, e.g., Shefrin and Thaler, 1988). Behavioral theories allow for the possibility that individuals may regret their bad habits and lack of foresight after the fact. Consequently, the notion of inadequate saving has a clear normative meaning within the context of these theories.

The evidence offered in this section suggests that most households without a college education do not behave in a manner consistent with optimal life cycle planning. These households save little relative to their simulated asset trajectories. Moreover, their estimated and simulated trajectories do not even exhibit the same qualitative patterns (refer once again to Figure 4).[8] Given the behavioral differences between households with and without college degrees, an important question arises: Is it possible to design policies that effectively stimulate saving at all levels of education and income?

III. PENSION POLICY

In recent years, asset accumulation in private pension plans has accounted for a substantial fraction of personal saving (see Bernheim and

---

[8] It could be argued that low-income individuals save less relative to simulated saving because they discount the future more heavily. Although a higher discount factor would reduce saving, it would not alter the qualitative features of the asset trajectories (unless discounting was high enough to prevent the accumulation of any significant assets for retirement).

Shoven, 1988, and Bosworth, Burtless, and Sabelhaus, 1991). This observation raises the possibility that policies affecting private pensions may have powerful effects on aggregate personal saving. Whether or not these effects would actually materialize in practice depends upon the manner in which workers would respond to an expansion of private pension coverage. Economic theory suggests that such an expansion would simply crowd out other forms of personal saving. The simulation results presented in section II illustrate this principle. However, previous studies of personal saving generally fail to find evidence for the hypothesis that private pensions reduce other forms of personal saving (see, e.g., the review in Shefrin and Thaler, 1988, especially pp. 622–624). Depending upon whether one credits the theoretical analysis or the empirical studies, one can reach dramatically different conclusions about the effect of pension policy on aggregate personal saving.

The analysis of section II raises an intriguing possibility: if the behavior of those with college education conforms to the predictions of the life cycle hypothesis, while the behavior of those without a college education does not, then perhaps private pensions do displace personal saving among the college educated, but do not displace personal saving among the rest of the population. In this case, pension policy could be an effective tool for stimulating total personal saving, as long as it is primarily used to provide incentives for expansion of coverage among lower-income (less-educated) workers.

To investigate the effect of pensions on household saving, we estimate equations that explain the median value of the wealth-to-wage ratio (henceforth, WWRAT) as a function of the husband's age (AGE), total household earnings (EARN), and a dummy variable summarizing the husband's private pension coverage (PENS).[9] We employ a cubic function of AGE to allow for flexible age-wealth trajectories. Because earnings may be related to the shape of the asset trajectory as well as to its absolute level, we also interact EARN with AGE. For similar reasons, PENS is interacted with AGE in most specifications.

For purposes of comparison with the previous literature, it is useful to begin with results for the entire data sample (all households, irrespective of educational attainment). The following estimated equation is consistent with the view that pensions fail to displace other forms of personal saving:

---

[9] Because our object is to explain median wealth rather than mean wealth, we employ quantile regression techniques (least absolute deviations), rather than more traditional regression techniques (least-squared deviations).

$$\text{WWRAT} = -4.72 + 0.411 \text{ AGE} - 0.115 \text{ (AGE)}^2/10 + 0.106 \text{ (AGE)}^3/10^3$$
$$\quad\quad\quad (1.34) \quad (0.098) \quad\quad (0.023) \quad\quad\quad\quad (0.017)$$

$$- 0.140 \text{ EARN}/10^4 + 0.581 \text{ EARN} \times \text{AGE}/10^6 - 0.0004 \text{ PENS.}$$
$$\quad (0.024) \quad\quad\quad\quad (0.045) \quad\quad\quad\quad\quad\quad (0.0379)$$

Note that the coefficient of the pension dummy is economically trivial and statistically insignificant.

The absence of a relationship between pension coverage and personal saving is sometimes interpreted as providing evidence that standard economic models do not faithfully represent the typical household's decision-making process. Proponents of the standard model, however, argue that the absence of a pension effect is a statistical artifact. Pension coverage is not random. A worker who is concerned about retirement may turn down job offers from employers who fail to provide attractive pension benefits. Conversely, a worker who gives little thought to retirement may be unwilling to accept a job that provides pension coverage if this offer entails a reduction in current disposable income. If these hypothetical facts are indeed descriptive of behavior, then those who are inclined to select jobs with pension coverage will tend to save more than those who are inclined to select jobs without pension coverage. For any particular individual, a private pension may displace other forms of saving; however, in the data, this pattern may be obscured by the fact that pension coverage is correlated with the inclination to save more. In other words, a sample selection effect may offset the saving-displacement effect.

Unless we can determine whether the absence of a pension effect is a behavioral phenomenon or a statistical artifact, we cannot predict the impact of a change in pension policy on personal saving. We suggest a method of distinguishing between these two hypotheses, based upon the following argument. It is certainly possible that, by coincidence, a sample selection effect exactly offsets the saving-displacement effect. However, the magnitude of the saving-displacement effect should vary systematically with age; specifically, the difference between the accumulated assets of those with pension coverage and those without pension coverage should increase with age. Although the sample selection effect may also vary with age, it seems highly unlikely that these two effects would exactly offset each other at *every* age.

We therefore estimate a new equation, in which an interaction term involving PENS and AGE is added to the list of explanatory variables. The estimated relationship is as follows:

$$\text{WWRAT} = -4.64 + 0.406 \text{ AGE} - 0.114 (\text{AGE})^2/10 + 0.105 (\text{AGE})^3/10^3$$
$$\phantom{\text{WWRAT} = }(1.47) \quad (0.108) \quad\quad (0.025) \quad\quad\quad (0.019)$$

$$-\ 0.137 \text{ EARN}/10^4 + 0.576 \text{ EARN} \times \text{AGE}/10^6 - 0.098 \text{ PENS}$$
$$\ \ (0.026) \quad\quad\quad\quad (0.049) \quad\quad\quad\quad\quad\quad (0.169)$$

$$+\ 0.310 \text{ PENS} \times \text{AGE}/10^2.$$
$$\ \ (0.373)$$

Taken individually, the coefficients of the pension variables lack statistical significance. In addition, the hypothesis that both coefficients equal zero is entirely consistent with the data.[10] In other words, private pension eligibility is not systematically related to either the level or the shape of the asset accumulation trajectory. Although, in principle, this could still reflect the offsetting effects of asset displacement and sample selection, it seems implausible that these effects would offset each other at every age. It appears more likely that there is little or no behavioral link between pension eligibility and personal saving.

Of course, the preceding results do not distinguish between households on the basis of education. In light of our previous findings, it is clearly important to make this distinction. We therefore estimate wealth trajectories separately for the two subgroups (college educated, not colleged educated) described in section II.

We obtain the following equation for households without a college education:

$$\text{WWRAT} = -3.60 + 0.313 \text{ AGE} - 0.086 (\text{AGE})^2/10 + 0.077 (\text{AGE})^3/10^3$$
$$\phantom{\text{WWRAT} = }(1.51) \quad (0.111) \quad\quad (0.026) \quad\quad\quad (0.020)$$

$$-\ 0.110 \text{ EARN}/10^4 + 0.406 \text{ EARN} \times \text{AGE}/10^6 + 0.008 \text{ PENS}$$
$$\ \ (0.044) \quad\quad\quad\quad (0.088) \quad\quad\quad\quad\quad\quad (0.176)$$

$$-\ 0.125 \text{ PENS} \times \text{AGE}/10^2.$$
$$\ \ (0.395)$$

Note that the coefficients of the pension variables are even smaller, both in terms of economic and statistical significance, than they were in the previous equation (based on the full sample). In order to illustrate the implications of this equation, we extrapolate asset trajectories for hypothetical

[10] The F statistic for the joint hypothesis that both coefficients equal zero is 0.78. One would obtain an F statistic of this magnitude or greater roughly 46% of the time, even if the true coefficients were zero.

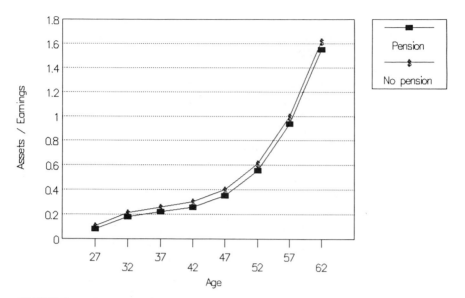

FIGURE 8. *Estimated Wealth Trajectories, No College.*

households with pension coverage and households without pension coverage.[11] Figure 8 exhibits these trajectories. Note that pension eligibility bears little or no relationship to the path of the wealth-to-wage ratio.

In contrast, we estimate the following equation for households with a college education:

$$\text{WWRAT} = \underset{(4.58)}{5.78} - \underset{(0.329)}{0.502}\ \text{AGE} + \underset{(0.077)}{0.126}\ (\text{AGE})^2/10 - \underset{(0.058)}{0.080}\ (\text{AGE})^3/10^3$$

$$+ \underset{(0.048)}{0.062}\ \text{EARN}/10^4 - \underset{(0.091)}{0.021}\ \text{EARN} \times \text{AGE}/10^6 + \underset{(0.563)}{0.899}\ \text{PENS} - \underset{(1.25)}{2.83}\ \text{PENS}$$

$$\times\ \text{AGE}/10^2.$$

Note that the coefficients of the pension variables in this equation are much more significant, both economically and statistically. The data decisively reject the hypothesis that both of these coefficients equal zero.[12]

---

[11] For the purpose of this calculation, the household's earnings are taken to be constant at $30,000. This figure is close to median age-adjusted earnings for households without a college education.

[12] The F statistic for this hypothesis is 5.60, which is significant at the 99% level of confidence.

Note also that the signs of all the other coefficients in the equation for college-educated households are exactly the reverse of the signs of these coefficients in the equation for households without college education. Clearly, the behavior of these two groups differs markedly.

In order to illustrate the implications of the estimated equation for college-educated households, we extrapolate asset accumulation trajectories for hypothetical households with private pensions and without private pensions.[13] Figure 9 depicts these trajectories. Note that those individuals who are eligible for pensions accumulate resources at a significantly slower rate than those individuals without pensions. Remarkably, at age 62, the gap between the assets of these two groups is almost identical in magnitude to the gap that emerges from our simulations (Figure 7). These patterns are strongly consistent with the view that private pensions displace other personal saving for college-educated households. It is unlikely that the observed relationship between pension coverage and saving results from spurious factors, because such factors would presumably also have produced the same patterns for less-educated households.[14] These results suggest that previous studies may have failed to find a significant saving displacement effect simply because they did not distinguish between households on the basis of education.

The contrast between Figures 8 and 9 points to a clear and important conclusion: private pensions displace personal wealth accumulation only when the head of the household is college educated. This is consistent with the findings of section II on the adequacy of personal saving. Indeed, our evidence tends to support a more general conclusion: college-educated households behave in the manner predicted by standard economic theories of saving, while households with less education do not.

It should be emphasized that past and current policies have been more successful at stimulating the expansion of pension coverage among college-educated workers than among those with less education. Analysis of the SCF data reveals that 75.2% of husbands with college degrees are covered by private pensions, in comparison to 55.7% of husbands without college degrees. In other words, the current system is quite effective at providing pensions to those who reduce other saving in response, but is substantially less effective at providing coverage to those individuals for whom pensions would represent incremental saving.

---

[13] For the purpose of this calculation, the household's earnings are taken to be constant at $50,000. This figure is close to age-adjusted median earnings for households with a college education.

[14] It is worth mentioning that there is some evidence of a small sample selection effect: the trajectory for households with pensions starts out slightly above the trajectory for households without pensions. However, this effect is not the dominant pattern in the data.

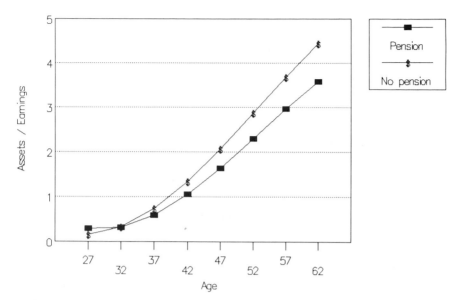

FIGURE 9. *Estimated Wealth Trajectories, College.*

Proposals to encourage or require portability of private pensions could have the effect of expanding pension coverage among lower-income workers. The absence of portability substantially reduces the benefits of pension coverage for workers with relatively little job stability. On average, these workers also have relatively low earnings. Portability would enhance the attractiveness of pensions to workers with little job stability and thereby increase the likelihood that these workers would obtain pension coverage.

A more drastic proposal would require employers to provide all workers with private pension coverage. Although this requirement would not be related to income, it would have a far greater impact on pension coverage among low-income workers than on pension coverage among high-income workers (roughly three-fourths of whom are already covered). In response to this requirement, those employers who had not previously provided pension coverage would probably reduce other forms of employee compensation. Our analysis suggests that newly covered workers with high earnings would simply adjust other personal saving to offset this change. In contrast, newly covered workers with lower earnings would reduce consumption. In effect, mandatory pension coverage would force lower-income households to increase saving.

Our analysis also raises concern about the recent growth of 401K plans. Participation in these plans is entirely voluntary. Many employers have substituted 401K plans for more conventional plans in an effort to reduce operating expenses. We would not expect this trend to have a significant impact on the total amount of saving done either by or on behalf of high-income workers. However, the elimination of compulsory contributions may significantly depress total saving by or on behalf of lower-income workers.

IV. TAX INCENTIVES FOR SAVING

The most commonly discussed strategies for stimulating personal saving entail reductions in capital income taxation. Economic theory suggests that households will respond to a higher after-tax rate of return by increasing future consumption relative to current consumption. However, the increase in anticipated future net worth resulting from higher rates of return may actually induce households to save less. Indeed, empirical estimates of the interest elasticity of saving (which measures the sensitivity of saving to the after-tax rate of return) vary widely (see, e.g., Boskin, 1978; Summers, 1981; and Hall, 1988).

Current policies provide saving incentives primarily to lower-income households. Eligibility for deductible IRAs, for example, is subject to an AGI cap. The existence of an AGI cap raises an important question: does the interest elasticity of saving vary systematically across income classes?

Simulations based upon the model described in section II suggest that higher-income households should be much more responsive than lower-income households to a change in the after-tax rate of return. According to these simulations, a 35-year-old, high-school-educated couple with pension coverage and annual earnings of $30,000 in 1991 should have saved roughly 1.5% of its earnings.[15] A permanent, one percentage point rise in the before-tax rate of return modestly increases this figure to 1.6%. In contrast, a 35-year-old, college-educated couple with pension coverage and annual earnings of $50,000 in 1991 should have saved roughly 4.8% of its earnings. The same permanent, one percentage point rise in the before-tax rate of return increases this figure by a much larger amount (both absolutely and proportionately), to 5.5%. Similar results hold for couples without pensions. For the representative high-school-educated couple, saving would fall from 5.6% of earnings to 4.5% of earnings in response to the higher rate of return; for the college-

---

[15] In this calculation, the rate of saving is defined as saving above and beyond reinvestment of capital income, divided by after-tax wage income.

educated couple, it would fall less (both absolutely and proportionately), from 9.2% to 8.8%.[16]

The contrast between the simulated responses of college-educated individuals and high-school-educated individuals becomes even more striking when one factors in the statistics on pension coverage mentioned at the end of section III. If one averages across those individuals with pensions and those individuals without pensions, the simulations imply that saving by college-educated households would increase by 10.2% in response to a permanent one percentage point increase in the before-tax rate of return, while the saving of households without college degrees would *fall* by 4.5%. Consequently, a policy that provides tax incentives for saving exclusively to lower-income households excludes those households that are most likely to increase saving in response to the policy; indeed, it is conceivable that such policies could actually reduce aggregate personal saving.

It is important to emphasize that this positive relationship between income and the interest elasticity of saving results from a natural economic consideration, rather than from some peculiar feature of the simulation model. It is natural to assume that, when planning for the future, most households are concerned first and foremost with assuring themselves of some minimum standard of living. As lifetime resources increase, households have more discretion to allocate resources over time in a way that increases consumption above and beyond this minimum standard. Saving to provide for minimum consumption is, in effect, saving for a fixed target. It is well known that an individual who saves to achieve some target will reduce saving in response to an increase in the rate of return (see, e.g., Bernheim and Shoven, 1988). In contrast, discretionary saving to finance consumption over and above the target responds positively to an increase in the rate of return. For low-income households, saving to achieve the minimum consumption target is probably far more important than saving to fund incremental consumption. Thus, target saving dominates the simulated behavior of these households, and produces a low or negative interest elasticity of saving. On the other hand, for high-income households, saving to fund incre-

---

[16] These simulations imply that the interest elasticity of saving tends to be higher when the household has private pension coverage. The explanation for this phenomenon is straightforward. An increase in the rate of return reduces the present discounted value of future income; in that sense, it makes the household poorer, and reduces current consumption. (This effect was originally noted by Summers, 1981). Because pension income is received after retirement, its present discounted value is more sensitive to the rate of return than is the present discounted value of future (preretirement) earnings. Thus, those individuals with pensions are more likely than those individuals without pensions to reduce current consumption in response to an increase in the rate of return.

mental consumption is probably far more important than saving to achieve the minimum consumption target. Consequently, incremental saving dominates the simulated behavior of these households and produces a high-interest elasticity of saving. In the appendix, we develop this argument mathematically and demonstrate for a simple model that the interest elasticity of saving rises with income.

Throughout this section, we have assumed that household behavior accords with standard economic theories. The preceding sections call this premise into question. However, this observation does not undermine our conclusion. We have found that the behavior of college-educated (high-income) households does correspond to the predictions of standard theories; consequently, for this group, it is likely that one would observe a substantial interest elasticity of saving. On the other hand, we have also found that the behavior of households without a college education (those with lower income) does not conform to standard economic theories. Although this finding reduces our faith in the applicability of our simulation results, it does not reverse our conclusions concerning the interest elasticity of saving. The notion that households will respond to a change in the after-tax rate of return is predicated upon the assumption that households rationally anticipate and plan for future economic contingencies. To the extend that this assumption proves incorrect, there is no particular reason to believe that low-income households will respond to a change in the after-tax rate of return.

Most current proposals to provide tax incentives for saving are patterned after IRAs. IRAs were established as part of the 1974 Employee Retirement Income Security Act, to give workers who were not covered by employer-provided pension plans added incentives to accumulate resources for retirement. In 1981, IRA eligibility was extended to all taxpayers. Subsequently, the Tax Reform Act of 1986 curtailed the tax deductibility of IRA contributions for high-income households.

Two prominent current policy initiatives would reverse the direction of the 1986 reforms and extend tax incentives for saving to households in higher-income brackets. The Bush Administration's Family Saving Accounts (FSAs) would allow single individuals with incomes below $60,000 and married couples with incomes below $120,000 to make contributions of up to $2,500 per person (not including children) to qualified accounts. The FSA proposal is an example of a "back-loaded" system: contributions are nondeductible, but accumulated funds are not taxed upon withdrawal. An alternative proposal, the Bentsen-Roth "super-IRA," would allow contributions of up to $2,000 per person (not including children) to either a traditional or a back-loaded IRA.

Unfortunately, there are sound conceptual reasons to doubt the effectiveness of extending eligibility for IRA-style accounts to higher-income households. First, contributions are capped. Under the current system, a single taxpayer, for example, can make no more than $2,000 in tax-deductible contributions. For any taxpayer who would have saved more than $2,000 in the absence of IRAs, the availability of an IRA does not affect the costs or the benefits that result from an additional dollar of saving and, therefore, provides no incentive on the margin for the tax-payer to increase saving. In such cases the IRA constitutes a "giveaway" of public funds, and its principal effect is to reduce federal tax receipts. In addition, the IRA may actually induce the taxpayer to spend more on current consumption, because it increases his or her total after-tax resources. For both of these reasons, the IRA would contribute to a lower rate of national saving. These concerns are of little significance for low-income households, because few of them would save more than $2,000 in the absence of the program. It is far more likely that high-income households would save more than the contribution limit. Thus, a standard IRA-style scheme may be a particularly ineffective method of providing high-income households with tax incentives for saving.

Second, even if a taxpayer would not (in the absence of IRAs) have saved more than the IRA contribution limit in a given year, he or she could take full advantage of the IRA deduction either by drawing down previously accumulated assets or by borrowing. Indeed, the *1992 Tax Guide for College Teachers and Other College Personnel* devotes a full page to the issue, "What if You're Short of Cash to Fund Your IRA?" (pp. 229–230). The guide describes an IRS private letter ruling that allows households to finance their IRAs by borrowing. Contributions funded either by shifting existing assets or by borrowing do not increase household saving. Instead, they depress national saving by reducing federal tax receipts, and add to the federal budget deficit. Once again, high-income households, who possess greater wealth, financial sophistication, and access to credit markets, are more likely than lower-income households to engage in borrowing or asset shifting and thereby defeat the purpose of the program.

Empirical evidence on the efficacy of IRAs is mixed. Gale and Scholz (1992) find little evidence that IRAs stimulated household saving between 1983 and 1986. Venti and Wise (1986, 1987, 1990, 1991) and Feenberg and Skinner (1989) argue that most IRA contributions during this period represent net increases in household saving. Joines and Manegold (1991) conclude that the effects of IRAs on household saving are unlikely to be as large as the estimates of Venti and Wise and may be as small as the estimates of Gale and Scholz.

An alternative proposal to promote household saving, based upon

"Premium Saving Accounts" (PSAs), is described in Bernheim and Scholz (1992). A PSA system would require each taxpayer to save in total some fixed amount (the "floor") before becoming eligible to make contributions to a tax-favored account. For each dollar saved in excess of the floor, the taxpayer would be eligible to contribute one additional dollar to the tax-favored account, up to some limit ("the ceiling"). These floors and ceilings would vary with AGI and certain types of capital income. As with IRAs, capital income accrued on balances held in PSA accounts would be exempt from taxation.[17]

The use of both floors and ceilings would create "windows" of program eligibility. Consider, for example, a husband and wife with a combined AGI of $80,000. They might face a floor of $8,000 and a ceiling of $12,000. Should they save less than $8,000 in the corresponding tax year, they would not be eligible to make any contributions to a tax-favored account. If, on the other hand, they saved $9,500, they would be eligible for favorable tax treatment on $1,500. If they saved more than $12,000, then they would be eligible to make the maximum contribution of $4,000 (the difference between $12,000 and $8,000).

The most important and distinctive feature of a PSA system is that floors and ceilings would vary with AGI. Eligibility windows could be positioned to maximize, within each income class, the number of households receiving tax breaks on the marginal dollar of saving. Thus, higher-income taxpayers would not be deprived of tax incentives for saving; rather, they would simply be required to save large fractions of their incomes than lower-income taxpayers before becoming eligible for the program. It would also be much more difficult for households to take advantage of tax-favored PSA accounts by shifting assets or by borrowing, because eligibility would be based upon total saving. An individual cannot increase total saving by shifting assets from one account to another or by borrowing in order to invest.[18]

To implement a PSA system, one needs to measure saving. Bernheim and Scholz (1992) propose the following measure:[19]

---

[17] With this essential structure, a PSA system could be either front-loaded or back-loaded. Penalties could be established to lock funds into tax-favored accounts for relatively short periods of time (e.g., seven years), or until some age close to retirement (perhaps age $59\frac{1}{2}$). Accounts could be established for specific purposes (e.g., retirement, purchase of a home, college education), or the accounts could be unrestricted.

[18] The administrative feasibility of monitoring total saving for each taxpayer is discussed in Bernheim and Scholz (1992).

[19] Many economists would define saving as the change in the stock of wealth between two points in time. If one adopts this definition, then saving is very hard to measure—one would need to assess the market value of all assets every year. The definition used in the text represents a compromise between economic logic and administrative feasibility.

1. Net purchases of assets (i.e., for assets on which investors receive capital gains and losses, total purchases minus total sales),

plus

2. The January 1 to January 1 change in cash account balances (e.g., bank accounts),

minus

3. The January 1 to January 1 change in total debt (e.g., mortgages and consumer credit).

In effect, saving is defined as the incremental personal resources that an individual diverts into investments in any given year, over and above reinvested capital gains.[20]

If this definition of saving is employed, then it is also important to adjust each taxpayer's eligibility floors and ceilings upward by the amount of capital income other than capital gains. In the absence of such an adjustment, the system would distort investors' choices among assets, causing them to tilt their portfolios toward assets that produce current income, rather than capital gains. See Bernheim and Scholz (1992) for a detailed discussion of this issue.

In the remainder of this section, we evaluate the effects of three distinct strategies for stimulating household saving: an IRA-like program with an AGI cap (henceforth referred to as the "standard IRA" system), an IRA-like program without an AGI cap (henceforth referred to as the "universal IRA" system), and a PSA system. We compare the cost-effectiveness of extending tax incentives for saving to higher-income taxpayers through universal IRAs and PSAs.

Table 1 contains illustrative eligibility schedules for a PSA system. We selected these particular schedules after examining the empirical distribution of saving. We restricted attention to a class of simple schedules and chose the schedules that provide maximum saving incentives.[21]

The schedules define eligibility windows for each level of AGI. In order to facilitate comparison with IRAs, we have adopted window widths of $2,000 per year for single households, $2,250 per year for married couples with one earner, and $4,000 per year for married couples with two earners. The lower end of the window (the floor) is determined by a two-part calculation. First, compute the value of an algebraic

---

[20] Note that it is possible to compute this measure of saving without assessing the value of unrealized capital assets because, by definition, unrealized gains are fully reinvested.

[21] An eligibility schedule belongs to this class if the floor is set equal to zero up to some level of AGI, beyond which the floor rises linearly with AGI. We also studied more complex schedules but discovered that it was difficult to improve significantly upon the simple schedule described in the text.

TABLE 1.
Deductible Contribution Formula.

If your income is	Deductible qualified contribution floor (added to capital income)	Deductible qualified contribution ceiling (added to floor)*
Married couples		
Less than $34,000	0	$2,250 or $4,000
Greater than $34,000	.167 × (Income − 34,000)	$2,250 or $4,000
Single households		
Less than $42,000	0	$2,000
Greater than $42,000	.34 × (Income − 42,000)	$2,000

* For the purpose of comparison with IRAs, married couples with one earner are allowed to contribute $2,250, and married couples with two earners can contribute $4,000. In the actual implementation of this proposal, we see no compelling reason to make this distinction.

expression involving AGI. We refer to this value as the "unadjusted floor"—it is identical for all taxpayers with the same level of AGI. Second, add capital income other than capital gains to obtain the "adjusted floor" (or simply, "the floor"). Table 1 indicates, for example, that a dual-earner married couple with an AGI of $30,000 and no capital income would have a floor of $0 and a ceiling of $4,000. In contrast, a couple with an AGI of $120,000 and dividend and interest income of $2,000 would have a floor of $16,362 (0.167 × $86,000 + $2,000) and a ceiling of $20,362. Figure 10 graphs the proposed eligibility schedule for married couples. Note that because the typical U.S. household saves very little, the floor is zero for lower-income households.

The standard and universal IRA systems differ from the PSA proposal in that the IRA systems anchor the eligibility window at $0 for all income classes, and no adjustment is made for capital income. The standard system phases out deductible contributions for couples with incomes between $40,000 and $50,000 and for single taxpayers with incomes between $25,000 and $35,000. The universal system allows all households to make deductible contributions.[22]

We will compare these plans on the basis of three criteria. The first criterion is a measure of effectiveness. Specifically, for each plan, we estimate the number of households that would receive a higher after-tax rate of return on the incremental dollar of investment. We refer to these households as the IMPACT GROUP. Our second criteria is a measure of wasteful subsidization. Specifically, for each plan, we estimate the num-

[22] The IRA-like proposals we simulate are superior to actual IRA schemes, because, in practice, IRA schemes are susceptible to tax arbitrage strategies involving borrowing and asset shifting, which our simulations do not capture.

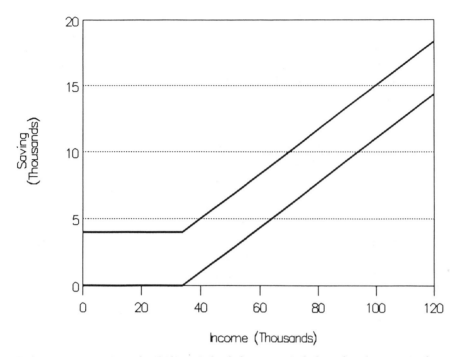

FIGURE 10. *PSA Eligibility Schedule, Married Couples (no capital income).*

ber of households that would make the maximum eligible contribution to a tax-favored account while continuing to receive the unsubsidized after-tax rate of return on the incremental dollar of investment. We refer to these households as the NO-IMPACT GROUP. Our third criterion is also a measure of wasteful subsidization: we calculate the budgetary cost of subsidizing the NO-IMPACT GROUP. We refer to this cost as the GIVEAWAY.

In evaluating these plans, it may be useful to consider other criteria, such as the ratio of the number of households in the IMPACT GROUP to the DOLLARS OF GIVEAWAY. A "bang-for-the-buck" ratio of this type would provide some indication of the cost-effectiveness of each proposal.

To calculate the size of the IMPACT GROUP, NO-IMPACT GROUP, and DOLLARS OF GIVEAWAY, we must predict the extent to which each household would participate in each plan. Our predictions are predicated on three behavioral assumptions. First, we assume that no household would make a contribution to any tax-favored account unless it would contribute to a universal IRA. Second, if a household would make a contribution to a universal IRA, then that same household would also, if eligible, contribute to either a standard IRA or a PSA. The justification for these first two assumptions is compelling: both proposals are identical to the universal IRA system, except that eligibility is more restricted.

Our third assumption concerns the magnitude of contributions. For each alternative proposal, we assume that an eligible household would make the maximum allowable contribution when two conditions are satisfied: the household would contribute to a universal IRA, and its total saving would exceed its eligibility ceiling. This third assumption is more problematic than the others. Saving in a tax-favored account may be an imperfect substitute for other forms of saving because, perhaps, of restrictions on early withdrawal. Thus, it is conceivable that some households would contribute less than the maximum amount even when these conditions are satisfied. In practice, it would be very difficult to identify these households with available data.

Obviously, our three assumptions are helpful only if we know whether or not households are inclined to make contributions to universal IRA accounts. During the period of universal IRA eligibility, this inclination can be inferred from actual behavior. Consequently, we base our calculations upon a sample of households surveyed in 1983 and 1986 for which data on IRA participation are available.

More specifically, we use the 1983 and 1986 waves of the SCF. Key variables are constructed as follows. Income is defined as the average of total household income for 1983, 1984, and 1985. Our measure of saving corresponds to the definition proposed earlier. To calculate the net change in assets exclusive of capital gains or losses, we calculate (by asset category) the average constant contribution needed to generate the balance in 1986, given the observed balance in 1983 and the average rate of return that prevailed during this period. Our asset categories include stocks and mutual funds, bonds, IRA and Keogh accounts, money market accounts, certificates of deposit, profit sharing and thrift accounts, the dollar cash value of whole life insurance, and other financial assets (for a more detailed discussion of the calculations, see Gale and Scholz, 1992). Changes in cash account balances (saving and checking accounts) and total debt are measured directly.

Table 2 provides background information on the saving propensities of households that contributed to IRA accounts. The top panel shows that, on average across income groups, total saving was positive for only 59.5 percent of participating couples. Among those households that saved, average saving ranged from $5,693 in the lowest income quintile

TABLE 2.*

Income quintiles	Percentage that save	Dollars	
		Average amount for HHlds that save	*Median amount for HHlds that save*
Panel A: average annual saving of married couples, IRA Contributors 1983–1986[†]			
Lowest	59.5	5,693	3,840
Second	61.5	12,741	6,839
Middle	58.5	11,140	5,432
Fourth	61.7	19,693	9,358
Highest	56.4	90,296	19,695
Full population	59.5	26,728	7,128
Panel B: average annual saving of single households, IRA Contributors 1983–1986[‡]			
Lowest	56.6	2,885	2,322
Second	58.7	5,015	5,841
Middle	70.7	4,402	2,475
Fourth	63.0	8,017	3,518
Highest	60.1	36,212	9,923
Full population	61.7	11,130	3,579

* Data are from the 1983–1986 Survey of Consumer Finances. Saving is defined in the text, income deciles are given in Table 1.
† The weighted number of couples that contributed to IRAs between 1983 and 1986 is 13,536,814.
‡ The weighted number of singles that contributed to IRAs between 1983 and 1986 is 3,252,938.

to $90,296 in the highest income quintile. These averages, however, are affected by the relatively small number of households that saved very large amounts. The third column of the table provides the saving of the typical (median) participating households with positive total saving in each income quintile. These figures range from $3,840 in the bottom quintile to $19,695 in the top quintile. The typical participating couple with positive saving accumulates $7,128 per year. The corresponding figure for single households is $3,579.[23]

Table 3 compares the effect of the policies on married couples. The top panel shows the size of the IMPACT GROUP. Overall, the PSA system provides incentives to 2.4 million couples, roughly 90 percent more than the IRA with AGI restrictions and 30 percent more than the universal IRA. The difference is particularly pronounced in the top income quintile. By definition, the IRA with AGI caps ignores these households.

23 Bosworth, Burtless, and Sabelhaus (1991) and Venti and Wise (1992) present tabulations on household saving from several microdatasets, including the Survey of Consumer Finances. The numbers on saving presented in Tale 2 differ from these other tabulations in that they apply only to those households saving positive amounts.

TABLE 3.*

A Comparison of Three Saving-Incentive Proposals, Married Couples.

Income quintile	IRA w/ AGI cap	Universal IRA	PSA
Impact group (in 1000s)			
Lowest	559	559	560
Second	344	344	377
Middle	353	550	602
Fourth	0	284	622
Highest	0	102	228
Full population	1,256	1,840	2,388
No-impact group (in 1000s)			
Lowest	1,039	1,039	921
Second	1,262	1,262	1,143
Middle	1,277	1,080	813
Fourth	0	1,420	773
Highest	0	1,416	817
Full population	3,578	6,218	4,467
Annual giveaway (in $1,000,000s)			
Lowest	465	465	401
Second	813	813	725
Middle	728	1,002	767
Fourth	0	1,631	858
Highest	0	1,950	1,119
Full population	2,006	5,861	3,870

* Simulations use data from the 1983–1986 Survey of Consumer Finances. Saving and column headings are defined in the text. The PSA schedule is given in Table 1.

Relative to the universal IRA, the PSA increases the number of couples receiving marginal incentives in the top income quintile by 122.4 percent.[24] Because, in this sample, over 60 percent of positive household saving is attributable to households in the top quintile of the income distribution, this improvement is particularly important.

The bottom two panels of Table 3 measure the NO-IMPACT group and the cost of these ineffective subsidies. The calculations show, for

[24] Because high-income households are more likely to increase saving in response to tax incentives, there is some justification for selecting an eligibility schedule that would maximize the IMPACT GROUP in the top income quintile, rather than the total IMPACT GROUP. This would be accomplished with a schedule that sets the floor equal to zero as long as AGI is below $45,000, and increases the floor by 17.7 cents for each dollar of AGI over $45,000. Relative to the universal IRA, this PSA schedule increases the number of couples receiving marginal incentives in the top income quintile by 266.1 percent. Surprisingly, the use of a schedule that maximizes the IMPACT GROUP for the top quintile, rather than the total IMPACT GROUP, reduces the total IMPACT GROUP only slightly (by roughly 9,000 households). However, it increases the NO-IMPACT GROUP by 9.7 percent.

TABLE 4.*

A Comparison of Three Saving-Incentive Proposals, Single Taxpayers.

Income quintile	IRA w/ AGI cap	Universal IRA	PSA
Impact group (in 1000s)			
Lowest	188	188	199
Second	105	105	150
Middle	136	173	173
Fourth	25	97	38
Highest	0	40	134
Full population	454	603	694
No-impact group (in 1000s)			
Lowest	196	196	185
Second	280	280	236
Middle	312	275	275
Fourth	290	304	263
Highest	0	350	197
Full population	1,078	1,405	1,155
Annual giveaway (in $1,000,000s)			
Lowest	66	66	62
Second	141	141	117
Middle	168	158	158
Fourth	85	188	163
Highest	0	292	151
Full population	460	845	650

* Simulations use data from the 1983–1986 Survey of Consumer Finances. Saving and column headings are defined in the text. The PSA schedule is given in Table 1.

example, that the PSA system would reduce the number of households in the NO-IMPACT group by 1.75 million (28.2 percent) and would reduce federal expenditures on ineffective subsidies by $2.0 billion (34.0 percent), relative to the universal IRA. In terms of cost-effectiveness, the PSA system increases the ratio of the IMPACT GROUP to the GIVE-AWAY by 96.5 percent overall, and by 287.2 percent (i.e., by a factor of almost four) in the top income quintile. The IRA with AGI caps also effectively reduces ineffective subsidies and budgetary cost, but it achieves this reduction by excluding the very households that are most likely to respond to tax incentives.

Table 2 reveals that participating single households saved considerably less than married households. Nevertheless, the gains from adopting the PSA system would still be substantial for single households. Table 4 indicates that the size of the IMPACT group would increase by 15.1 percent overall, and by 235.4 percent in the top-income quintile, relative to the universal IRA proposal. Moreover, both the size of the

NO-IMPACT group and the GIVEAWAY would fall relative to the universal IRA proposal. The result is a 49.7 percent increase in overall cost-effectiveness (the ratio of the IMPACT group to GIVEAWAY), and a 551.3 percent increase in cost-effectiveness for the top quintile, relative to the universal IRA proposal.

These comparisons of IRA and PSA proposals incompletely incorporate behavioral responses. For example, households saving strictly less than the PSA eligibility floor might increase their saving in order to become eligible for PSAs. It is also possible that these proposals will differentially affect saving for psychological reasons. Indeed, those who believe that IRAs significantly stimulated private saving often suggest psychological explanations, such as the following: (1) IRAs were aggressively marketed by financial institutions; (2) IRAs provided taxpayers with an effective way of earmarking funds for retirement, thereby facilitating the division of funds into distinct "mental accounts," some of which are psychologically more difficult to invade; (3) the existence of a sizable early withdrawal penalty effectively locked saving into IRAs, thereby helping households to impose self-discipline; and (4) the IRA eligibility limit provided households with a saving "target." Empirical evidence suggests that the fourth effect was particularly important (many households contributed exactly $2,000, the widely publicized contribution limit, even in cases where they were actually eligible to contribute more). The PSA system, like a universal IRA program, would preserve all these features. Indeed, the fourth effect would probably be strengthened with PSAs, because the proposal would provide many taxpayers with more ambitious targets.

V. CONCLUSIONS

The evidence presented in this paper supports the view that many Americans, particularly those without a college education, save too little. Our analysis also indicates that it should be possible to increase total personal saving among lower-income households by encouraging the formation and expansion of private pension plans. It is doubtful that favorable tax treatment of capital income would stimulate significant additional saving by this group. Conversely, the expansion of private pensions would probably have little effect on saving by higher-income households. However, these households are more likely to increase saving significantly in response to favorable tax treatment of capital income. Currently, eligibility for IRAs is linked to an AGI cap, and pension coverage is more common among higher-income households than among low-income households. The most effective system for promoting personal saving would have precisely the opposite features.

Extending tax incentives for saving to higher-income households is problematic. We have discussed three competing policy options: IRAs with AGI caps, the universal IRA, and the PSA. Our analysis reveals that the PSA system is a more cost-effective vehicle for providing saving incentives to all households, particularly those in the top quintile of the income distribution.

Pension policies and tax policies do not exhaust the full range of strategies for stimulating personal saving. One particular class of policies not discussed here merits further attention. An accumulating body of evidence, including that contained in sections II and III of this paper, suggests that the behavior of many households (particularly those with lower income) are not well described by traditional economic theories. Consequently, it may be possible to design more effective policies by educating the population or by exploiting the psychology of saving. The Japanese appear to have had considerable success with such a strategy during the postwar period (see Horioka, 1988, and Bernheim, 1991). The development of a framework for analyzing policies of this type is an important research priority.

APPENDIX: HOUSEHOLD INCOME AND THE INTEREST ELASTICITY OF SAVING

Consider a two-period model, in which an individual maximizes

$$u(c_1, c_2) = \alpha^{-1} \left[\left(c_1 - m \right)^\alpha + \beta \left(c_2 - m \right)^\alpha \right],$$

subject to

$$c_1 + \frac{c_2}{1 + r} = w + \frac{w\mu}{1 + r},$$

where c_t denotes consumption in the tth period of life ($t = 1.2$), r is the after-tax rate of return, w is earnings in the first period, $w\mu$ is earnings in the second period (the reader should construe this as pension income, where $\mu < 1$ is the replacement rate), m is minimum consumption, and α is the (constant) elasticity of marginal utility with respect to consumption. Optimization requires

$$c_2 - m = \gamma \left(c_1 - m \right),$$

where

$$\gamma \equiv [\beta(1 + r)]^{\frac{1}{1-\alpha}}.$$

Substituting this expression into the budget constraint and solving for first period saving ($s = w - c_1$), we obtain

$$s = (w - m) - \frac{(1 + r)(w - m) + (w\mu - m)}{1 + r + \gamma}.$$

From this equation, we derive an expression for the interest elasticity of saving:

$$\varepsilon_s \equiv \frac{r}{s}\frac{ds}{dr} = -\frac{r\left[1 - \left(\dfrac{\gamma\xi}{(1 + r)(1 - \alpha)}\right)\right]}{1 + r + \gamma},$$

where

$$\xi = \frac{(1 + r)(w - m) + (w\mu - m)}{\gamma(w - m) - (\mu w - m)}.$$

It is then apparent that

$$\frac{d\varepsilon_s}{dw} = \left[\frac{r\gamma}{(1 + r)(1 - \alpha)(1 + r + \gamma)}\right]\frac{d\xi}{dw}.$$

It follows that the sign of $d\varepsilon_s/dw$ is the same as the sign of $d\xi/dw$. But

$$\frac{d\xi}{dw} = \frac{m(1 + r + \gamma)(1 - \mu)}{[(\gamma - \mu)w + m(1 - \gamma)]^2},$$

which is positive if and only if $\mu < 1$. Thus, as long as income replacement during retirement is less than complete, the interest elasticity of saving rises with income.

REFERENCES

Avery, Robert B. and Gregory E. Elliehausen (1988), "1983 Survey of Consumer Finances: Technical Manual and Codebook." Mimeo, Board of Governors of the Federal Reserve System, August.

————, and Arthur B. Kennickell (1988). "1986 Survey of Consumer Finances: Technical Manual and Codebook," Mimeo, Board of Governors of the Federal Reserve System, November.

Bernheim, B. Douglas (1991). *The Vanishing Nest Egg: Reflections on Saving in America.* Twentieth Century Fund, New York, NY.

———— (1992a), "Is the Baby Boom Generation Preparing Adequately for Retirement? Summary Report." Mimeo, Princeton University, August.

———— (1992b). "Is the Baby Boom Generation Preparing Adequately for Retirement? Technical Report." Mimeo, Princeton University, August.

———— (1992c). "A Discussion of Two Papers on Saving." Mimeo, prepared for the Economics of Aging Conference in Caneel Bay, Princeton University, May.

————, and John Karl Scholz (1992). "Premium Saving Accounts: A Proposal to Improve Tax Incentives for Saving." Mimeo, Princeton University and the University of Wisconsin—Madison, September.

————, and John B. Shoven (1988). "Pension Funding and Saving." In *Pensions in the U.S. Economy*, Zvi Bodie, John B. Shoven, and David A. Wise, eds., 85–111. Chicago: University of Chicago Press and NBER.

————, and Oded Stark (1988). "Altruism Within the Family Reconsidered: Do Nice Guys Finish Last?" *American Economic Review* 78, 1034–1045.

Bernstein, Allen (1991). *1992 Tax Guide for College Teachers and Other College Personnel.* Washington D.C.: Academic Information Services Inc.

Boskin, Michael (1978). "Taxation, Saving, and the Rate of Interest." *Journal of Political Economy* April, 3–27.

Bosworth, Barry, Gary Burtless, and John Sabelhaus (1991). "The Decline in Saving: Evidence from Household Surveys." *Brookings Papers on Economic Activity*, 1, 183–241.

Diamond, Peter A. (1977). "A Framework for Social Security Analysis." *Journal of Public Economics* December, 275–298.

Feenberg, Daniel R., and Jonathan Skinner (1989). "Sources of IRA Saving." In *Tax Policy and the Economy*, Lawrence Summers, ed., 25–46. Cambridge, MA: The MIT Press.

Feldstein, Martin (1992). "College Scholarship Rules and Private Saving." NBER Working Paper No. 4032, March.

Gale, William G., and John Karl Scholz (1992), "IRAs and Household Saving." Mimeo, UCLA and University of Wisconsin—Madison.

Hall, Robert (1988). "Intertemporal Substitution in Consumption," *Journal of Political Economy* 96, 337–357.

Hamermesh, Daniel S. (1984). "Consumption During Retirement: The Missing Link in the Life-Cycle." *Review of Economics and Statistics* February, 1–7.

Hausman, Jerry A., and Lynn Paquette (1987). "Involuntary Early Retirement and Consumption." In *Work, Health and Income Among the Elderly.* G. Burtless, ed., 151–175. Washington D.C.: Brookings Institution.

Horioka, Charles Y. (1988). "Why is Japan's Private Saving Rate So High?" In *Recent Developments in Japanese Economics.* R. Sato and T. Negishi, eds. Tokyo: Harcourt Brace Jovanovich Japan/Academic Press.

Hubbard, R. Glenn, Jonathan Skinner, and Stephen P. Zeldes (1992). "Precautionary Saving and Social Insurance." Mimeo, Columbia University, April.

Joines, Douglas H., and James G. Manegold (1991). "IRA and Saving: Evidence From a Panel of Taxpayers." Mimeo, U.S.C.

Kotlikoff, Laurence J., Avia Spivak, and Lawrence H. Summers (1982). "The Adequacy of Saving." *American Economic Review* December, 1056–1069.

Lazear, Edward P. (1992). "Some Thoughts on Savings." Hoover Institution Working Paper #E-92–17, June.

Manski, Charles F. (1993). "Dynamic Choice in a Social Setting: Learning From the Experience of Others." *Journal of Econometrics*, 58, 121–136.

Organization for Economic Cooperation and Development (1989). *OECD Economic Outlook, Historical Statistics, 1960–1989*, Organization for Economic Cooperation and Development: Paris, France.

Shefrin, Hersh M., and Richard H. Thaler (1988). "The Behavioral Life Cycle Hypothesis." *Economic Inquiry* 26, 609–643.

Summers, Lawrence (1981). "Capital Taxation in a Life Cycle Growth Model." *American Economic Review* September, 533–544.

——— (1985). "Issues in National Savings Policy." National Bureau of Economic Research Working Paper #1710, Cambridge, MA, September.

Venti, Steven F., and David A. Wise (1986). "Tax-Deferred Accounts, Constrained Choice and Estimation of Individual Saving." *Review of Economic Studies* LIII, 579–601.

———, and ——— (1987). "IRAs and Saving." In *The Effects of Taxation on Capital Accumulation*. Martin Feldstein, ed., 7–48. Chicago: University of Chicago Press and NBER.

———, and ——— (1989). "Aging, Moving, and Housing Wealth." In *The Economics of Aging*. David A. Wise, ed. Chicago: University of Chicago Press and NBER.

———, and ——— (1990). "Have IRAs Increased U.S. Saving?: Evidence from Consumer Expenditure Surveys." *Quarterly Journal of Economics* 105, 661–698.

———, and ——— (1991). "The Saving Effect of Tax-Deferred Retirement Accounts: Evidence from SIPP." In *National Saving and Economic Performance*, B. Douglas Bernheim and John B. Shoven, eds., 103–128. Chicago: University of Chicago Press and NBER.

———, and ——— (1992). "Government Policy and Personal Retirement Saving." *Tax Policy and the Economy* 6, 1–41.

THE UNEMPLOYMENT INSURANCE PAYROLL TAX AND INTERINDUSTRY AND INTERFIRM SUBSIDIES

Patricia M. Anderson
Department of Economics, Dartmouth College

Bruce D. Meyer
Department of Economics and Center for Urban Affairs and Policy
Research, Northwestern University and NBER

EXECUTIVE SUMMARY

Unemployment insurance (UI) in the U.S. is financed through a payroll tax that is imperfectly experience rated, and thus only partially reflects a firm's use of the system. As a result, certain firms and industries receive many more dollars in unemployment benefits than they pay in taxes. We document that the same patterns of large interindustry subsidies have persisted for over 30 years, and we find that these subsidies are due mostly to differences in layoff rates across industries. Agriculture, mining, manufacturing, and particularly construction receive subsidies, while trade, finance, insurance and real estate, and services consistently pay more in taxes than they receive. Additionally, using previously unexamined firm level data, we document a persistent pattern of interfirm subsidies across several years. Together, these results indicate that UI benefit payments

This paper was prepared for the 1992 NBER conference on Tax Policy and the Economy. We would like to thank James Poterba and seminar participants at Northwestern University for their comments, and Sherryl Bailey, John Steinman, and numerous officials of state employment security agencies for help in obtaining data. Meyer is grateful for support by the NSF through grants SES-8821721 and SES-9024548.

are predictable, thus weakening arguments for incomplete experience rating that focus on its insurance value to firms faced with large layoff costs. We also find that the efficiency costs of the cross-subsidies to less stable industries may be large, but such calculations depend on differences between marginal and average subsidies that are difficult to estimate.

Unemployment insurance (UI) in the United States is financed through an experience-rated payroll tax. That is to say, the tax rate for a firm partly depends on the benefits paid to its employees. While the bulk of the literature on the incentive effects of UI explores the relationship between UI benefits and unemployment durations, a growing strand of the literature focuses on this system of financing benefits through an experience-rated payroll tax.[1] This UI payroll tax is quantitatively important, currently raising over $20 billion annually. However, certain industries and firms receive many more dollars in unemployment benefits than they pay in taxes, with this subsidization occurring at the expense of other industries and firms. While such a pattern of cross-subsidies is expected in an insurance program at a given point in time, in fact the patterns of subsidies persist, year after year, for the same industries and firms. This continuous cross-subsidization will distort the efficient allocation of resources and increase the aggregate level of unemployment and its accompanying societal costs. Thus, it is important to understand not only the size and patterns of interindustry and interfirm subsidies, but also the degree and source of their persistence. It is also important to know the patterns of UI subsidies, because these likely affect the political economy of support by different industries and firms for UI reform.

Because state UI programs vary in many dimensions, we present evidence for a large number of states. We begin by documenting interindustry subsidies for the last dozen years using aggregate data. We find that the same industries receive subsidies in almost all states and that the subsidies are often very large. The subsidies have only fallen slightly since the changes in the UI finance under the Tax Equity and Fiscal Responsibility Act of 1982 (TEFRA) were implemented in 1985. However, this fall can at least partly be attributed to the reduction in subsidies typically found in better economic times. Even with such reforms, and despite the many changes in the economy in the past decades, there is also a very close correlation between the subsidies received during the last twelve years and those received thirty years ago.

---

[1] Atkinson and Micklewright (1991) is an excellent recent survey of the literature on UI incentive effects, while important early works on UI financing includes Becker (1972), Brechling (1977), Feldstein (1978), and Topel (1983). See Topel (1990) and Hamermesh (1990) for recent work.

We also analyze the sources of these interindustry subsidies by examining the relative importance of temporary and permanent layoff rates, unemployment durations, and wage and benefit levels. We find that the subsidies are directly attributable to higher temporary layoff rates and, to a lesser extent, to higher permanent layoff rates. Higher industry UI benefits per worker are also partly responsible, but relatively higher tax rates and taxable wages in these industries and lower unemployment durations tend to reduce the subsidy.

While this study and previous studies use industry data to group firms with presumably similar subsidies, industry data are really a proxy for firm data. Firms within the same industry (especially a broadly defined industry) may differ dramatically. In the past, however, firm panel data on UI benefits received and taxes paid have not been available. We use such data and find that the variation in use of UI is as great within industry as it is across industries. While the same firms tend to receive subsidies year after year, these firms are not confined to those industries that receive subsidies overall. Additionally, many firms in subsidized industries consistently pay more in taxes than they receive in benefits.

Thus, at both the firm and industry level, the patterns of redistribution are predictable, such that the unemployment insurance system has a strong element of persistent subsidization. This subsidization reduces labor costs and, thus, the cost of production for unstable industries and firms, and increases it for stable ones. In the case of an interindustry subsidy, it is unlikely to lead to higher industry profits, because entry into the industry would tend to compete away any above-average profits. Rather, the lower costs are likely to be reflected in lower prices, which allows unstable sectors to expand output and employment.[2] Because our industry groups are broad, part of what we call interfirm subsidies are really industry subsidies at a finer level and are likely to be reflected in product prices. Again, the result is an expansion of unstable firms, which is subsidized by net taxes on more stable ones. However, part of the firm level subsidies likely increases profits without affecting the allocation of resources across sectors.

The degree of persistence of firm level subsidies is important when one is determining how closely experience rated tax payments should reflect UI benefits received. While UI insures workers against job loss, incomplete experience rating of UI also insures firms against having to pay the full UI costs of a large layoff. The rationale for this second type of

---

[2] Deere (1991) examines evidence for such an effect at the broad industry level, concluding that employment in construction is substantially increased, while that in services is decreased.

insurance to firms is diminished, however, if the frequency of UI claims at a given firm is highly predictable. Thus, our findings of strong persistence in firm use of UI suggest that the firm level insurance costs of tighter experience rating (at least for the large firms we examine) may be smaller than previously thought.

The patterns of UI subsidies also are likely to affect the political economy of support by different industries and firms for changes in UI legislation. Because several billion dollars are currently transferred between industries, and these transfers would be affected by many changes in the UI system, support for reforms is likely affected by these subsidies. The paper proceeds with a brief summary of experience rating systems, before presenting empirical findings on the persistence and causes of interindustry and interfirm subsidies. We then estimate the efficiency costs resulting from the subsidies. The final section then offers some conclusions.

I. A BRIEF SUMMARY OF EXPERIENCE RATING SYSTEMS

There are many possible ways to find UI benefits, including using general revenues, employee contributions, employer contributions, or any combination of these.[3] The United States has chosen to finance its system mainly through a tax on employers, with the tax rate based on some measure of the firm's past experience with the UI system. While overall the tax is only 1.1 percent of total wages and 2.1 percent of taxable wages, the maximum rate (which varies by state) is typically over 6 percent and in several states reaches 10 percent. Currently, employers must pay a 6.2 percent tax on the first $7,000 of each employee's wages to the federal government.[4] However, the law also provides for a credit of 5.4 percent to all employers paying state taxes under an experience-rated UI system. Thus, while each state is free to implement its system as it wishes, there is a strong incentive to implement an experience-rated system, and all states have done so.

These state experience rating systems take many forms, but the two most common are reserve ratio (thirty states) and benefit ratio experience rating (fifteen states).[5] In a reserve ratio system, a firm's tax rate is a

---

[3] Atkinson and Micklewright (1991) discuss the systems currently used in some major OECD countries.

[4] Many states have tax bases higher than $7,000 for the state portion of the tax.

[5] See National Foundation for Unemployment Compensation & Workers' Compensation (1990). Michigan and Pennsylvania are counted as benefit ratio states even though they have hybrids of reserve ratio and benefit ratio systems.

decreasing function of the difference between taxes paid and benefits received divided by average covered payroll. Typically, payroll is averaged over the past three years, while taxes paid and benefits received are summed over all past years and are not discounted. In a benefit ratio system, a firm's tax rate depends on the ratio of average benefits paid to average taxable wages, where both are generally averaged over only the last three years.

Under either system, firm tax rates change in steps as these ratios change. However, for most firms in almost all states, the tax rates do not rise sufficiently when the ratios fall to cause firms to pay the full UI costs of laying off a worker. Additionally, statutory minimum and maximum tax rates imply that there are large ranges at the top and bottom of the tax schedule over which a firm's layoff behavior has no effect on its tax payments. Provisions such as these result in the experience rating being incomplete, so that a firm laying off an employee can expect to pay back less in future taxes than the full cost of the benefits received by that employee. As a result, the system provides an incentive to use temporary layoffs to adjust to demand fluctuations.[6] Because each state system attempts to balance taxes and benefits over the long run, firms with unstable employment are effectively subsidized by the more stable firms.

In order to clarify the effects of recent changes in experience rating, we describe in general terms how the range of rates and tax base interact to determine the tightness of experience rating. In order for benefit payments to affect a firm's tax payments, the tax rate needs to be able to change in response to a firm's layoffs. Thus, a wider range of rates is generally associated with tighter experience rating.[7] In addition, a given change in the tax rate will have a greater effect on future tax payments if the taxable wage base is higher.

Until reaching the maximum tax rate, a firm that consistently receives more in benefits than it pays in taxes will face higher future tax payments as it moves up the tax schedule. The more likely it is that a firm is at the maximum rate, the looser is the experience rating. Once at the maximum rate, if a firm receives more benefits, it does not pay additional taxes to compensate and, thus, receives a pure subsidy. The more likely this is to occur, the looser is the experience rating. Thus, one

---

[6] This is in comparison with a perfectly experience rated system. The choice of some experience rating over no experience rating does encourage employment stabilization.

[7] However, given a fixed range of rates, there is a tradeoff between the size of the changes in tax rates in response to changes in benefits and the fraction of firms that will be subject to some change. This situation should make it clear that the range in rates is not a complete characterization of the incentives of a tax schedule.

useful way of summarizing the extent of experience rating is the maximum level of firm unemployment that is consistent with taxes equaling benefits for a maximum rate firm. Here unemployment is measured as the fraction of a firm's workforce that is unemployed on average. Let τ_{max} be the maximum tax rate; let b be UI benefits at an annual rate, that is, fifty-two times the weekly benefit; and let W be the taxable wage base. Then the maximum unemployment rate consistent with balancing benefits and taxes is $\mu_{max} = \frac{W\tau_{max}}{b}$. Thus, it is an interaction of the tax rates and taxable wage base that helps determine the tightness of experience rating. Consider the case where annual wages always exceed the tax base. Then a proportional increase in all tax rates[8] and cut in the tax base by the same proportion would leave incentives unchanged. Note that the μ_{max} would be unaffected by these changes. The last dozen years have seen roughly these two countervailing changes.

The Effects of TEFRA

A provision of TEFRA that became effective in 1985 raised the gross federal UI tax rate from 3.4 percent to 6.2 percent and the creditable portion of the federal unemployment tax from 2.7 percent to 5.4 percent. For employers to receive the full credit for federal taxes paid, a state's maximum tax rate had to be at least 5.4 percent. In response, many states followed by raising their maximum UI tax rates. As reported in the first two lines of Table 1, states sharply increased their maximum tax rate and their range of rates between 1982 and 1985. The result was a big jump up in the maximum unemployment rate consistent with balancing taxes and benefits, as seen in the fourth row of the table. By this measure, then, TEFRA succeeded in tightening experience rating. While the higher maximum rates and larger ranges of rates were mostly still in place in 1992, the tighter experience rating created by the changes of TEFRA has been largely eroded by a taxable wage base that has declined in real terms. The federal UI taxable wage base, which was originally the same as the Social Security wage base, has only been raised irregularly since 1935. While the Social Security tax base is $55,500 for 1992, the UI tax base is only $7,000. While states can determine their own tax base for the state part of the UI tax, and sixteen states now index their tax bases, most still follow the federal pattern. UI benefits, however, have generally kept pace with inflation. These trends can be seen clearly in the 17-percent decrease in the ratio of the taxable wage base to the average UI

---

[8] In reserve ratio states, this statement requires a proportional increase in all tax rates for a given difference between past benefits and taxes (the numerator of the reserve ratio), because the denominator of the reserve ratio depends on the taxable wage base.

TABLE 1.
Summary Measures of State Experience Rating for Selected Years.

	1982	1985	1990	1992
Average of all 50 states				
Maximum tax rate	5.20	7.04	6.63	6.75
Range of rates	4.26	6.05	6.16	6.16
Ratio of taxable wage base to average benefits	1.11	1.21	1.07	1.01
Maximum unemployment rate consistent with equal benefits and taxes	5.62	8.46	7.09	6.75
Average of 22 states with industry data				
Maximum tax rate	5.02	7.31	6.78	6.93
Range of rates	4.08	6.28	6.33	6.38
Ratio of taxable wage base to average benefits	1.09	1.17	1.05	0.99
Maximum unemployment rate consistent with equal benefits and taxes	5.42	8.54	7.14	6.88

Sources: Highlights of State Unemployment Compensation Laws, National Foundation for Unemployment Compensation & Workers' Compensation, various years; and ET Handbook 394 and Supplements, U.S. Department of Labor.
Notes: The numbers are employment weighted averages of the numbers for the individual states. Average benefits are 52 times average weekly benefits. The maximum unemployment rate consistent with equal benefits and taxes is the product of the maximum tax rate and the ratio of the taxable wage base to average benefits. The 1992 average benefit numbers are extrapolated using the 1985–1990 trend. See the text for further explanation.

benefit between 1985 and 1992, reported in the third line of Table 1. Because $\mu_{\max} = \frac{W\tau_{\max}}{b}$, this decline in $\frac{W}{b}$ has resulted in the maximum unemployment rate consistent with a balancing of benefits and taxes falling dramatically since 1985. Thus, most of the strengthening of experience rating under TEFRA has been eroded in recent years because of a federal taxable wage base that has been fixed in nominal terms and, thus, fallen in real terms since 1983, while real benefits have remained approximately constant.

II. INDUSTRY LEVEL EVIDENCE ON PERSISTENT CROSS-SUBSIDIES

To establish the extent of interindustry subsidies, we examine a large number of states over as long as twelve years. It is important to examine a large number of states given their diversity of experience rating systems and industrial bases. We also examine as long a period as possible to determine subsidies that are persistent, rather than because of a single transitory downturn. In order to do this, we wrote to each of the fifty states, requesting data on taxes collected and benefits paid since 1980 by industry. About half of the states supplied some data, with slightly fewer providing data in a usable form. Thus, the bottom half of Table 1 reports information for twenty-two states that have a variety of experience rating systems and industry distributions, and account for just over 55 percent of total UI-covered employment for the United States. The summary measures indicate that our twenty-two states follow the same time pattern as the other states and have slightly higher taxes and tighter experience rating.

Table 2 gives our main summary statistics for the twenty-two states. For each of eight industries, we report two numbers: the ratio of benefits received to taxes paid and the average annual subsidy to the industry (in millions of dollars) caused by incomplete experience rating. A number greater than one for the benefit/tax ratio indicates the industry received a subsidy, and below it will be a positive number for the average annual subsidy. A number less than one for the benefit/tax ratio indicates that the firm was a subsidizer, so that the subsidy number below is negative. For each state we also indicate the years of data we have available, where the average number of years is 10.8, and the minimum is eight. The industry benefit/tax ratio we report is the relative benefit/tax ratio defined as $\frac{B_i/T_i}{R}$, where B_i is UI benefits received by employees in industry i over the period, and T_i is taxes paid by firms in industry i, and R is $\Sigma_i B_i / \Sigma_i T_i$. We have divided by R, the overall state ratio of benefits to taxes, because this ratio often deviates from one over long periods of time.[9] We calculate the average annual subsidy to the industry as $B_i - T_i R$. This subsidy measure accounts for the overall state fund balance by allocating any excess or deficit of taxes over benefits to the industries in proportion to the amount paid in, before calculating the difference between taxes and benefits for each industry. The resulting number, then, represents the interindustry subsidy that would result if the state collected exactly the same amount in taxes as it paid in benefits over the time period, but if at the same time there was no change in the relative tax structure.

In Table 2, there is a striking tendency of the same industries in different states to receive subsidies. In all twenty-two states, construction receives a positive subsidy, and in all but Connecticut, Minnesota, and Vermont, manufacturing also receives one. Agriculture and mining also receive generally positive subsidies. At the other extreme, trade and also finance, insurance, and real estate (FIRE) always receive negative subsidies, that is, they are always subsidizers. In all but New York, transportation and communication subsidizes other indus-

---

[9] There are a number of reasons for long-term differences between benefits and taxes. In some cases we have only charged benefits, which are often much less than total benefits. In addition, state fund balances also go through long-term swings as benefit and tax schedules and unemployment change.

tries,[10] while services has a negative subsidy in twenty of twenty-two states. The benefit/tax ratio in construction varies from 1.14 in Tennessee to over 2.0 in Connecticut and Ohio. While agriculture usually receives a modest subsidy, in California the benefit/tax ratio is over 2.0.

In addition to pointing out the predictability of the interindustry subsidies, Table 2 also shows that the magnitudes of these subsidies are no small matter. Even in a very small state such as Maine, $6.1 million is transferred annually to manufacturing, and another $4.1 million is received by construction, with $5.1 million coming from trade, $2.6 million from services, and $2.0 million from FIRE. In Minnesota, the average annual subsidy to construction is $43.5 million, and in the much larger state of Pennsylvania, the subsidy to construction is over $100 million, with the loss to trade being almost $80 million. The largest subsidy in the table is a $112.8 million annual subsidy to agriculture in California.

Table 3 reports several summary measures for our twenty-two states as well as estimated U.S. totals and benefit/tax ratios from thirty years ago. The first line of the table reports the average of the benefit/tax ratios, which vary from 1.66 in construction to 0.56 in FIRE. Note that these numbers imply that construction receives about two-thirds more in benefits than it pays in taxes, while FIRE receives about half of what it pays in. For our twenty-two states together, the total subsidy to construction is over $650 million annually, and the subsidy to manufacturing is almost $290 million. Trade and services are the largest losers in these cross-subsidies, transferring a combined $900 million annually to other industries. If we inflate these numbers by the ratio of total U.S. covered employment to that in our twenty-two states, our results suggest that nationally almost $1.2 billion are transferred to construction, while trade and services pay nearly $1.6 billion more than they receive. These estimated U.S. totals are reported in the third line of Table 3 and should be treated as rough estimates, because states differ along many dimensions that could make this extrapolation inaccurate.

The fourth line of Table 3 reports the industry benefit/tax ratios for the years beginning with 1985, the first year of the TEFRA provisions. While the cross-subsidies are clearly smaller than they are during the full period, they are only slightly smaller. A decrease would have been expected anyway, because the interindustry subsidies tend to fall in expansionary periods.[11] It is not surprising that the legislation did not appreciably re-

---

[10] Even the New York numbers would indicate that transportation and communication subsidized other industries were it not for the over $80 million in benefits paid because of a 1989 NYNEX strike.

[11] See Munts and Asher (1981).

TABLE 2.

Ratio of Benefits Received to Taxes Paid and Average Annual Subsidy (in millions of dollars) by Major Industry for 22 States.

State and years	Industry and 2-digit Standard Industrial Classification (SIC) codes							
	Agriculture 01–09	Mining 10–14	Construction 15–17	Manufacturing 20–39	Transport 40–49	Trade 50–59	FIRE 60–67	Services 70–89
Alabama 1980–1990		1.09	1.26	1.05	0.70	0.85	0.61	1.00
		0.29	5.65	3.67	−2.44	−5.01	−2.22	0.06
California 1981–1990	2.03	1.33	1.41	1.20	0.86	0.72	0.67	0.76
	112.79	3.39	76.66	89.55	−13.87	−120.72	−40.15	−107.65
Connecticut 1984–1991	1.53		2.16	0.95	0.75	0.79	0.59	0.78
	1.55		27.07	−3.16	−2.33	−8.90	−6.44	−7.78
Georgia 1981–1984, 1986–1990	1.17	0.89	1.23	1.00	0.86	0.91	0.71	1.06
	0.34	−0.07	6.30	0.38	−1.69	−4.34	−3.17	2.25
Hawaii 1980–1991	1.42		1.73	1.14	0.95	0.67	0.72	0.71
	0.62		7.39	0.60	−0.24	−3.70	−1.14	−3.54
Kentucky 1980–1991		1.57	1.36	1.07	0.81	0.75	0.50	0.70
		8.92	10.10	5.20	−2.02	−10.24	−3.66	−8.30
Louisiana 1980–1991	1.27	1.30	1.73	1.05	0.88	0.67	0.55	0.65
	0.95	6.41	38.06	2.92	−3.22	−21.30	−5.91	−17.90
Maine 1980–1990	1.40	1.93	1.60	1.29	0.65	0.62	0.27	0.71
	0.35	0.05	4.09	6.12	−0.92	−5.12	−1.99	−2.58
Minnesota 1980–1991	1.40	2.09	1.79	0.88	0.85	0.71	0.54	0.78
	1.81	7.87	43.49	−11.71	−2.67	−19.68	−6.96	−12.15
Missouri 1980–1985, 1988–1991	1.13	1.39	1.55	1.24	0.84	0.74	0.55	0.67
	0.29	0.58	15.17	16.92	−2.42	−13.52	−5.16	−11.86
Nevada 1980–1991	0.82	0.98	1.59	1.17	0.82	0.79	0.76	0.91
	−0.12	−0.05	7.25	0.80	−0.74	−2.99	−0.92	−3.23

State								
New York 1980–1989			1.79	1.22	1.12	0.76	0.66	0.78
			74.39	60.43	7.34	−56.17	−31.71	−54.28
North Dakota 1980–1991		1.47	1.77	1.06	0.63	0.61	0.32	0.70
		1.21	6.10	0.31	−1.15	−3.86	−1.25	−1.65
Ohio 1980–1990	1.37	1.84	2.14	1.11	0.92	0.58	0.37	0.60
	0.29	7.27	97.93	39.99	−3.30	−73.09	−22.60	−48.42
Oregon 1980–1990	1.28	2.13	2.09	1.28	0.74	0.75	0.53	0.71
	2.21	0.77	17.58	20.45	−4.51	−15.73	−7.03	−11.52
Pennsylvania 1983–1991	1.00	1.94	1.82	1.08	0.86	0.67	0.49	0.80
	0.00	16.36	107.55	33.39	−8.70	−79.08	−34.24	−37.45
Tennessee 1983–1988, 1990	1.18	1.56	1.14	1.13	0.81	0.95	0.66	0.71
	2.18	0.95	3.22	8.09	−1.46	−1.69	−2.24	−6.89
Texas 1980–1991	1.02	1.21	1.45	1.05	0.86	0.85	0.84	0.80
	0.02	9.26	46.60	7.81	−6.20	−24.57	−7.28	−25.56
Utah 1981–1991	0.99	1.62	1.60	1.04	0.77	0.75	0.59	0.75
	−0.07	2.75	7.67	0.73	−1.43	−4.46	−1.78	−3.48
Vermont 1980–1991	1.17	2.07	1.97	0.96	0.60	0.71	0.46	0.87
	0.06	0.20	4.34	−0.46	−0.62	−2.03	−0.69	−0.80
West Virginia 1980–1991	0.75	1.72	1.77	1.03	0.60	0.47	0.32	0.58
	−0.20	16.47	14.57	0.98	−3.77	−16.08	−3.51	−8.46
Wisconsin 1980–1990	1.30	1.99	1.88	1.04	0.92	0.70	0.43	0.61
	1.34	1.39	37.44	6.93	−1.40	−20.10	−8.25	−17.34

Notes: The upper number for each state and industry is the ratio of benefits paid to taxes received, adjusted for the overall state ratio of benefits to taxes. The lower number is the average annual subsidy to the industry (in millions of dollars) caused by incomplete experience rating. A positive number indicates that the industry received a subsidy, while a negative number indicates that the industry subsidized other industries.

TABLE 3.
Summary Measures of Subsidies for 22 States and the United States by Major Industry.

	Agriculture 01–09	Mining 10–14	Construction 15–17	Manufacturing 20–39	Transport 40–49	Trade 50–59	FIRE 60–67	Services 70–89
				Industry and 2-digit Standard Industrial Classification (SIC) codes				
Average benefit/tax ratio, 22 states in Table 2	1.01	1.37	1.68	1.09	0.81	0.73	0.55	0.76
Sum of annual subsidies, 22 states in Table 2 (millions of $)	124.41	84.03	658.61	289.94	–57.75	–512.39	–198.31	–388.53
Subsidy sum inflated to give U.S. total (millions of $)	224.08	151.34	1186.26	522.23	–104.02	–922.90	–357.18	–699.80
Post-1985 average benefit/tax ratio	1.09	1.40	1.60	1.05	0.87	0.76	0.63	0.79
Average benefit/tax ratio, 10 states, 1957–1967		1.36	1.66	1.07	0.66	0.75	0.48	0.77

Sources: Authors' calculations using data supplied by state employment security agencies. See Table 2 for the individual state data. The data on 10 states for 1957–1967 are derived from Becker (1972) as reported in Deere (1991).
Notes: The subsidy sum inflated to give a U.S. total is the 22-state total divided by the fraction of covered employment represented by these 22 states (55.5 percent).

duce the subsidies, because the effects of the changes were quickly eroded away, as discussed earlier.

These results are very much in accord with past research on the subject by Becker (1972), which uses data from the 1950s and 1960s, and by Munts and Asher (1981), which uses data from the 1970s. The statistics presented in the latter are not strictly comparable to those in Tables 2 and 3, but the authors conclude that construction, manufacturing, and agriculture are most likely to receive subsidies, and that trade and FIRE are most likely to be subsidizers. Becker (1972) provides information that is detailed enough to allow us to construct relative benefit/tax ratios by industry in the same manner as Table 2.[12] We calculate these statistics for the six states that are also available in our new data (California, New York, Ohio, Oregon, Pennsylvania, and Utah) and directly compare the two. While separated by over two decades, the ratios are remarkably similar, with a correlation of 0.83 for the forty-two state-industry observations. We can similarly compare an industry average across all ten states in Becker's data with an industry average for all twenty-two of our states. These numbers for the period 1957–1967 are reported in the last line of Table 3. The correlation of these averages for the seven industries is 0.99. Thus, taken together with these past studies, Tables 2 and 3 imply a striking pattern of interindustry subsidies that has persisted for well over thirty years.

III. CAUSES OF PERSISTENT SUBSIDIES FROM THE UNEMPLOYMENT INSURANCE SYSTEM

The previous section documented the existence of persistent subsidies resulting from the UI financing system. Given that the interindustry subsidies range in the hundreds of millions of dollars, it is important that we understand their causes. In order to focus on the source of these subsidies, we can decompose the benefit/tax ratio into several key parts. To this consider that this ratio can be expressed as

$$\frac{B_i/T_i}{R} = \frac{(n_i d_i b_i)/(t_i w_i)}{(ndb)/(tw)} .$$

(1)

Here n_i is the total number of UI claims in industry i, d_i is the duration of these claims, and b_i is the average weekly benefit amount, so that the product of these three terms is total industry benefits. Similarly, t_i is the average tax rate and w_i is total taxable wages in the industry, which

[12] See Becker (1972), pp. 336–337.

together determine total UI taxes paid. The unsubscripted variables are the equivalent state level variables. Equation (1) can be then rewritten to express the benefit/tax ratio as the product of five ratios:

$$\frac{B_i/T_i}{R} = \left(\frac{n_i}{n}\right)\left(\frac{d_i}{d}\right)\left(\frac{b_i}{b}\right)\left(\frac{t}{t_i}\right)\left(\frac{w}{w_i}\right). \tag{2}$$

Decomposing the benefit/tax ratio in this way allows for a simple interpretation of the relative contribution of UI incidence, duration, benefit levels, tax rates, and taxable wages to the overall subsidy. If a given ratio is greater than one, then it is a source of higher subsidies, while if the ratio is less than one, the opposite is true.

While the interpretation of such a decomposition is thus quite straightforward, the data used in Tables 2 and 3, though, like those of the previous studies, do not have the level of detail necessary to perform this decomposition. Data from eight states that were part of the Continuous Wage and Benefit History (CWBH) project, however, do provide this information.[13] The data consist of UI administrative wage and benefit records for a sample of between 5 and 20 percent of the states' covered workers. We have taken a sample of approximately 150,000 wage records from each state, and matched them with the benefit records by the quarter in which the UI was initiated. Because the wage records contain information on both wages and tax rates, we can compute total UI taxes paid and compare this to benefits received. Additionally, by noting when the firm identifier given on the employee wage record changes, we can identify permanent and temporary separations.[14]

For each industry in each state and for the state overall, we calculate the average incidence, duration, benefits, tax rate, and taxable wages over all the firms. The ratio of industry to state then gives us the sources of the benefit/tax ratio. Each ratio can be thought of as representing the value for an average firm in the industry, standardized by the value for an average firm in the state overall. Additionally, we further subdivide incidence, characterizing claims as arising from either permanent layoffs or from temporary layoffs.[15]

---

[13] See Anderson and Meyer (1993) for a fuller description of this data set.

[14] In the final data set, the years 1978–1983 are available for Georgia, 1978–1982 for Missouri, 1980–1983 for Washington, 1979–1981 for Idaho, and 1981–1983 for Louisiana, New Mexico, Pennsylvania, and South Carolina.

[15] Note that the benefit/tax ratio calculated from the components for this representative firm will not be identical to the ratio for the industry as a whole, but rather is an approximation of that ratio. However, there is a very high correlation of 0.97 between the two measures.

In Table 4, we summarize the results of the decomposition. The numbers in columns [1] to [5] correspond to the five component ratios given in equation (2). The component ratios were calculated separately for each state, and the table presents the average for that industry across the eight states. Recall that a number less than 1 indicates that the component is responsible for decreasing the benefit/tax ratio, while a number greater than 1 indicates that the component is responsible for increasing the benefit/tax ratio. Thus, while the interpretation of the benefit/tax ratio given in column [6] is analogous to those given in Tables 2 and 3, here it is calculated simply as the product of columns [1] through [5].[16] Columns [7] and [8], which decompose incidence into permanent and temporary layoffs, are calculated in a similar manner to column [1]; thus, they are state-industry averages divided by the state average, which are then averaged over all eight states.

First note that as was true in Tables 2 and 3, construction, manufacturing, and mining are being subsidized, and FIRE, trade, services, and transportation and communication are subsidizers. Unlike in those tables, though, in Table 4, agriculture appears as a relative subsidizer. However, there are only a small number of observations for this industry in the CWBH data, making it somewhat less reliable. Several patterns in the sources of the cross-subsidies are evident from Table 4. First, it is clear that the major determinant of an above average subsidy is an above average rate of UI-compensated layoffs. The largest (and smallest) numbers in the table appear in columns [1], [7], and [8]. Especially important to manufacturing, and to a lesser extent to mining and construction, is the above-average incidence of UI-compensated spells that end in recall. This temporary incidence is almost three times that of the average, and close to ten times that for an industry such as retail trade where temporary layoffs are well below average. While the largest variance across industries is found in column [8], that of column [7] is also very large. Thus, while high rates of temporary layoffs are a leading cause of net positive subsidies, above-average rates of permanent layoffs resulting in UI are also to blame, especially in construction. In fact, manufacturing and construction produce this type of UI spell one and a quarter to two times as often as the average.

In manufacturing, the higher overall incidence of UI is accompanied by spells of shorter duration, which work to slightly decrease the sub-

---

[16] Note that column [6] is not the actual average over all eight states, but again represents an approximation based on the experience of an "average" firm from those states. The two measures are very closely related, though, having a correlation of 0.995.

TABLE 4.
Decomposition of Industry Benefit/Tax Ratios (average for 8 CWBH states).

	Overall incidence [1]	UI duration [2]	UI benefits [3]	Tax rate [4]	Taxable wages [5]	Benefit/tax ratio [6]	Type of Incidence	
							Perm [7]	Temp [8]
Agriculture	0.70	0.96	0.88	0.90	1.65	0.87	0.74	0.78
Construction	1.53	1.04	1.09	0.79	1.15	1.58	2.20	1.23
FIRE	0.25	1.20	0.95	1.17	0.81	0.27	0.51	0.12
Manufacturing	2.15	0.92	0.99	0.99	0.77	1.50	1.27	2.62
Mining	1.22	1.13	1.18	1.09	0.79	1.40	0.91	1.36
Retail Trade	0.34	1.18	0.88	1.07	1.27	0.49	0.62	0.23
Services	0.38	1.22	0.92	1.05	1.13	0.50	0.65	0.27
Transportation and communica-tion	0.45	1.18	1.01	1.13	0.81	0.49	0.64	0.42
Wholesale trade	0.54	1.25	0.99	1.09	0.86	0.63	0.87	0.38

Note: Columns [1]–[3] are industry/state ratios, while colums [4] and [5] are state/industry ratios, so that [6] = [1]*[2]*[3]*[4]*[5]. Columns [7] and [8] are industry/state ratios. Numbers above 1 indicate that this component works to increase the benefit/tax ratio, while numbers less than 1 indicate that this component works to decrease the benefit tax ratio. See text for a complete explanation of the decomposition.

sidy. This is not the case for construction and mining, though, where both duration and incidence contribute positively to the subsidy. The exact opposite is true in agriculture, where both duration and incidence contribute negatively to the subsidy. For all the remaining industries, a lower incidence of UI is somewhat offset by longer durations. In general, though, there is not as much variation across industries in the effects of duration as there is in those of incidence.

In column [5] we see that there is quite a bit of variation in the effect of the taxable wage base. Thus, for example, the high incidence of benefits in manufacturing is somewhat mitigated by a high taxable wage base, thereby decreasing the overall subsidy. This is not the case for construction, however, where the taxable wage base is below average, leading to an increase in the subsidy. Construction is also unique in that this lower taxable wage base does not then result in below average benefit levels, but rather both the taxable wage base and the benefit level (column [3]) contribute to above average benefit/tax ratios. In the other industries, there is a weak tendency for above-average benefits, and taxable wage bases go hand in hand, each partially offsetting the effect of the other on the total benefit/tax ratio.

The main reason taxable wages and benefit levels are not perfectly correlated is that the taxable wage base and the wage base used for determining benefit levels are calculated differently. The weekly benefit level is generally determined as a percentage of high quarter earnings (subject to a maximum), while the taxable wage base is the first X dollars from the employer in a given year, where X is usually around $6,000 or $7,000. It is easy to see why a highly variable industry such as construction would be particularly helped by this system. For example, in Georgia in 1980, to qualify for UI, a worker needed to earn 1.5 times the high quarter earnings in the base period. The maximum weekly benefit of $90 would then be received by anyone with high quarter earnings of $2,225 or more. In a stable industry, we would expect base period earnings to be close to four times the high quarter earnings, implying that in qualifying for the maximum weekly benefit, the worker most likely reached the maximum taxable wage base of $6,000. For a construction worker, however, the high quarter earnings are likely to be very much higher than earnings in other quarters when work is slack. It would be possible, then, to receive the maximum weekly benefit, while having a taxable wage base that is as low as $3,338. While it is likely that base period earnings are in fact more than the minimum of 1.5 times the high quarter earnings, it is clear that they can be considerably below average without a corresponding decrease in weekly benefits.

Column [4] shows the effect of the tax rate component. The fact that there is not much variation in this effect, given the variation in incidence, points to a key determinant of the persistent subsidization. While the effect of incidence is highly positively correlated with the overall subsidy, the opposite is true for the effect of tax rates. This is due to the design of state experience rating systems, whereby tax rates are higher for firms with more use of the UI system. As Table 4 makes clear, though, the increases in tax rates are not nearly sufficient to offset the effects of increased UI receipt. Thus, the failure of the tax rates to rise along with UI incidence leads to a persistent pattern of subsidization. In insurance terms, the premiums paid by firms do not accurately reflect the risk of loss.

An examination of the state level data on the sources of the cross-subsidies confirms the averages of Table 4. For the seventy-two state-industry cells (eight states times nine industries), we calculate covariances of the benefit/tax ratio with the source ratios given in equation (2), as well as the components representing the two types of layoffs. All of the covariances except that with the taxable wage base are significantly different from zero. As expected, the layoff variables have by far the highest covariances with the benefit/tax ratio, 0.43 for temporary layoffs and 0.22 for permanent layoffs (0.36 for overall incidence). All other covariances have the expected signs, but are less than 0.04. In general, then, these results indicate that the averages of Table 4 capture the main relationships in the data.

Overall, the results of the decomposition show that high rates of temporary layoffs for certain industries are the main reason for persistent interindustry subsidies. The relative importance of temporary layoffs compared to permanent layoffs further indicates that cross-subsidies are due not so much to permanent shocks to certain firms in an industry, but rather more to temporary or seasonal changes that lead to short-term employment adjustment. This is an important point, because the insurance value to firms of imperfect experience rating is dependent upon the unpredictability of UI payments. One can also conclude that a key reason for the persistent subsidies is that tax rates do not vary sufficiently to compensate for the differences in layoffs. While imperfect experience rating is a major cause of subsidization, the results also imply that the divergence between the wages on which benefits are based and taxable wages is a significant contributor. Higher benefits and higher taxable wages do not always go hand in hand, because benefit levels are not based on taxable wages, but rather on high quarter wages, and are subject to maxima and minima.

IV. FIRM LEVEL EVIDENCE ON PERSISTENT SUBSIDIES

Past work on UI subsidies, such as that by Becker (1972) and Munts and Asher (1981), focused on broad industry groups, because taxes paid and benefits received by laid-off employees were not available at the firm level.[17] However, the firm is the appropriate unit to analyze because experience rating is done at the firm level. In this section, we once again make use of the newly available CWBH data set that provides just this information, to investigate the persistence of firm-level subsidies. Our data on firm-level subsidies come from the administrative records of two of the states that participated in the CWBH project. For both Georgia and Washington, we have the UI wage and benefit records for a 10 percent sample of the state's covered workers, and those data cover a period greater than three years. For Georgia the years 1978–1983 are available, while for Washington the time period covered is 1980–1983. In order to be reasonably certain that this 10 percent sample would accurately reflect a firm's UI experience, we limit our data set to records from those firms that had over 1,000 employees at least some time during the period covered by our data. Nonetheless, there is likely to be a good deal of measurement error in our data on firm-level benefit payments.

While Georgia and Washington were chosen mainly because they afforded the longest time spans to examine, they also allow us to contrast two vastly different experience rating systems. In Washington, a truly experience-rated tax schedule only goes into effect if the overall state balances exceed a certain level. Because this was never the case during the time period we examine, all firms were assessed a flat-rate tax of 3 percent. By contrast, in Georgia there are forty-three different tax rates, ranging from 0.07 percent to 5.71 percent in the years 1979–1981, and from 0.06 percent to 5.38 percent in the remaining years. In our data, only 0.3 percent of the firm year observations are at the minimum tax rate, and 2.3 percent are at the maximum. Thus, most of the firms in Georgia face a sloped tax schedule. For all but a few rates, this slope is about 0.44 for the 1979–1981 period, and 0.41 for the other years. These are relatively steep slopes not only in comparison to the zero slope of Washington, but also in comparison to other states with more traditional schedules. Anderson and Meyer (1992) show that in 1981, 93 percent of Georgia employment was at firms who could expect to pay back over $0.80 in higher future

---

[17] Marks (1984) approaches the problem at the firm level, but he only looks at persistence in tax rates.

taxes for each dollar in benefits received. The next closest state was Louisiana, with only 58 percent of employment at such firms. One should note that these measures of the tightness of experience rating partly depend on the types of firms in a state and their behavior. However, our measure of experience rating in section 1, the maximum unemployment rate consistent with paying some cost of additional layoffs, is also considerably above average for Georgia during this period. Thus, a comparison between Georgia and Washington is also a comparison between a state with very tight experience rating and one with effectively no experience rating.

We can use the sample of CWBH data discussed in the previous section to compare these large firms with firms in the state overall. While the general patterns of the industry distribution are fairly similar across the two samples, manufacturing is overrepresented in this large firm sample, as is transportation and communication, with most other industries underrepresented. Construction stands out especially in this regard.[18] Based on the state sample, the large firms that we use in our sample account for approximately a quarter of total employment in each state. In Georgia, these firms receive 32 percent of the UI benefits, while in Washington, they receive only 21 percent.

For each firm year, we calculate the total amount of UI taxes (state and federal) a firm pays, based on our sample of wage records. We then match any UI benefits received by these workers to the firm employing the worker in the quarter that the benefits were initiated. This allows us to calculate total benefits initiated by the firm's actions for the year and to compare them with total taxes paid. As with the industry group data, in order to account for the effects of the business cycle, we standardize the benefit/tax ratio for each firm by dividing by the overall state benefit/tax ratio for that year.[19] Comparing this relative benefit/tax ratio across years then allows us to determine if the same firms are consistently subsidized (or subsidizing) over time. Recall that the argument for UI as firm insurance would imply that large benefit outlays are unpredictable, and, hence, the redistribution implied by insurance principles only would result in no consistent patterns.

Table 5 provides a first indication that, in fact, the redistribution caused by the UI payroll tax may significantly depart from the pure insurance model. Note first that a significant number of firms are either not subsidized at all or are subsidized in almost every year. For example,

[18] About 45% of the Georgia firm sample is in manufacturing compared with 28% for the state sample, while for Washington the comparison is 34–20%. For both states, only 2% are in construction compared with 7% in the state sample.

[19] These yearly ratios were obtained from the sample of CWBH data discussed in the previous section.

TABLE 5.
Distribution of Firms, Employment, and UI Benefits by Number of Years Subsidized.

Number of years subsidized*	Number of firms	Percent		
		Firms	*Employment*	*Benefits*
Georgia				
0	52	24.88	34.71	6.21
1	43	20.57	19.97	8.85
2	35	16.75	13.88	12.68
3	27	12.92	11.34	14.07
4	26	12.44	11.19	22.15
5	12	5.74	4.92	21.58
6	14	6.70	3.98	14.47
Washington				
0	113	64.94	59.63	18.90
1	19	10.92	25.72	26.32
2	7	4.02	3.16	11.57
3	13	7.47	4.69	10.55
4	22	12.64	6.81	32.67

* Subsidized is defined as (UI benefits/UI taxes)$_{firm}$/(UI benefits/UI taxes)$_{state}$ for the year being greater than 1.

in Georgia 45 percent of the firms are subsidized at most one of the six years, with another 7 percent always subsidized. In Washington, the patterns are much stronger, with 65 percent of the firms never being subsidized and another 13 percent always being subsidized, so that over three-quarters of the firms are at the extremes. Table 5 also presents the percentage of total employment and total UI benefits represented by firms in each category. In both states, over one-third of UI benefits are received by employees at firms that are subsidized in all, or in all but one, of the years. At the same time, though, these firms account for only a small fraction of employment. In fact, in Washington they account for just 12 percent of employment, while receiving 43 percent of benefits. Similarly in Georgia, 9 percent of the employment receives 36 percent of the benefits. Thus, a clear pattern of redistribution is emerging.

Table 6 provides a quick summary of the persistence of subsidies from year to year. The top row of each panel gives the probability that a firm will receive a subsidy in later years, given that it does now. Similarly, the second row of each panel gives the probability that a firm will subsidize other firms in later years, given that it does now. The numbers indicate that there is some tendency for firms to continue over time in their current situation, although this is much more pronounced for firms not

TABLE 6.
*Conditional Probability of a Firm Being Observed in Later Years with
Same Subsidy Status as in Current Year.**

	Probability still receiving/ not receiving subsidy		
	1 year later	3 years later	5 years later
Georgia			
Receiving subsidy in year 1	0.63	0.53	0.49
	(399)	(216)	(67)
Not receiving subsidy in year 1	0.79	0.70	0.73
	(743)	(441)	(142)
Washington			
Receiving subsidy in year 1	0.77	0.68	—
	(127)	(38)	
Not receiving subsidy in year 1	0.93	0.91	—
	(417)	(137)	

Note: Row counts in parentheses
* Subsidy status is determined by (UI benefits/UI taxes)$_{firm}$/(UI benefits/UI taxes)$_{state}$ for the year being greater than 1 (receiving subsidy) or less than 1 (not receiving subsidy).

receiving subsidies and for firms in Washington. A useful way to summarize this persistence is to calculate the probability of receiving a subsidy for firms that received one in the past minus the probability of receiving one for those that did not in the past. With no persistence, these differences in probabilities would be zero. For Georgia, this difference in probabilities is 0.42, 0.23, and 0.22 after one, three, and five years, respectively. For Washington, the comparison is more striking, with the difference in probabilities being 0.70 and 0.59 after one and three years, respectively. Thus, knowing a firm's subsidy status today is a very good predictor of its subsidy status in the future.

To help in understanding this persistence more fully, the transition matrices in Tables 7 and 8 provide a more detailed picture of the patterns of redistribution effected by the UI payroll tax in Georgia and Washington. In these tables, firms are classified according to whether their benefit/tax ratio is 0–0.5 (very small), 0.5–1 (small), 1–2 (large), or over 2 (very large). Given that a firm is currently in a certain class, the matrices give the probabilities that the firm will be in each of the classes in later years. The probability of remaining in the same class is thus reported by the diagonal elements.[20] If one turns first to the results for Georgia in

[20] Note that the conditional probabilities presented in Table 6 are equivalent to the diagonals of a transition matrix of this sort where there are only two classes: 0–1 (no subsidy) and over 1 (receives subsidy).

TABLE 7.
1-, 3-, and 5-Year Transition Matrices for Georgia Firms.

		Benefit/tax ratio 1 year later			
		0–0.5	0.5–1	1–2	Over 2
	0 to 0.5	0.62	0.24	0.09	0.06
		(287)	(109)	(40)	(26)
Benefit/tax	0.5 to 1	0.32	0.36	0.21	0.12
ratio		(89)	(100)	(58)	(34)
in year 1	1 to 2	0.19	0.23	0.31	0.28
		(38)	(47)	(63)	(57)
	Over 2	0.13	0.20	0.24	0.43
		(26)	(38)	(47)	(83)

		Benefit/tax ratio 3 years later			
		0–0.5	0.5–1	1–2	Over 2
	0 to 0.5	0.53	0.21	0.13	0.13
		(149)	(59)	(36)	(36)
Benefit/tax	0.5 to 1	0.26	0.37	0.19	0.18
ratio		(42)	(59)	(31)	(29)
in year 1	1 to 2	0.22	0.28	0.22	0.28
		(26)	(34)	(26)	(34)
	Over 2	0.20	0.24	0.28	0.28
		(19)	(23)	(27)	(27)

		Benefit/tax ratio 5 years later			
		0–0.5	0.5–1	1–2	Over 2
	0 to 0.5	0.44	0.28	0.19	0.09
		(43)	(27)	(18)	(9)
Benefit/tax	0.5 to 1	0.31	0.42	0.18	0.09
ratio		(14)	(19)	(8)	(4)
in year 1	1 to 2	0.39	0.22	0.15	0.24
		(16)	(9)	(6)	(10)
	Over 2	0.08	0.27	0.23	0.42
		(2)	(7)	(6)	(11)

Note: Row probabilities may not add to 1 because of rounding; cell counts in parentheses; benefit/tax ratio is defined as (UI benefits/UI taxes)$_{firm}$/(UI benefits/UI taxes)$_{state}$ for the year.

Table 7, there is substantial evidence for persistence of extreme benefit/ tax ratios. The probability that a firm with a benefit/tax ratio over 2 will receive a subsidy five years later is 0.67, while for a firm that previously had a benefit/tax ratio below 0.5, the probability of receiving a subsidy five years later is only 0.28. A stronger degree of persistence of very large benefit/tax ratios is observed in Table 8 for Washington, where the

TABLE 8.
1- and 3-Year Transition Matrices for Washington Firms.

		Benefit/tax ratio 1 year later			
		0–0.5	*0.5–1*	*1–2*	*Over 2*
	0 to 0.5	0.83	0.13	0.03	0.01
		(280)	(44)	(9)	(5)
Benefit/tax	*0.5 to 1*	0.44	0.35	0.11	0.09
ratio		(35)	(28)	(9)	(7)
in year 1	*1 to 2*	0.10	0.20	0.42	0.27
		(6)	(11)	(23)	(15)
	Over 2	0.11	0.06	0.15	0.68
		(8)	(4)	(11)	(49)
		Benefit/tax ratio 3 years later			
		0–0.5	*0.5–1*	*1–2*	*Over 2*
	0 to 0.5	0.82	0.11	0.05	0.03
		(97)	(13)	(6)	(3)
Benefit/tax	*0.5 to 1*	0.50	0.33	0.11	0.06
ratio		(9)	(6)	(2)	(1)
in year 1	*1 to 2*	0.21	0.21	0.21	0.37
		(4)	(4)	(4)	(7)
	Over 2	0.16	0.05	0.21	0.58
		(3)	(1)	(4)	(11)

Note: Row probabilities may not add to 1 because of rounding; cell counts in parentheses; benefit/tax ratio is defined as (UI benefits/UI taxes)$_{firm}$/(UI benefits/UI taxes)$_{state}$ for the year.

probability that a firm with a benefit/tax ratio over 2 will obtain a ratio over 2 again one year later is 0.68, and it is 0.58 for three years later. Here, the probability that a firm with a benefit/tax ratio over 2 will receive a subsidy three years later is 0.79, while for a firm that previously had a benefit/tax ratio below 0.5, this same probability is only 0.08.

If one looks at those firms with very small benefit/tax ratios in Washington, the persistence is just as striking as it is for those with very large ratios. The probability that a firm with a benefit/tax ratio under 0.5 will obtain a ratio under 0.5 again one year later is 0.83, while it is 0.82 for three years later. By contrast, for Georgia the probabilities are 0.62 for one year, 0.53 for three years, and 0.44 for five years. As large as some of these probabilities are, it is important to note that the presence of measurement error will cause us to understate the persistence in the benefit/tax ratios. This is due to the fact that random errors that cause the computed benefit/tax ratio to fluctuate around its true mean will lead to the erroneous appearance of changes in the ratio.

Firm and Industry Components of the Benefit/Tax Ratio

Past work on benefit tax/ratios makes comparisons across industries but ignores any variation across firms, within industry. The last findings show that there are persistent interfirm subsidies, but they do not indicate if the subsidies could be predicted based on the industries in which the firms are located, or if other firm characteristics are responsible. It is thus informative to explore what fraction of the variance in benefit/tax ratios is industry-specific, what fraction is firm-specific, and what cannot be attributed to firm or industry. In order to explore this question, we write the benefit/tax ratio for firm j in industry i in year t as

$$R_{ijt} = \alpha_t + \beta_i + \gamma_{ij} + \epsilon_{ijt}, \tag{3}$$

where α_t captures changes from year to year in the benefit/tax ratio, β_i captures differences between industries, γ_{ij} captures differences between firms within an industry, and ϵ_{ijt} captures the variation over time for a given firm.

There are several ways to estimate the relative contribution of industry, firm, and other factors to the variance of the benefit/tax ratio. There is no unique decomposition of the variance of R_{ijt}. Using the firm-level benefit/tax ratio (adjusted for the state average) as the dependent variable, we estimate equation (3) on the Georgia and Washington data. We use year, industry class, and firm dummy variables for the α's, β's, and γ's. The change in the adjusted R^2 provides a simple summary measure of the fraction of the variance in R_{ijt} explained by the different factors. In Georgia, industry dummy variables add an additional 7 percent to the variance explained by year only, firm dummy variables add an additional 11 percent, and 82 percent of the variance is left unexplained. In Washington, industry dummy variables add an additional 28 percent to the variance explained, while firm dummies add an additional 32 percent, leaving 40 percent unexplained.[21] When two-digit industry group rather than major industry class is used, the inclusion of firm dummy variables still results in a large increase in adjusted R^2. In Georgia, two-digit industry explains 11 percent of the variance, with firm explaining an additional 7 percent. For Washington, 38 percent of the variance is explained by two-digit industry, and firm explains another 22 percent. Thus, by this simple measure, across-firm differences are important, even within two-digit industry groups.

---

[21] Year dummies essentially explain none of the variance. This finding is expected, because standardizing by the state ratio should remove the effects of the business cycle.

A second way of decomposing the variance in R_{ijt} is to directly estimate the variance of the different components of R_{ijt} in equation (3). Again, netting out the time period dummies, the α_t's, we can write the variance of R_{ijt} as

$$Var[R_{ijt} \mid \alpha_t] = \sigma_\beta^2 + \sigma_\gamma^2 + \sigma_\epsilon^2, \tag{4}$$

where σ_β^2, σ_γ^2, and σ_ϵ^2 are the variances of β_i, γ_{ij}, and ϵ_{ijt}, respectively. There are several standard ways to estimate the σ's in the previous equation, with no single preferred methods, so we try two.[22]

There are several conclusions from this exercise that agree quite closely with the results from the comparison of adjusted R^2's earlier. The estimated variances, σ_β^2 and σ_γ^2, are about equal, indicating that there is about the same amount of variance within industries as there is between industries. As before, this comparison still holds when one looks at two-digit industries rather than industry divisions.[23] It is also clear that a relatively large fraction of the variance remains unexplained, especially in Georgia. In Washington, though, this residual variance is slightly smaller than the fraction explained by industry and firm. A large part of this unexplained variance, however, is likely due to measurement error, because our benefit/tax ratios are based on a 1/10 sample of employees. We should note that part of the variance that we attribute to firms might be accounted for if we used still narrower industry groups. Nonetheless, the evidence does suggest that the variance across firms (within industry) is as great as that across industry and, hence, that a substantial source of cross-subsidization is ignored in work done at the industry level.

This key finding that there is a considerable amount of persistence in interfirm subsidies, which are not explained by industry alone, has several implications. First, given the magnitude of the interindustry subsidies, this indication that they are only half of the story implies that the cross-subsidy problem is likely to be much greater than past evidence at the broad industry level has suggested. Second, the key argument against more complete experience rating revolves around the idea of insuring the firm against losses from a large benefit payout. As with any

---

[22] We estimate the σ's using the method of maximum likelihood, and the MIVQUE0 method developed by Hartley, Rao, and LaMotte (1978).

[23] In fact, the fraction of the variance in the benefit/tax ratio attributed to firms rather than industries often rises when one examines 2-digit industries. This surprising result occurs because the estimates of the industry variance are fairly imprecise when one examines industry divisions because one is essentially estimating a variance using only a few observations.

insurance plan, patterns of interfirm subsidies are expected at a point in time. However, to the extent that these patterns are predictable year after year, the insurance value of the subsidies is lessened. Our findings, then, suggest that the loss in insurance value from tightened experience rating is likely to be smaller than previously thought.

5. EFFICIENCY LOSSES FROM CROSS-SUBSIDIES

Much of the past work on UI financing has focused on the distortionary effect of imperfect experience rating on firm layoff decisions. For example, Topel (1983) concludes that 30 percent of layoff unemployment may be due to incomplete experience rating. We would expect imperfect experience rating to also affect the level of employment at firms. Because most firms' tax payments do not equal the UI costs of their layoffs, incomplete experience rating increases the cost of labor of some firms and decreases it for others. Subsidized firms will then increase their size at the expense of firms paying more than their share in taxes. This section estimates the efficiency loss from this distortion of labor costs. We find that these costs are not especially large if the marginal subsidy is not very different from the average subsidy. However, there is little evidence to examine this difference. If the relevant marginal subsidy is much higher, then the welfare costs of the cross-subsidies could be substantial.

The societal losses stemming from the distortion of labor costs across industries can be summarized by measures of deadweight loss (DWL). Topel (1990) provides the only discussion we know of deadweight losses from UI subsidies. Without actual data on benefits and tax payments, however, Topel estimates the subsidy based only on average industry unemployment. He estimates that the DWL caused by the subsidy to construction alone is $300 million annually and that accounting for the difference between marginal and average subsidies (a point discussed later) could make the losses much larger. However, while we are interested in comparing the current UI system to a perfectly experience-rated system, Topel compares the current system to the situation of no unemployment insurance. As a result, his measure of the UI employment subsidy includes the effect of the nontaxation of UI benefits that was in force prior to 1987.[24] If one uses Topel's method for calculating the DWL, but accounts for the taxation of benefits, the resulting DWL is $86 million rather than $300 million. This difference should be kept in mind when one compares our results to those in Topel (1990).

---

[24] His estimates also implicitly assume that UI benefits are valued dollar for dollar by workers and the firm.

We begin by providing estimates of the efficiency loss assuming that all firms in a given industry in all states have the same subsidy rate, and that the marginal subsidy is the same as the average. If one defines S as the dollar subsidy to an industry over its total payroll, the deadweight loss as a fraction of payroll for a given industry can be approximated as $DWL = 0.5\epsilon S^2$ where ϵ is the elasticity of labor demand for firms in that industry.[25] In Table 9, we present the average industry subsidies from Table 3, both as a dollar value per employee and as a fraction of the total industry payroll. We then estimate a dollar value for the deadweight loss triangle, based on 1985 average industry payroll and a value of 1 for the elasticity of labor demand.[26] In general the absolute value of the subsidies is relatively small when compared to industry employment and payroll. Only in construction does the subsidy amount to even a full percentage point of payroll, and for most other industries it is less than half of 1 percent. Similarly, annual subsidies per employee are under $100 for all but mining and construction. The overall deadweight loss estimate of Table 9 is $10.24 million with $6.22 million of the total loss coming from construction alone.[27] However, as discussed further later, there are several reasons why these estimates are likely to understate severely the true efficiency losses.

One obvious problem with these estimates is that they reflect only the loss from the labor misallocation across industries, while, as we have shown earlier, the across-firm variation within industry is equally if not more important. A simple example will serve to illustrate how important this difference is. Imagine an industry made up of equal numbers of two types of firms: one type always receives a 5 percent subsidy, and the other always provides a 5 percent subsidy. While there will be no subsidy calculated at the industry level (and, hence, no misallocation), there is actually a deadweight loss equal to 0.125 percent of payroll at each and

[25] To see this, consider that the welfare triangle over total payroll can be defined as $DWL = (0.5 \, \Delta W \Delta N)/WN$, where W is the average wage, N is employment for a given industry, and Δ means the change in the variable following. Noting that $\epsilon = (\Delta N/N)/(\Delta W/W)$ and $S = \Delta W/W$ leads to the expression given.

[26] Industry payroll figures are from the Monthly Labor Review. Hamermesh (1986) reviews estimates of labor demand elasticities, finding that industry-level constant-output elasticities range from 0.3 to 1.0, while allowing output to vary leads to estimates between 0.4 and 2.6. Because firm demand should be closer to the latter, we use 1.0 as an estimate of the elasticity. Additionally, because the DWL is proportional to ϵ, one can easily multiply the given DWL by an alternate elasticity if desired.

[27] Given our $6 million number, one might wonder how Topel arrived at his $300 million figure. We indicated that his figure would be $83 million now that benefits are taxable. He also appears to have assumed values for the construction industry unemployment rate and the maximum tax rate that are extreme and increase the subsidy. In addition, he appears to have left out the 0.5 in the DWL formula earlier.

TABLE 9.
Estimated Deadweight Loss from Labor Misallocation.

	Employment (1000's)	Weekly earnings (dollars)	Subsidy as a percentage of the annual wage bill	Dollar value of subsidy per employee	Dollar value of deadweight loss
Mining	930	520	0.60	162.73	455,468
Construction	4,687	464	1.05	253.10	6,220,557
Manufacturing	19,314	386	0.13	27.04	351,773
Transportation	5,242	450	−0.08	−19.84	44,080
Trade	23,100	219	−0.35	−39.95	1,621,519
FIRE	5,953	289	−0.40	−60.00	713,000
Services	21,974	256	−0.24	−31.85	835,685
Total					10,242,082

Note: Employment and Earnings numbers are annual averages for 1985 and are from *Monthly Labor Review* (1986).

every firm (assuming $\epsilon = 1$). We can use our firm-level data to estimate how this across-firm misallocation compares to that across industries. Looking at our firms in Georgia, and summing taxes, benefits, and payroll across all firms within an industry, we obtain average subsidies that are very close to those in Table 9.[28] However, using the firm-level information to calculate the deadweight loss at each firm, and then summing across all firms in each industry, results in a dollar value for the deadweight loss that is 4.56 times larger than the one calculated based on industry averages.[29] Thus, because firms within industries vary substantially as to their subsidy status, looking only at the across industry misallocation severely understates the extent of the efficiency losses.

A very similar source of understatement is our use of the average U.S. subsidy rather than state-level subsidies. Just as relying on total industry subsidies rather than firm-level subsidies loses a source of variation, so too does using a national average. Annual payroll is available at the state level for manufacturing establishments, though, allowing us to gauge the importance of this type of aggregation. When we calculate a separate deadweight loss value for each of the twenty-two states and then sum them together, we estimate a loss that is 1.66 times that obtained using

[28] We use Georgia rather than Washington because its experience rating system is more representative of the United States.

[29] The six-year average of taxes, benefits, and payroll are used for each firm. This measure is likely to somewhat overstate the firm-level DWL, since some of the firm variability will be due to the sampling error inherent in looking at only a six-year period.

the average subsidy over these states.[30] Again, we appear to understate the deadweight loss in Table 9.

A third problem is more difficult to summarize but no less important. All of the previous discussions are based on the assumption that the average subsidy that we are able to calculate is identical to the marginal subsidy that is appropriate for firm decisions. However, the marginal subsidy may well be much greater than the average subsidy. Because the deadweight loss increases with the square of the subsidy, this difference could be very significant. For example, consider the case of a seasonal firm that lays off a fraction x of its workers for one-half of the year.[31] For the case of a 40 percent replacement rate (about the average), total UI benefits are 40 percent of the labor costs of the marginal seasonal employee's wage bill (this is calculated as $(0.4)(\frac{1}{2})/(\frac{1}{2})$). Because the UI tax is rarely more than 2 percent of average wages, nearly all of this 40 percent would be a marginal subsidy to seasonal employment. For now, then, we will ignore UI taxes completely. By contrast, the average subsidy at this firm is $(x(0.4)(\frac{1}{2}))/(x(\frac{1}{2}) + (1 - x))$.[32] If seasonal workers are one-tenth of employment ($x = .1$), for example, then the marginal subsidy is 40 percent, while the average subsidy is 2.1 percent. Again, because the DWL is proportional to the square of the subsidy, the difference between average and marginal can have a large impact on the efficiency losses.

Unfortunately, it is difficult to gauge overall how much the marginal subsidy is likely to differ from the average. We might expect the divergence to be especially large in seasoning industries such as retail trade, construction, and some types of services and manufacturing. This understatement will be more of a problem the smaller x is, because in general if only a fraction x of the workforce is seasonal, the marginal subsidy will be more than $1/x$ times greater than the average measured subsidy.[33] It is important to note, though, that the marginal subsidy should probably only apply to the fraction of the workforce that is seasonal. Overall, though, this relationship is one more reason to believe that the small

[30] For our sample, the $290 million subsidy to manufacturing represents about 0.13 percent of total payroll in those twenty-two states, and implies a deadweight loss of about $194,000. Note that the larger dollar value given in Table 9 reflects having inflated the numbers for our twenty-two states to represent the United States as a whole. Using the individual state subsidies results in a total deadweight loss of almost $322,000.

[31] This example is a slightly modified version of one in Topel (1990). With a 40 percent replacement rate, most states' potential duration rules would allow a person to receive UI for just under one-half of the year. Thus, this example is close to the extreme case.

[32] Note that if $x = 1$, this simplifies to the expression given earlier.

[33] See the previous formula. For small x, the ratio is approximately $2/x$.

deadweight loss estimates of Table 9 are gross underestimates of the true loss, especially in some key industries.

To assess the overall effect of the previous three adjustments to the national industry level deadweight loss estimates of Table 9, we must combine the effects of the difference between firm and industry, state and nation, and marginal and average subsidies. The Georgia estimates of the difference between firm and industry subsidies suggested that the firm DWL estimates are 4.56 times higher. Similarly, the manufacturing industry data imply state subsidies 1.66 times higher than those using the U.S. average. Combining these factors with the subsidy estimates of Table 9 yields a total U.S. deadweight loss estimate of $77.51 million annually. While this is a substantial loss, it is fairly small relative to the $20 billion annual cost of UI. We have very little basis to assess the additional effect on the deadweight loss estimates of the difference between marginal and average subsidies. We can, however, say that if the marginal subsidies are z times higher than the average subsidies (but apply to $1/z$ of the workforce), the implied annual DWL is $z(77.51)$ million. Because z could be fairly large, the true deadweight loss caused by incomplete experience rating could be substantial.[34]

Besides this deadweight loss from the misallocation of resources, there are also losses from increased unemployment. This loss occurs because the firms whose expansion is most subsidized are those for whom unemployment is the highest, and marginal subsidies are the greatest for employees who are regularly unemployed. If one notes that the percentage change in employment implied by a subsidy is simply $S\epsilon$, it is straightforward to calculate the change in employment implied by a subsidy. For example, based on the information in Table 9, employment in construction is 1.05 percent, or 49,000, greater than it would be in the absence of a UI subsidy. If these 49,000 workers have the same average unemployment rate as the industry overall, construction industry unemployment would rise by 6,400. However, it is reasonable to assume that the additional workers hired because of the subsidy will experience more unemployment than the average worker. In the most extreme case, the additional workers are unemployed half the year. In this case the increase in unemployment in construction would be about 24,500

---

[34] To be consistent with the average subsidies we observe, a marginal subsidy higher than the average must apply to only some fraction of employment. This assumes that all firms in a subsidized industry receive subsidies and that the same labor demand elasticity applies to all sectors of all firms' employment. For example, if the marginal subsidy in an industry is five times the average, then it could only apply to $\frac{1}{5}$ of the industry workforce. Thus, the DWL in that industry would rise by a factor of 5 because the DWL per employee would rise by the factor of 5^2 but only apply to $\frac{1}{5}$ of the industry employment.

workers. Some of this increase would be offset by a decline in unemployment in industries with decreases in employment, but this calculation suggests there are moderate increases in unemployment caused by the cross-subsidies.

Overall, it is clear that there are efficiency losses in the current UI tax system, which stem from the fact that there is a tax on employment at relatively stable firms and a subsidy for relatively unstable firms. This misallocation implies that aggregate output could be increased by redirecting resources. Additionally, the subsidies lead to increased unemployment rates, given the larger workforces at the less stable firms. Although it remains difficult to measure the exact size of these losses even with our new data, it is clear that looking only at national industry level cross-subsidization will lead to a severe underestimation of the loss.

VI. CONCLUSIONS

In this paper, we present several key findings on the nature of the interindustry and interfirm subsidies generated through the UI payroll tax. We document that the same patterns of large interindustry subsidies have persisted for over thirty years, and we find that these subsidies are due mostly to differences in layoff rates across industries. It is especially temporary layoff rates, combined with tax rates, that do not reflect these differences in layoffs that are responsible. This importance of temporary layoffs (relative to permanent changes in employment) indicates to a large extent that the benefit payments are predictable. Thus, it is a finding that weakens arguments for incomplete experience rating as insurance for firms against large layoff costs. While high temporary layoff rates that are not matched by higher tax rates are the main contributor to large interindustry subsidies, we also find that the divergence between the levels of wages on which taxes and benefits are calculated contributes to the subsidies, albeit to a lesser extent.

Our exploration of interfirm subsidies provides more evidence on the predictability of benefit payments. Using previously unexamined firm level data, we document a persistent pattern of benefit/tax ratios over several years. We find that a firm currently receiving a subsidy from the UI system is much more likely to be still receiving a subsidy three to five years later than a firm that is not currently subsidized. This result implies that to a significant degree, the interfirm subsidies are regular transfers, rather than insurance for firms, thus further weakening the argument for incomplete experience rating. An additional finding of our work with firm level data is that much of the variation across firms in UI benefit receipt and tax payments is not captured by industry data. Thus, past work performed at the industry level is likely to have revealed only a fraction of the cross-subsidies carried out by the UI payroll tax.

The interindustry and interfirm subsidies that we document will have real effects on the economy. First, subsidized firms and industries will be larger, while those doing the subsidizing will be smaller. This misallocation of resources leads to a deadweight efficiency loss. While even with our new data sources it is difficult to attach an exact dollar value to this loss, we argue that it may be substantial. Additionally, there is an effect on aggregate unemployment, because it is just those workers who are most likely to be regularly unemployed who are most subsidized. Again, the data is not available to arrive at precise estimates of the effect, but we find that UI cross-subsidization may be responsible for substantial unemployment in such industries as construction.

REFERENCES

Anderson, Patricia M., and Bruce D Meyer (1992). "The Incentives and Cross-Subsidies of the UI Payroll Tax" (with Patricia Anderson). Working paper, March 1992.

————, and ———— (1993). "Unemployment Insurance in the United States: Layoff Incentives and Cross-Subsidies." *Journal of Labor Economics* 11.

Atkinson, Anthony B., and John Micklewright (1991). "Unemployment Compensation and Labor Market Transitions: A Critical Review." *Journal of Economic Literature* 24, 1679–1727.

Becker, Joseph M. (1972). *Experience Rating in Unemployment Insurance: An Experiment in Competitive Socialism.* Baltimore: The Johns Hopkins University Press.

Brechling, Frank (1977). "The Incentive Effects of the U.S. Unemployment Insurance Tax." In *Research in Labor Economics,* vol. 1. Ronald Ehrenberg, ed. Greenwich, CT: JAI Press.

Deere, Donald R. (1991). "Unemployment Insurance and Employment." *Journal of Labor Economics* 9, 307–324.

Feldstein, Martin S. (1978). "The Effect of Unemployment Insurance on Temporary Layoff Unemployment." *American Economic Review* 68, 834–846.

Hamermesh, Daniel S. (1986). "The Demand for Labor in the Long Run." In *Handbook of Labor Economics,* Orley C. Ashenfelter and Richard Layard, eds. Amsterdam: North-Holland.

———— (1990). "Unemployment Insurance Financing, Short-Time Compensation, and Labor Demand." *Research in Labor Economics* 11, 241–270.

Hartley, H. O., J. N. K. Rao, and L. LaMotte (1978). "A Simple Synthesis-Based Method of Variance Component Estimation." *Biometrics* 34, 233–244.

Marks, Denton (1984). "Incomplete Experience Rating in State Unemployment Insurance." *Monthly Labor Review* 107, 45–49.

Munts, Raymond C., and Ephraim Asher (1981). "Cross-Subsidies Among Industries From 1969 to 1978." *Unemployment Compensation: Studies and Research,* 277–297.

National Foundation for Unemployment Compensation & Workers' Compensation (various years). *Highlights of State Unemployment Compensation Laws.* Washington, DC: NFUCWC.

Topel, Robert H. (1983). "On Layoffs and Unemployment Insurance." *American Economic Review* 73, 541–559.

——— (1990). "Financing Unemployment Insurance: History, Incentives, and Reform." In *Unemployment Insurance.* W. Lee Hansen and James F. Byers, eds. Madison, WI: University of Wisconsin Press.

INCOME INEQUALITY AND THE INCOMES OF VERY HIGH-INCOME TAXPAYERS: EVIDENCE FROM TAX RETURNS

Daniel R. Feenberg
NBER

James M. Poterba
Massachusetts Institute of Technology and NBER

EXECUTIVE SUMMARY

This paper uses tax return data for the period 1951–1990 to investigate the rising share of adjusted gross income (AGI) that is reported on very high income tax returns. We find that most of this increase is due to a rise in reported income for the one quarter of one percent of taxpayers with the highest AGIs. The share of total AGI reported by these taxpayers rose slowly in the early 1980s, and increased sharply in 1987 and 1988. This pattern suggests that at least part of the increase in the income share of high-AGI taxpayers was due to the changing tax incentives that were enacted in the 1986 Tax Reform Act. By lowering marginal tax rates on top-income households from 50% to 28%, TRA86 reduced the incentive for these households to engage in tax avoidance activities. We also find substantial differences in the growth of the income share of the

We are grateful to Caitlin Carroll for research assistance; to David Cutler, Jerry Hausman, Lawrence Katz, Sylvia Nasar, Sherwin Rosen, and Joel Slemrod for helpful comments; and to the National Science Foundation for research support.

highest one quarter of one percent of taxpayers, and the share of other very high income taxpayers. This casts doubt on the view that the increasing inequality of reported incomes at very high levels is driven by the same factors that have generated widening wage inequality at lower income levels.

The evolution of U.S. income distribution has recently attracted enormous academic and popular attention. Systematic studies of labor earnings based on large household surveys, such as those by Bound and Johnson (1992), Katz and Murphy (1992), Levy and Michel (1991), and Murphy and Welch (1992), have demonstrated that labor earnings, the most important component of income for all but the highest income households, became more unequal during the 1980s. The returns to college education rose, and the real earnings of low-skill individuals declined relative to those of better-trained workers.

The most controversial feature of the income distribution, however, is the apparent increase in the share of income accruing to a small group of very high-income households: those in the top 1 percent of the income distribution. A widely publicized calculation, described in Krugman (1992), suggests that very high-income households received a disproportionate share of the real income growth in the U.S. economy during the last decade.

Measuring the income and wealth of high-income households is extremely difficult. The economic lives of the rich, especially the rich who are not famous, are something of a mystery. Mandel (1992) estimates that there are only a few thousand highly visible, highly compensated individuals in the U.S. economy—athletes, top executives at large companies, and partners at major law firms and investment banks. Various sources suggest that the compensation received by these individuals rose rapidly during the last decade. Yet whether the experiences of this group generalize to the nearly one million households in the top 1 percent of the income distribution remains an open question. Information from income tax returns remains the most reliable, if imperfect, source of information about the economic activities of this group.

One class of explanations for the apparent increase in the relative incomes of high- versus low-income households focuses on changes in economic institutions or structure that might raise wages or capital incomes for the high-income group. Slemrod (1993) argues that increasing globalization of economic activity may raise the incomes of high-ability individuals by more than that of the less able. The rise of new financial institutions and practices during the last fifteen years—for example, takeovers and leveraged buyouts—may also have expanded the opportunities for a small group of individuals to earn very high incomes. This explanation for rising incomes of top "performers" follows the analysis of superstar compensation developed by Rosen (1981) and explored further in Frank and Cook (1992).

An alternative explanation for the growth of reported income inequality focuses on changes in taxpayer incentives to report taxable income, rather than defer income recognition or otherwise shelter accruing income. Because high-income households derive more of their income from portfolio investments and self-employment than households elsewhere in the income distribution, they are likely to have more opportunity to engage in legal tax avoidance, and more discretion in deciding how, and how much, of their income is reported to the Internal Revenue Service (IRS), than their lower-income counterparts. The tax reforms of 1981 and 1986 lowered marginal tax rates on high-income households, reducing their incentives to engage in various forms of tax avoidance. Taxpayers at the top of the income distribution faced marginal tax rates as high as 70 percent in 1980, while in 1988, their marginal tax rates were capped at 28 percent.

The suggestion that recent tax reforms induced changes in reported taxable income, even if they did not affect taxpayer behavior, lies at the center of the recent debate on whether the tax reforms of the 1980s increased labor supply (see Bosworth and Burtless, 1992, and Lindsey, 1987a, 1988). Because the Congressional Budget Office (CBO) data on income distribution, the data underlying the Krugman (1992) calculation, rely on tax returns for data on the incomes of high-income households, changes in taxpayer reporting behavior could directly affect estimates of income inequality at top income levels.

This paper presents new evidence on the changing share of adjusted gross income (AGI) reported by very high-income taxpayers. We focus primarily on the comparison of annual income distributions for the years 1951–1990 and limit most of our analysis to the top one-half of 1 percent of taxpayers. We document the changing composition of income reported by these households, and we try to provide some evidence on the importance of tax-induced changes in income reporting in contributing to this group's rising share of AGI. We do not explore the variation in the relative incomes of households elsewhere in the income distribution, a subject that has also attracted substantial controversy (see Nasar, 1992, and Roberts, 1992). For studying the distribution of incomes below the top tier, tax returns are not the best source of information. Not all low-income households file tax returns, and even for those who do, tax returns do not include information on most transfer payments.

This paper is divided into six sections. The first describes our methods for using tax return data to estimate the share and composition of income accruing to high-income taxpayers, whom we label *Top AGI Recipients* (TARs). Section II describes the impact of the major tax reforms in 1981 and 1986 on the incentives for high-income taxpayers to report taxable income. The third section presents time series information on the share of AGI, as well as various AGI components such as wages and salaries, dividends, interest, and capital gains, reported by these taxpayers. We find that most of the increase in the share of income reported by taxpayers in the top fifth of the income distribution is accounted for by an increase in the share of reported income in the top *one quarter of 1 percent* of taxpayers.

Our results also suggest that the increase in reported income inequality is not simply an artifact of capital gains realizations in the 1980s, but reflects changes in the distribution of most other income sources as well. The share of income reported by top income taxpayers rose throughout the 1980s, but we find the sharpest increase in 1987 and 1988, the years following a significant decline in marginal tax rates. We therefore conclude that changes in decisions about how much taxable income to report have contributed to the observed increase in the reported incomes of high-income households. Unfortunately, we cannot estimate the share of the reported income increase that is due solely to changes in taxpayer reporting practices.

Section IV presents data on the composition of reported income for high-income households. Wages and salaries became substantially more important, and capital income less important, between 1970 and the mid-1980s. We find that this trend began roughly in 1969, when the top marginal tax rate on earned income fell from 77 percent to 50 percent. The fifth section investigates the extent to which the changing income share of top-income taxpayers can be attributed to changes in the composition of factor rewards in the aggregate economy, rather than to shifts within the distribution of each type of factor income. We find that high stock market returns during the 1980s would have raised the income share of top-income taxpayers even if the ownership of stock had remained fixed at its 1979 levels. The actual share of income received by these households rose faster than the changing distribution of aggregate factor rewards would have predicted. The changing mix of factor incomes is particularly unsuccessful in explaining the rapid growth in the share of AGI reported by high-income households in the years following the 1986 Tax Reform Act. The final section concludes and suggests several avenues for further work.

I. ESTIMATING THE INCOME OF VERY HIGH-INCOME HOUSEHOLDS

The CBO publishes widely cited estimates of the U.S. income distribution (1992a, 1992b). This distribution is defined in terms of adjusted family income (AFI). AFI is similar to AGI as defined by the federal income tax, but it also includes cash transfer payments and imputed corporate taxes, and excludes some business losses that can be deducted when taxpayers compute AGI.

Table 1 shows the CBO's estimates of the share of AFI accruing to households in the top fifth of the income distribution during the period 1977–1988. The estimates show a rising share of income accruing to this group, and in particular show that the top 1 percent of households account for a very large share of the total increase for the top quintile. In 1977, the estimates suggest that the top 20 percent of all households received 45.6 percent of adjusted family income, while in 1988 the analogous group received 51.4 percent of the total. The share received by the top one percent of households, however, rose from 8.3 percent (1977) to 13.4 percent (1988). This 5.2 percent increase is 90 percent of the 5.8 percent increase for the top 20 percent. The lower panel in Table 1 shows the share of wages and salaries accruing to the top 20 percent and the top 1 percent of households. The highest 1 percent accounts for two-

TABLE 1.
CBO Income Distribution Estimates, 1977–1988.

	Percent			
	1977	*1980*	*1985*	*1988*
Share of adjusted family income received by				
Top 20%	45.6	46.7	50.1	51.4
81–90%	15.6	15.7	15.7	15.3
91–95%	10.1	10.1	10.4	10.1
95–99%	11.6	11.7	12.4	12.6
Top 1%	8.3	9.2	11.6	13.4
Share of wages and salaries received by				
Top 20%	42.1	43.5	45.8	47.7
81–90%	17.7	17.8	17.9	17.5
91–95%	10.5	10.7	11.2	11.1
95–99%	9.8	10.3	11.2	11.4
Top 1%	4.1	4.7	5.5	7.7

Source: Congressional Budget Office (1992b). The statistics in the top panel are also reported in the U.S. House of Representatives *1992 Green Book* (p. 1521).

thirds of the gain in the share of wages and salaries reported by the top 20 percent of households.

An income distribution can be defined over households, as in the CBO estimates, individuals, or taxpayers.[1] Each of these three options has advantages and drawbacks. Focusing on households can be misleading because demographic changes can shift the characteristics and number of households. Between 1960 and 1989, the average number of individuals per U.S. household declined from 3.3 to 2.6. The shares of single-person households, and of households headed by a single adult with children, have increased significantly in recent decades. Because these households have lower incomes on average than other households, the share of income accruing to a given fraction of households at the top of the income distribution should increase as a result of this demographic change.[2] Focusing on individuals also raises difficult issues, such as the treatment of spouses and children. Do they receive a proportional share of household income? If so, then if a single high-income taxpayer marries a lower-income earner, she may drop out of the high-income category. The birth of children to high-income households could have the same effect.

Defining the income distribution in terms of a given share of tax returns, the natural choice given our reliance on tax data, can also yield spurious results. The number of tax returns filed varies with changes in the tax law. The 1986 Tax Reform Act was expected to remove almost six million low-income households from the tax rolls, although in practice it had a far smaller effect (see Hausman and Poterba, 1987 and Slemrod, 1992). By shrinking the number of taxpayers, such a reform would lower the number of tax returns in the top percentile of the taxpayer distribution. Because the taxpayers removed from the tax rolls typically have very low incomes, this change would reduce the share of income reported by the top percentile of taxpayers. This could bias comparisons between income distribution statistics, even for adjacent years, when the tax system is in flux.

Our approach to identifying the top of the income distribution begins with tax returns filed in 1989. We select the one-half of 1 percent of these returns with the highest AGI; there were 558,778 tax returns in this

---

[1] In 1989, of ninety-three million households in the United States, sixty-six million were "family households." There were 113 million tax returns filed in 1989.

[2] While this may contaminate comparisons of the top of the household income distribution in widely separated years, it is unlikely to have a large effect on comparisons of the income distribution over short time periods.

group.[3] We define this number of returns as N_{1989} and then compute an analogous number of returns in other years by multiplying N_{1989} by the ratio of the adult *population* in each year to that in 1989. Our procedure, which follows McCubbin and Scheuren (1988), indexes the number of high-income tax returns to the aggregate population, rather than the number of tax returns filed or the number of households. We define the top N_t taxpayers in each year as "Top AGI Recipients" (TARs). They represent roughly half as many households as the CBO's top 1 percent of the income distribution.[4]

A. Estimating Income Shares Using the Treasury Tax Model

In each year since 1968, the U.S. Treasury has released a data file containing an anonymous sample of individual tax returns, the Treasury Tax Model data base, which can be used to estimate the total income of high-income taxpayers. This data file over-samples high-income tax returns, providing reasonably accurate information on this group's income.

Table 2 shows the number of tax returns at different income levels in the 1989 Tax Model and indicates the sampling weights associated with returns in each group. There are nearly 12,000 returns with incomes of more than $1,000,000 in the data base. The probability that a tax filer with taxable income in this range would be included in the data file is approximately one in five. There are a similar number of tax returns with taxable incomes between $50,000 and $100,000, but each return filed in this income group has less than a 1 in 1,000 chance of being included on the data file. The Treasury Tax Model data bases for each year since 1979 are part of the NBER TAXSIM program, and we use these data files to tabulate the distribution of both AGI and various AGI components for these years.[5]

---

[3] Our reported income share for high-income households would not change if a top income taxpayer married someone with no income, although it would increase if a high-income taxpayer married another income recipient. It is also possible that marriages or divorces between individuals with high, but not very high, incomes could affect the income reported by the TAR group.

[4] Although our data set on federal tax returns does not include information on the state in which the tax filer resides, we can compare the number of federal income tax returns above various threshold income levels with state revenue statistics. They show some, but not extreme, concentration of tax returns. In 1989, for example, New York residents filed 3.7 percent of all federal income tax returns, but 12.9 percent of all returns with AGI in excess of $1 million.

[5] We compute the changing shares of AGI reported in each year, despite the fact that the *definition* of AGI changes when, for example, the capital gains exclusion is eliminated. This is partly for comparison with the widely cited results from the CBO. Our results also focus on several components of AGI with constant definitions through time.

TABLE 2.
Tax Returns Included in the Treasury Tax Model Data Base.

Income class	Number of returns	Average sample weight
<50K	53,680	1,794
50–100K	11,947	1,087
100–200K	4,561	455
200–500K	6,705	91
500–1,000K	7,700	15
>1,000K	11,996	5

Source: Authors' tabulations from 1989 Tax Model Data File.

B. *"Interpolating" Incomes for High-Income Taxpayers*

For years prior to 1979, we rely on aggregate data published by the Treasury Department in *Statistics of Income: Individual Income Tax Returns* (SOI) to estimate the income of TARs.[6] The SOI tables show the number of tax returns, and reported AGI, in various taxable income intervals. The reported AGI categories for high-income taxpayers have remained fixed in nominal terms for nearly three decades, with taxpayers divided into those with AGIs of 100–200K, 200–500K, 500–1,000K, and more than one million dollars. Estimating the amount of AGI reported by a given share of taxpayers therefore requires interpolating the IRS data.

To estimate the total income accruing to the top 0.5 percent of taxpayers, we interpolate AGI within categories below $1 million. We estimate a Pareto distribution for high-income tax returns and use our estimated distribution to estimate the total income accruing to top AGI recipients (TARs). The Pareto is a two-parameter distribution that is widely used in modeling the distributions of income and wages (see Johnson and Kotz, 1970).

We present the details of our interpolation procedure in an appendix but illustrate our method in Figure 1. This figure shows our estimated Pareto distribution for 1990, a year when our estimate of the income threshold for the top 0.5 percent of taxpayers (Y^*) was $258,499. In this case, we can determine from the reported IRS data that the AGI threshold for the top 0.5 percent of taxpayers lies between $200,000 and $500,000. We use the reported information on the fraction of tax returns with AGI above $200,000, and on the fraction with AGI above $500,000, to estimate the parameters of a Pareto distribution. We then use this estimated distribution to estimate Y^*.

---

[6] To ensure comparability over time, in any of our tables or figures that show results for the 1951–1990 period, we also interpolate during the 1979–1990 period when we could make more precise estimates using the Tax Model data base.

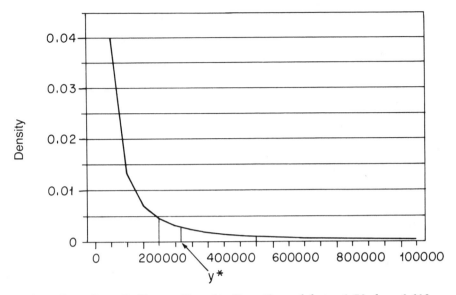

FIGURE 1. *Sample Pareto Density Function: alpha = 1.59, k = 6,619 (1990 parameters).*

Table 3 describes the results of our interpolation procedure. The first and second columns present our estimates of the cutoff income level for the Top AGI Recipients. Figure 2 plots this income threshold, which increased only 10 percent in real terms between 1970 and 1985, but in the four years, 1985–1989, it increased by nearly 50 percent, or almost $85,000 ($1991). The late 1980s, therefore, appears to be the period of most rapid change in the reported income distribution at high incomes.

The third and fourth columns in Table 3 show the number and share of tax returns that are included in our high-income group. These columns show the net effect of indexing the number of TARs to the adult population, rather than to the number of tax returns filed.[7] In the years since 1986, the share of returns in the TAR group varies very little. Between 1986 and 1987, it declined by .02 percent. There is very little change in the share of tax returns in the TAR group between 1975 and 1986, although there is some evidence that the number of tax returns grew more slowly than population for the period 1955–1975. Our TAR

---

[7] Indexing to the number of returns filed would make the last column of Table 3 equal to 0.005 in all years.

FIGURE 2. *High-Income Threshold for TARs: 1951–1990.*

TABLE 3.
Income Thresholds for "Top AGI Recipients," 1955–1990.

Year	High-income threshold		Returns above threshold	
	Current dollars	*1991 Dollars*	*Number (000s)*	*Percent of total*
1955	28,466	144,801	334	0.0057
1960	31,290	144,098	355	0.0058
1965	39,836	172,197	384	0.0057
1970	49,594	173,978	410	0.0055
1975	61,721	156,204	441	0.0054
1980	104,611	172,895	502	0.0054
1981	111,670	167,274	510	0.0054
1982	117,797	166,258	517	0.0054
1983	125,448	171,546	523	0.0054
1984	137,723	180,566	529	0.0053
1985	150,996	191,189	535	0.0053
1986	171,195	212,727	541	0.0053
1987	199,436	239,059	548	0.0051
1988	238,652	274,762	554	0.0051
1989	251,338	276,066	558	0.0050
1990	258,499	269,376	564	0.0050

Source: Authors' calculations using data from annual publications of *Statistics of Income: Individual Tax Returns.* Data in column three are in thousands of returns. The definition of the "high income threshold" is the income level that excludes only the $0.005* (\text{Adult Population}_t)/(\text{Adult Population}_{1990})$ highest-income tax returns.

group includes a larger share of tax returns in 1960 (0.58 percent) than in 1970 (0.55 percent), 1980 (0.54 percent), or 1990 (0.50 percent). This should tend to *increase* the share of reported income accruing to the TAR group in the early years of our data period, and yield a downward bias in our estimate of the trend in the TAR income share over time.

II. TAX CHANGES AND INCENTIVES FOR REPORTING TAXABLE INCOME

Tax policy parameters such as marginal tax rates can affect the amount of income reported on tax returns either by inducing real changes in individual behavior, such as changes in the number of hours that individuals work, or by inducing changes in the reporting of a given income stream. Because taxpayers can use a variety of tax avoidance techniques to defer or reclassify their income, the tax base is sensitive to decisions about how much income to report. This section provides a brief overview of the changing tax avoidance incentives facing high-income taxpayers.

A. *Earned Income*

The two most significant changes in the tax rates on earned income of high-income taxpayers took place in 1969 and 1986. The Tax Reform Act of 1969 capped the marginal tax rate on earned income at 50 percent, at a time when the top marginal tax rate on unearned income was 70 percent (77 percent including the Vietnam war surtax). The top marginal tax rate on earned income remained at 50 percent through 1986, although rates just below those of top income taxpayers were reduced by the Economic Recovery Tax Act of 1981 (ERTA). The Tax Reform Act of 1986 (TRA86) reduced the top marginal tax rate on earned as well as unearned income from 50 percent to 28 percent, further lowering the incentives to (legally) avoid taxes.

Declining marginal tax rates reduced the incentives to engage in a variety of tax avoidance practices. One simple avoidance strategy involves transforming earned income into fringe benefits, ranging from company cars and conference "vacations," to health and life insurance policies. There is a large literature, summarized in Woodbury and Hammermesh (1992), suggesting that the demand for fringe benefits is sensitive to the marginal tax rate on earned income. A related strategy involves deferring earned income, and the associated taxes, to later years. Over long horizons, income could be deferred with retirement plans or deferred compensation arrangements.[8]

Some taxpayers may also have used income-retiming strategies over shorter tax-planning horizons, moving wages and salaries income from 1986 to 1987 or 1988, and capital gain realizations from later years to 1986. Taxpayers with some control over the timing of when clients are billed for their services, and those who receive large bonuses or otherwise lumpy earned income, faced strong incentives in 1986 to find ways to avoid recognizing income until lower tax rates became effective in later years. Deferring income by fourteen months, from December 1986 to January 1988, could raise a taxpayer's after-tax income by 44 percent (from $0.50 on the dollar to $0.72). This provided powerful incentives to engage in a wide range of income-retiming activities, which are unfortunately difficult to measure from tax returns or other public data sources.[9]

A particularly significant dimension of TRA86 was its change in the incentives for using Subchapter C corporations to avoid recognizing personal income. Before 1986, a dollar reported as individual income faced a tax burden of $0.50, while a dollar earned by a Subchapter C corporation faced a marginal tax rate of 46 percent, with somewhat lower rates on the first $100,000 of income. Corporate income could bear subsequent individual-level taxes if it was distributed as wages or dividends, although there were strategies, for example, bequeathing stock in a closely held business, that could reduce such taxes.

After TRA86 was fully phased in, the top personal income tax rate was below the corporate tax rate. A dollar of income reported directly on an individual income tax return faced a tax burden of 28 percent starting in 1988, compared with at least 34 percent if it was earned by a Subchapter C company. As Gordon and Mackie-Mason (1990) explain, these tax changes reduced the incentive to use corporations to shelter income, and they could have led to an increase in reported income for high-income taxpayers. Anecdotal evidence of the potential importance of this effect is provided by Scholes and Wolfson (1992), who note that there were 225,000 S-corporation elections in the last three weeks of 1986, compared with only 75,000 elections in the entirety of 1985.

---

[8] In the first few years of a low-tax rate regime, such as 1987 and 1988, it is even possible that individuals who had previously deferred income by contributing to retirement plans would *withdraw* plan assets, also leading to an increase in reported income.

[9] Scholes, Wilson, and Wolfson (1992) document the importance of retiming of *corporate* income around this tax change, which reduced the statutory corporate tax rate from 46 percent to 34 percent.

B. Capital Income

The tax changes that were enacted in 1981 reduced the top tax rate on unearned income other than capital gains from 70 percent to 50 percent. TRA86 further reduced this top rate to 28 percent. The tax rules affecting capital gains are more complex. Between 1969 and 1978, 60 percent of long-term capital gains could be excluded from taxable income, implying a top marginal tax rate of 28 percent (70%*.4). For some taxpayers, however, because the excluded portion of capital gains was considered a tax preference item for the minimum tax, the marginal rate on realized gains could exceed 40 percent (see Lindsey, 1987b). This situation was changed by the Tax Reform Act of 1978 (TRA78), which excluded capital gains from the set of minimum tax preference items, effective January 1, 1979. In addition, the 1978 reform lowered the share of long-term gains that was included in taxable income from 50 percent to 40 percent for gains realized after October 31, 1978. These changes reduced the maximum statutory tax rate on long-term capital gains to 28 percent beginning with the 1979 tax year. The preannounced reduction in top marginal rates at the highest incomes led to significant delay in the realization of capital gains by TARs. The 1981 tax reform, ERTA, further reduced the marginal tax rate on gains for top income taxpayers, because the reduction in marginal tax rates to 50 percent coupled with the 60 percent exclusion generated a top capital gains tax rate of 20 percent.

The Tax Reform Act of 1986 *raised* the top marginal rate on capital gains from 20 percent to 28 percent, because it eliminated the partial exclusion of long-term gains from taxable income. Because the 1986 changes were legislated to take effect in 1987, there was a strong incentive for taxpayers with accrued but unrealized gains to realize these gains in 1986. This "retiming" of gains is a striking feature of the time series on gain realizations (see Auerbach, 1988).

This brief summary of the tax rates facing high-income households suggests that there have been important changes over time in the after-tax income gains associated with tax avoidance strategies.[10] We now consider the detailed information on income reports by these households, to investigate whether there is evidence that such changes in taxpayer behavior took place.

---

[10] The discussion has focussed on legal tax avoidance strategies, although some taxpayers may resort to illegal strategies such as income underreporting. Poterba (1987) provides evidence on the potential sensitivity of evasion for capital gains, an important income source for high-income households, with respect to marginal tax rates.

III. THE SHARE OF INCOME RECEIVED BY TOP AGI RECIPIENTS

This section reports our basic findings on the changing concentration of reported income among high-income taxpayers. Figure 3 shows our estimate of the share of AGI accruing to TARs in each year between 1951 and 1990.[11] The AGI share of this group declined during the 1950s and 1960s, was roughly stable during the 1970s, and increased during the 1980s. The share of AGI reported by roughly the top one-half of 1 percent of taxpayers rose from 6 percent in 1981 to over 12 percent in 1988. The sharpest increase in AGI concentration occurred between 1985 and 1988, when the income share of this group rose from 8 percent to 12 percent. The TAR share of AGI also fell more than a full percentage point in 1989 and 1990, which could be consistent with an active role for short-term and one-time income retiming strategies in the years immediately following enactment of TRA86.

One possible explanation for the rising concentration of AGI among top income recipients is that capital gains realizations rose during the 1980s, and that they are a highly concentrated form of income. Figure 4 shows the share of AGI *excluding capital gains* reported by the top AGI recipients. The figure focuses on the period since 1979, and shows that while the nongain AGI share of this group rose by almost one percentage point between 1979 and 1986, it rose by more than three percentage points between 1986 and 1988. This figure suggests that capital gains are *not* the explanation for the broad trend in the concentration of AGI. It also demonstrates, however, that there was a rapid increase in reported noncapital gain income among TARs in the years immediately following TRA86. This is consistent with the view that these taxpayers reported more of their income in taxable form when marginal tax rates declined.

Although most of our analysis focuses on the top one-half of 1 percent of tax returns, we also examined reported AGI for several other subsets of the high-income population. The first two columns of Table 4 report the AGI share for the top one-tenth and one-quarter of 1 percent of tax returns. The middle column reports data for the top one-half of 1 percent of taxpayers, the TAR group that we focus on elsewhere. The two rightmost columns show the share of AGI reported by the top 1 and 2 percent

---

[11] We have not made the various adjustments to AGI that the Congressional Budget Office uses in computing "economic income" of households. For households in our AGI class, the most important CBO modifications are exclusion of some losses on real property, arguably the result of tax shelter investments, and the inclusion of some corporate tax payments as a component of taxpayer income.

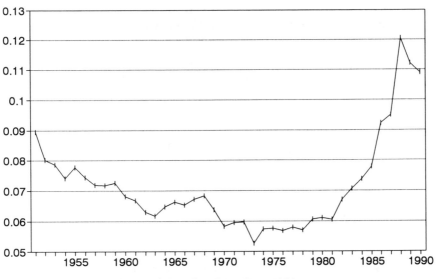

FIGURE 3. *TAR Share of Total AGI: 1951–1990.*

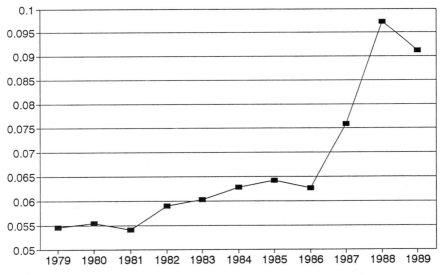

FIGURE 4. *Share of Nongain Income to TARs: 1979–1989 (ranked by nongain income).*

TABLE 4.
The Share of Income Accruing to Very High-Income Taxpayers,
1979–1989.

Year	Fraction of the income distribution (%)				
	Top 0.001%	*Top 0.0025%*	*Top 0.005%*	*Top 0.01%*	*Top 0.02%*
Panel A: Adjusted Gross Income					
1979	2.61	4.18	6.05	8.81	12.90
1980	2.63	4.24	6.12	8.91	13.05
1981	2.63	4.19	6.03	8.76	12.85
1982	3.14	4.81	6.73	9.51	13.66
1983	3.38	5.10	7.04	9.84	13.99
1984	3.66	5.41	7.36	10.14	14.29
1985	3.83	5.66	7.66	10.49	14.64
1986	4.74	6.71	8.84	11.79	16.05
1987	4.90	7.10	9.44	12.64	17.12
1988	6.75	9.38	12.02	15.41	19.93
1989	5.96	8.43	11.00	14.37	18.94
Panel B: Adjusted Gross Income Excluding Capital Gains					
1979	2.19	3.66	5.45	8.14	12.15
1980	2.24	3.74	5.54	8.24	12.29
1981	2.20	3.66	5.40	8.04	12.05
1982	2.54	4.08	5.90	8.59	12.64
1983	2.66	4.21	6.02	8.68	12.73
1984	2.87	4.46	6.28	8.94	12.96
1985	2.95	4.58	6.42	9.09	13.10
1986	2.83	4.43	6.26	8.95	13.00
1987	3.65	5.53	7.60	10.52	14.75
1988	5.09	7.37	9.73	12.85	17.18
1989	4.62	6.80	9.12	12.27	16.66

Source: Authors' tabulations using U.S Treasury Individual Tax Models for years 1979–1989.

of taxpayers for the years 1979–1989. These estimates are based on the Treasury Tax Model data bases.

Table 4 shows that even within the top 2 percent of the taxpayer distribution, the gains in reported AGI during the 1980s were highly concentrated. The share of AGI reported on the top 2 percent of tax returns rose by 6.04 percent between 1979 and 1989, but more than half of this increase, 3.35 percent, was reported on the top one tenth of 1 percent of tax returns (roughly 100,000 tax returns). More than two-thirds of the increase in AGI for the top 2 percent was reported by the top one-quarter of 1 percent of taxpayers. These findings are consistent with Krugman's (1992) "fractal" hypothesis about the shape of the income distribution.

Figure 5 makes the same point with a slightly different approach. It

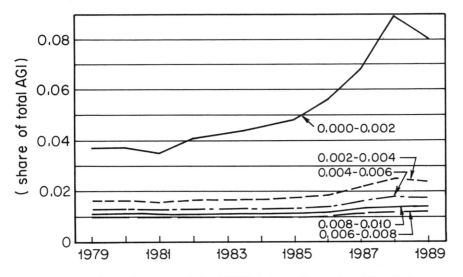

FIGURE 5. *Distribution of AGI Within Top Percent: 1979–1989.*

shows the share of AGI reported by five nonoverlapping groups: the top
0.2 percent, the *next* 0.2 percent, etc. The top line is the share of AGI
reported by the top one-fifth of 1 percent of taxpayers. It shows a sharp
increase between 1986 and 1988, and declines slightly in 1989. There has
been a relatively small increase in the AGI shares for all groups below
the top one-fifth of 1 percent of taxpayers.[12] This casts doubt on the view
that the factors responsible for the increase in reported incomes among
high-income taxpayers, especially in the 1986–1988 period, are the same
factors that were responsible for the widening of the wage distribution
over a longer time period. Figure 5 also underscores the importance of
the post-1986 period in contributing to the changes in reported income
concentration during the 1980s.

The lower panel of Table 4 reports similar calculations for AGI excluding capital gains. The same pattern emerges, with more than half of the
increase in nongain AGI for the top 2 percent of taxpayers accruing to
the top 0.1 percent of taxpayers. Comparing the upper and lower panels
of Table 4 provides interesting evidence, however, on the relative timing
of the concentration of gain and nongain income. While the share of
total AGI, including gains, reported by the top 0.1 percent of taxpayers

---

[12] Our tabulations focus on the distribution of income for taxpayers in each year, not the
distribution of the *same* taxpayers over time. Thus, the taxpayers in the top AGI category in
one year may be different from those in this category in the next year. Slemrod (1991)
provides some evidence on the persistence of income for high-income taxpayers.

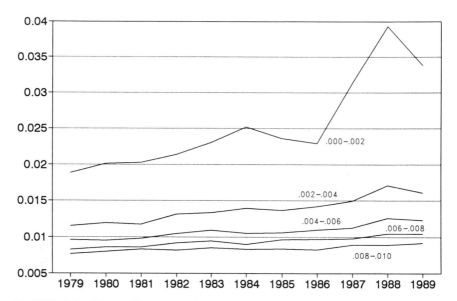

FIGURE 6. *Wage Shares Within the Top Percentile: 1979–1989.*

rose from 2.6 percent to 3.8 percent between 1979 and 1985, the share of nongain income increased less than one percentage point, from 2.2 percent to 2.95 percent. In the post-1986 period, however, the nongain income share for this group grew faster than its share of total AGI. Capital gain realizations, therefore, were a more important factor in the concentration of AGI in the early than in the late 1980s.

We can also perform a similar analysis for components of income. Figure 6 presents data on the share of wages and salaries accruing to taxpayers in the top 1 percent of the taxpayer distribution.[13] There is some growth in the share of wages for each of the high-income groups between 1979 and 1989, but a dramatic increase in the share of wages for the top 0.2 percent of taxpayers. Three-quarters of this increase occurs between 1986 and 1988, and the sharp break in the trend growth rate in 1986 is strongly suggestive of a link between TRA86 and this pattern of reported income.

Figure 7 presents similar data for a longer time period. This data series is based on aggregate IRS data, and shows the share of wages and salaries reported by top AGI Recipients. While the rapid increase in wage concentration after 1986 is unusual by historical standards, the trend toward rising concentration of wages and salaries began in the

---

[13] We continue to sort taxpayers by total AGI in preparing this figure.

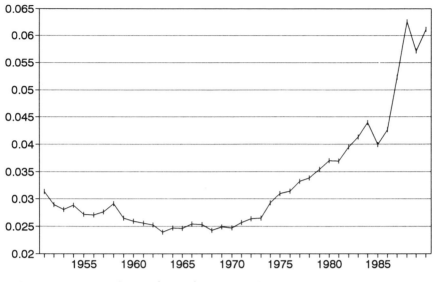

FIGURE 7. *TAR Share of Total Wages: 1951–1990.*

early 1970s. The wage share of the TARs rose by nearly 1.5 percentage points between 1970 and 1980, by another 0.5 percent between 1980 and 1985, and then by more than two percentage points in the two years after the Tax Reform Act of 1986. The beginning of the trend toward rising wage and salary concentration is roughly coincident with the Tax Reform Act of 1969, which reduced the top tax rate on earned income from 77 percent to 50 percent. We suspect that the large increase in reported TAR wages and salaries in the years after 1986 reflects, at least in part, a reporting response to lower marginal tax rates.[14]

Our findings suggest that whatever forces were behind the rising concentration of reported income in the high-income ranks during the 1980s, they were strongly concentrated within a small group of taxpayers, and strongly concentrated in the years after 1986. Without much more precise information on the financial and tax-planning activities of high-income taxpayers, it is impossible to determine how much of the increase in reported income was due to changes in tax avoidance behavior; how

[14] The difference between Slemrod's (1993) conclusion that there is no evidence for a high-income "Laffer curve," and our finding supporting a positive elasticity of reported taxable income with respect to tax rate reductions, can be traced to the data we analyze. Slemrod examines data on relatively few years between 1962 and 1988, and does not focus on the short-term changes that take place between tax years 1985 and 1988. His methodology is therefore designed to detect long-term trends, rather than high-frequency fluctuations such as those associated with income retiming.

FIGURE 8. *Wage Share of AGI Among the TAR: 1951–1990.*

much was due to changes in real behavior such as labor supply; and how much was due to changing returns to the factors, labor and capital, that high-income taxpayers own. This is a central goal for future work.

IV. THE INCOME COMPOSITION OF HIGH-INCOME TAXPAYERS

The previous section considered the high-income taxpayers' share of total AGI, AGI excluding capital gains, and wages and salaries. This section explores the fraction of total income reported by top-income taxpayers that is from various income sources, and asks how this income mix has changed over time.

Figure 8 shows wage and salary income as a share of AGI for TARs over the 1951–1990 period. This share rose during the 1970s, from one-third to one-half of the AGI for this group.[15] During the 1980s, however, while the concentration of wage income increased, the wage share of income for the TARs actually declined. This is not just an artifact of rising capital gain

---

[15] The U.S. House Ways and Means Committee (1991) reports data from the Congressional Budget Office on the top 1 percent of the income distribution for households. The increase in the share of wage income, from 34.2 percent in 1977 to 38.4 percent in 1988, is less pronounced in part because of the larger set of households included in the CBO's "top 1 percent" group.

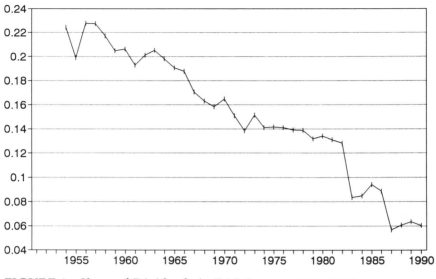

FIGURE 9. *Share of Dividends in TAR Income: 1951–1990.*

realizations; if the figure were redrawn with the share of wages in nongain AGI, it would look almost identical. Figure 8 also shows a very sharp decline, by over ten percentage points, between 1985 and 1987.

Figure 9 reports an analogous calculation for dividend income. The stylized view that high-income taxpayers derive most of their income from dividend payments has become increasingly inappropriate during the last three decades. TARs drew roughly one-quarter of their taxable income from dividends in the early 1950s, but only 6 percent of their AGI from this source in 1989.[16] Figure 10 shows that the share of dividends received by high-income taxpayers has also fallen. In the late 1980s, the top 0.5 percent of taxpayers reported roughly one-quarter of the dividends on all tax returns, compared with nearly half of all dividends in the late 1950s. These calculations are based on taxable dividends, and therefore exclude dividends received on equity held in IRAs, 401(k)s, and other tax-sheltered forms. It is difficult to argue that the growth of such investment vehicles is large enough to explain the pattern in Figure 10.

The analogous time series for interest income, shown in Figure 11, displays a rather different pattern. The share of interest income received TARs declined between 1951 and the early 1960s, was stable at about 10 percent until 1986, and then rose by almost five percentage points be-

[16] One factor that may partly explain this trend, especially in the 1980s, is the rise of money market mutual fund shares, which may generate dividends for lower-income households.

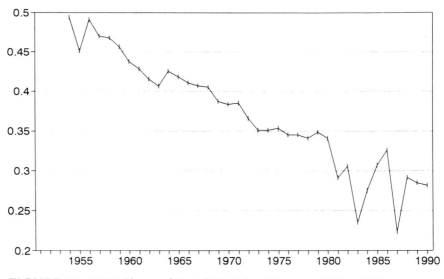

FIGURE 10. *TAR Share of Total Dividend Income: 1954–1990.*

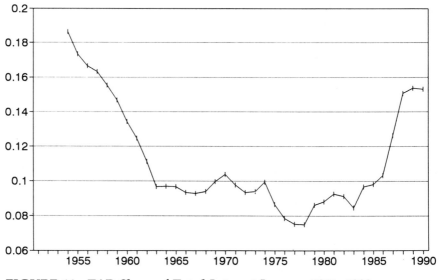

FIGURE 11. *TAR Share of Total Interest Income: 1951–1990.*

tween 1986 and 1988. Because clientele models of asset ownership suggest that the relative tax rates of different investors play a key role in determining portfolio composition, the post-1986 changes may reflect the changing relative marginal tax rates of TARs and other investors. TRA86 reduced the tax penalty associated with holding interest-bearing securities at top-income brackets. This legislated tax reduction was reinforced by declining inflation rates in the late 1980s, which further reduced the effective tax burden on interest income received by high-income households.

The next source of income we consider is capital gains. Figure 12 shows that the share of all capital gains reported by top-income taxpayers was stable at approximately 45 percent throughout the 1950s and 1960s, but fell to only 20 percent in the late 1970s. This was a period when, as we noted previously, the marginal tax rate on capital gains received by high-income taxpayers could exceed 40 percent. The share of capital gains reported by these taxpayers rose during the 1980s, to just over 50 percent in the second half of the decade.

The sharp decline in the top AGI recipients' share of capital gains in 1978 reflects behavioral response to the preannounced reduction in capital gains tax rates that was enacted in TRA78. Because the minimum tax provisions that affected realizations in calendar year 1978, but not 1979, only affected very high-income households, only these households had

FIGURE 12. *TAR Share of Net Capital Gains: 1951–1990.*

an incentive to delay gain realizations from 1978 to 1979. Consequently, their share of reported gains fell sharply in 1978 and rebounded in 1979.

This example highlights a more general point about the interpretation of our data on TAR shares of various income sources. These shares are sensitive to *relative* tax incentives, and the relative opportunities to respond to these incentives, that face taxpayers at different places in the income distribution. In 1978, when only top-income households had an incentive to delay gains, their share of total gains changed dramatically. This should be contrasted with the relatively stable TAR share of gain realizations around the enactment of TRA86. In 1986, taxpayers throughout the income distribution had an incentive to realize gains to avoid prospective marginal rate increases. The total volume of realized gains rose sharply, but the *share* of these gains realized by high-income households was not very different from the share in other years.

We consider one further income category, income from Subchapter S corporations. Figure 13 shows that the share of profits from these companies reported by TARs rose during the 1980s, but the most rapid increase occurred between 1981 and 1984. Subchapter S profits are now highly concentrated at top income levels: taxpayers in the top 0.1 percent of the distribution reported more than half of all Subchapter S income in the

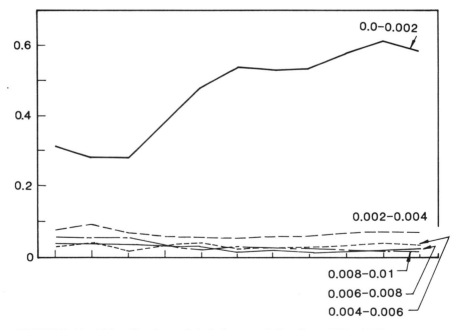

FIGURE 13. *Distribution of Subchapter S Profits: 1979–1989.*

1987–1989 period. The increase in the share of Subchapter S income was also very concentrated, with relatively little increase in the share of this income reported by taxpayers just below the top 0.1 percent.

Although the share of Subchapter S income reported by TARs did not rise appreciably in the years after TRA86, the total amount of such income did increase sharply (see Gordon and Mackie-Mason (1990)). Our tabulations of Subchapter S income reported in the Treasury Tax Model data files suggest this income category doubled between 1985 and 1988, and accounted for more than $40 billion in 1988. Because TARs (the top 0.5 percent of taxpayers) receive approximately 70 percent of Subchapter S income, the 1985–1988 increase explains approximately $14 billion of the reported income growth for this group.

V. THE CHANGING MIX OF FACTOR INCOMES AND INCOME INEQUALITY

Some types of income are distributed less equally than others. The distribution of reported AGI may become more unequal if the inequality of some AGI components increases, or the relative importance of some particularly unequally distributed components increases.[17] In this section we investigate whether the changing mix of income components during the 1980s can explain much of the increasing concentration of AGI that we observed in previous sections.

We investigate this question by constructing a counterfactual income distribution for each year of the 1980s. We maintained the 1979 distribution of each type of income across tax returns but allowed the level of each income type to vary from year to year as the aggregate *Statistics of Income* data suggest.[18]

Table 5 presents the results of our calculations, which suggest that the shifting mix of factor incomes did contribute to an increase in the concentration of AGI during the 1980s. If the distribution of each income type had remained at its 1979 level, but the mix of income types had changed as it did, the share of AGI accruing to TARs would have increased from 6.05 percent in 1979 to 7.69 percent by 1988. This is substantially less than the actual increase, to 12.02 percent. Our predicted income share tracks the actual income share much better for the years before 1986 than

---

[17] Karoly (1993) shows how to formally decompose one measure of aggregate income inequality, the Gini coefficient, into a weighted sum of Gini coefficients for the various income components.

[18] In cases where an income source can be negative, for example with Schedule C or E income, we varied and distributed positive and negative income separately.

TABLE 5.
Actual Income Shares versus Forecast Shares Using 1979 Factor Distributions.

Year	Adjusted gross income (%)		AGI excluding capital gains (%)	
	Actual	*Forecast*	*Actual*	*Forecast*
1979	6.05	6.05	5.45	5.45
1980	6.12	5.84	5.54	5.35
1981	6.03	5.73	5.40	5.26
1982	6.73	5.72	5.90	5.22
1983	7.04	5.88	6.02	5.23
1984	7.36	5.95	6.28	5.27
1985	7.66	6.15	6.42	5.41
1986	8.84	6.97	6.26	5.34
1987	9.44	7.15	7.60	5.57
1988	12.02	7.69	9.73	6.11
1989	11.00	7.52	9.12	6.00

Source: Authors' calculations using annual data from U.S. Treasury *Statistics of Income: Individual Tax Returns* publications, as well as the U.S. Treasury Individual Tax Model for years 1979–1988. Cell contents indicate the share of aggregate income on tax returns going to top AGI recipients.

in the 1987–1988 period. We also present results for a similar exercise with AGI excluding capital gains, which yields similar results. These estimates suggest that the rising share of income reported by TARs during the last decade cannot simply be attributed to a shifting mix of income components, but rather reflects some shift in the underlying distribution of these components as well.

VI. CONCLUSIONS AND FURTHER RESEARCH

Our analysis of tax return data suggests that the rising share of AGI reported on high-income tax returns in the last decade is largely due to an increase in the share of AGI reported by only a few tenths of 1 percent of the taxpaying population. The changes through time in the reported incomes of taxpayers near the top of the income distribution, even those in the "lower half" of the top 1 percent of all taxpayers, are substantially different than the changes for the highest income taxpayers, especially in the years following the 1986 Tax Reform Act. This suggests that the rapid growth in reported incomes at very high-income levels may not be part of a general trend toward a widening income distribution, but rather may reflect other factors including a tax-induced change in the incentives that high-income households face for reporting taxable income. Our evidence casts doubt on the view, presented forcefully in Barlow, Brazer, and Morgan's (1966) study, that tax incentives have little effect on the decisions of high-income households.

Our results are not inconsistent with the widely documented pattern of growing wage inequality in recent years. Many of the studies that find widening wage disparities are based on the Current Population Survey (CPS), however, so they have little or no information on the incomes of top-income households. Income items are "top-coded" at $100,000 in the CPS. The widening inequality observed throughout the wage distribution creates a strong presumption that wages and salaries at the very top of the income distribution have increased relative to those elsewhere. Yet those studies do not suggest that the period after 1986 was marked by sharp acceleration in the dispersion of earning power. The finding that the growth in AGI for very high-income taxpayers was most rapid in the post-1986 years suggests that the underlying determinants of reported AGI for this group may be significantly different from the determinants of relative incomes at lower incomes.

There are many directions in which our work can be extended. Our analysis focuses on *pretax* incomes, rather than the *after-tax* incomes that provide individuals with command over resources. Computing effective tax rates on different taxpayers requires various imputations of taxes on firms and workers, as in Kasten, Sammartino, and Toder (1993) or CBO (1992b), and we have not attempted this complex task.

The most pressing research priority involves searching for sources of data other than tax returns that provide information on the accruing incomes of high-income individuals. There are some sources of information on compensation for highly paid individuals. These include the data set on chief executive officer pay compiled by Joskow, Rose, and Shepard (1993), as well as surveys of earnings by lawyers and doctors that are carried out by professional organizations. These data sets may permit some analysis of how tax reforms have affected the mix of compensation, while also providing further evidence on the trends in earnings, if not total income, for high-income taxpayers.

TECHNICAL APPENDIX: INTERPOLATION USING THE PARETO DISTRIBUTION

The Pareto distribution specifies that the probability that a randomly chosen taxpayer's income, y, is greater than x is:

$$Pr(y > x) = (k/x)^{\alpha}. \tag{1}$$

The two parameters are k, the minimum income that the Pareto distribution applies to ($k > 0$), and α, the exponent that determines the shape of the distribution.

Our objective is to estimate the total income of roughly the top 0.5 percent of taxpayers. Reported data on the number of tax returns and total AGI for taxpayers in different AGI categories provide us with exact income totals for several groups of high-income taxpayers. We can therefore identify the income range where the threshold for the top 0.5 percent of taxpayers will fall. To estimate the precise threshold, we estimate the parameters of the Pareto distribution using information on the reported income cutoffs that bracket the actual threshold in each year.[19] Denote these cutoff incomes as y_1 and y_2, and the associated probabilities that a taxpayer's income will fall *below* these cutoffs as F_1 and F_2, respectively. Equating these observed probabilities with those implied by the Pareto distribution yields

$$1 - F_1 = (k/y_1)^\alpha \tag{2a}$$

and

$$1 - F_2 = (k/y_2)^\alpha. \tag{2b}$$

Solving these two equations yields an estimate of α:

$$\hat{\alpha} = \log\ [(1 - F_1)/(1 - F_2)]/\log\ [y_2/y_1]. \tag{3}$$

Given this value for $\hat{\alpha}$, our estimate of k is

$$\hat{k} = y_1(1 - F_1)^{(1/\alpha)}. \tag{4}$$

A discussion of some of the issues involved in estimating parameters of the Pareto distribution can be found in Johnson and Kotz (1970) and Quandt (1966). Ryoo and Rosen (1992) present a recent application of the Pareto distribution to relatively high incomes.

Table A-1 shows our parameter estimates for each year between 1951 and 1990. The parameter k is measured in current dollars and corresponds to the income level below which the Pareto distribution would not apply. The estimates of $\hat{k}$ are surprisingly small. We found that the Pareto distribution fit the actual distribution very poorly in the range of

---

[19] McCubbin and Scheuren (1988) discuss an alternative approach to interpolation from the published SOI data.

TABLE A-1.
Estimated Pareto Distribution Parameters,
1951–1990.

Year	$\hat{\alpha}$	$\hat{k}$
1951	1.83	1061
1952	1.79	967
1053	1.89	1159
1954	1.90	1205
1955	2.08	1720
1956	2.03	1661
1957	2.06	1731
1958	2.08	1782
1959	1.98	1685
1960	2.17	2124
1961	2.18	2240
1962	2.20	2366
1963	2.20	2503
1964	2.15	2454
1965	2.11	2505
1966	2.13	2713
1967	2.12	2919
1968	2.22	3558
1969	2.32	4006
1970	2.46	4725
1971	2.44	4892
1972	2.38	4959
1973	2.43	5587
1974	2.38	5674
1975	2.38	5891
1976	2.37	6342
1977	2.35	6621
1978	2.36	7445
1979	2.27	7324
1980	2.26	7904
1981	2.24	8293
1982	2.13	7614
1983	2.04	7174
1984	2.04	7876
1985	1.99	8036
1986	1.96	8711
1987	1.73	6830
1988	1.54	5390
1989	1.62	6845
1990	1.59	6698

Source: Authors' estimates using the method described in the text.

$\hat{k}$, but fit well at high incomes. The α parameter, which determines the rate at which the density of households declines as one moves to higher incomes, rises between the early 1950s and 1970, and then declines for the following two decades.

The income threshold y^* that only $100s\%$ of all taxpayers have incomes above satisfies the equation $s = (\hat{k}/y^*)^{\hat{a}}$, so $y^* = \hat{k}s^{-1/\hat{a}}$. Our estimate of the total income accruing to taxpayers with incomes above y^* is therefore

$$Y_{top} = N \int_{y^*}^{\infty} x\, f(x)\, dx = N \int_{y^*}^{\infty} \hat{a}\hat{k}^{\hat{a}} x^{-\hat{a}} dx, \tag{5}$$

where N denotes the total number of tax returns. When we need to interpolate particular types of income rather than AGI, we assume that the amount of income in each category (w_i) is related to AGI (y) according to a power function, $w_i = cy^{\delta}$. For example, total wages and salaries received by taxpayers with incomes above y_1, which we shall denote w_1, is given by:

$$w_1 = N \int_{y_1}^{\infty} cx^{\delta}\alpha k^{\alpha} x^{-\alpha-1} dx. \tag{6}$$

Evaluating this expression and a similar equation for w_2 using our estimates of k and α yields two equations in two unknowns, δ and c. Solving yields:

$$\delta = \log[w_1/w_2]/\log[y_1/y_2] + \alpha \tag{7}$$

and

$$c = w_1(\alpha - \delta)/N\alpha k^{\alpha} x^{\delta-\alpha}. \tag{8}$$

Because the actual amount of wage income above y_2 is a published aggregate, only the amount of wages between y^* and y_2 needs to be approximated.

We performed several validation exercises on our estimated Pareto distributions and found that they fit the actual income data reasonably well in the neighborhood of y^*. For years since 1979, we can compare our estimate of the share of income accruing to top-income taxpayers with the more accurate estimates from the public use version of the Treasury Individual Tax Model. Table A-2 presents the results of this validation exercise. The largest error in our estimate of the share of total income accruing to high-income taxpayers is 0.44 percent, in 1982, and the next largest error is 0.36 percent in 1986. That year's exceptional level of

TABLE A-2.
Actual and Estimated Income Share of Top AGI Recipients, 1979–1989.

	Percent		
Year	*Estimate using treasury tax model micro-data*	*Estimate using pareto distribution interpolation*	*Absolute difference*
1979	6.04	6.06	0.02
1980	6.12	6.11	0.01
1981	6.03	6.05	0.02
1982	6.27	6.71	0.44
1983	7.04	7.06	0.02
1984	7.35	7.38	0.03
1985	7.65	7.78	0.13
1986	8.83	9.23	0.36
1987	9.44	9.49	0.05
1988	12.02	12.05	0.03
1989	11.00	11.21	0.21

Source: Authors' calculations using annual data from U.S. Treasury *Statistics of Income: Individual Tax Returns* publications, as described in the text, as well as the U.S. Treasury Individual Tax Model for years 1979–1988.

capital gain realizations may contribute to our error, particularly if realized capital gains are not distributed according to a Pareto distribution.

References

Auerbach, Alan J. (1988). "Capital Gains Taxation in the United States: Realizations, Revenue, and Rhetoric." *Brookings Papers on Economic Activity* 2, 595–631.

Barlow, Robin, Harvey Brazer, and James Morgan (1966), *Economic Behavior of the Affluent,* Washington: Brookings Institution.

Bosworth, Barry, and Gary Burtless (1992). "Effects of Tax Reform on Labor Supply, Investment, and Saving." *Journal of Economic Perspectives* 6 (Winter), 3–25.

Bound, John, and George Johnson (1992). "Changes in the Structure of Wages During the 1980s: An Evaluation of Alternative Explanations." *American Economic Review* 82, 371–392.

Frank, Robert, and Phillip Cook (1992). "Winner Take All Markets." Mimeo, Cornell University Department of Economics.

Gordon, Roger, and Jeffrey Mackie-Mason (1990). "Effects of the Tax Reform Act of 1986 on Corporate Financial Policy and Organizational Form." In *Do Taxes Matter?* 91–131. J. Slemrod, ed. Cambridge: MIT Press.

Hausman, Jerry A., and James M. Poterba (1987). "Household Behavior and the Tax Reform Act of 1986." *Journal of Economic Perspectives* 1, 101–126.

Johnson, Norman L., and Samuel Kotz (1970). *Distributions in Statistics: Continuous Univariate Distributions—1.* New York: John Wiley.

Joskow, Paul L., Nancy L. Rose, and Andrea Shepard (1993). "Political and

Regulatory Constraints on CEO Compensation." *Brookings Papers on Microeconomic Activity* (forthcoming).

Karoly, Lynn A. (1993). "Trends in Income Inequality: The Impact of, and Implications for, Tax Policy." In *Tax Progressivity*, J. Slemrod, ed., forthcoming.

Kasten, Richard, Frank Sammartino, and Eric Toder (1993). "Trends in Federal Tax Progressivity, 1980–1993." In *Tax Progressivity*, J. Slemrod, ed., forthcoming.

Katz, Lawrence F., and Kevin M. Murphy (1992). "Changes in Relative Wages, 1963–1987: Supply and Demand Factors." *Quarterly Journal of Economics* 107, 35–78.

Krugman, Paul (1992). "The Right, the Rich, and the Facts: Deconstructing the Income Distribution Debate." *The American Prospect* (Fall 1992).

Levy, Frank, and Richard C. Michel (1991). *The Economic Future of American Families.* Washington, DC: The Urban Institute Press.

Lindsey, Lawrence (1987a). "Individual Taxpayer Response to Tax Cuts: 1982–1984, With Implications for the Revenue-Maximizing Tax Rate." *Journal of Public Economics* 33, 173–206.

———— (1987b). "Capital Gains Rates, Realizations, and Revenues." In *The Effects of Taxation on Capital Accumulation*, 69–97. M. Feldstein, ed. Chicago: University of Chicago Press.

———— (1988). "Did ERTA Raise the Share of Taxes Paid By Upper-Income Taxpayers? Will TRA86 be a Repeat?" In *Tax Policy and the Economy*, vol. 2, 131–160. Lawrence Summers, ed.

McCubbin, Janet, and Fritz Scheuren (1988). "Individual Income Tax Structures and Average Tax Rates: Tax Years 1916–1950." *Statistics of Income Bulletin*, vol. 8 (Winter 1988–89).

Mandel, Michael (1992). "Who'll Get the Lion's Share of the Wealth in the 1990s?" *Business Week* (June 8), 86–88.

Murphy, Kevin M., and Finis Welch (1992). "The Structure of Wages." *Quarterly Journal of Economics* 107, 285–326.

Nasar, Sylvia (1992). "However You Slice the Data, the Richest Did Get Richer." *New York Times* (May 11, 1992).

Poterba, James M. (1987). "Tax Evasion and Capital Gains Taxation." *American Economic Review* 77, 234–239.

Quandt, Richard (1966). "Old and New Methods of Estimation and the Pareto Distribution." *Metrika* 10, 55–82.

Roberts, Paul Craig (1992). "Income Data . . . Untitled." *Washington Times* (May 11).

Rosen, Sherwin (1981). "The Economics of Superstars." *American Economic Review* 71 (December), 845–858.

Ryoo, Jaewoo and Sherwin Rosen (1992), "The Market for Engineers," mimeo, University of Chicago Center for the Study of the Economy and the State.

Scholes, Myron, and Mark Wolfson (1992). *Taxes and Business Strategy: A Planning Approach* (Englewood Cliffs: Prentice Hall).

————, Peter Wilson, and Mark A. Wolfson (1992). "Firms' Responses to Anticipated Reductions in Tax Rates: The Tax Reform Act of 1986." NBER Working Paper 4171.

Slemrod, Joel (1991). "Taxation and Inequality: A Time-Exposure Perspective." In *Tax Policy and the Economy*, vol. 6, 105–127. J. Poterba, ed. Cambridge: MIT Press.

—— (1992), "Did the Tax Reform Act of 1986 Simplify Tax Matters?" *Journal of Economic Perspectives*, 6, 45–58.

—— (1993). "On the High Income Laffer Curve." In *Tax Progressivity*, J. Slemrod, ed., forthcoming.

U.S. Congress, Congressional Budget Office (1992a). "CBO's Method for Simulating the Distribution of Combined Federal Taxes Using Census, Tax-Return, and Expenditure Micro-Data." Mimeo, Washington, DC.

U.S. Congress, Congressional Budget Office (1992b). *Measuring the Distribution of Income Gains*. Washington, DC: CBO.

U.S. House of Representatives, Committee on Ways and Means (1991). *1991 Green Book: Background Material and Data on Programs Within the Jurisdiction of the Committee on Ways and Means*. Washington, DC: Government Printing Office.

U.S. Treasury Department, Internal Revenue Service (1991). "Individual Income Tax Returns: Preliminary Data, 1989." *Statistics of Income Bulletin* 10 (Spring 1991), 7–21.

——, —— (1992). "Individual Income Tax Returns: Preliminary Data, 1990." *Statistics of Income Bulletin* 11 (Spring 1992), 11–23.

——, —— (various years). *Statistics of Income: Individual Income Tax Returns*. Washington, DC.

Woodbury, Stephen, and Daniel Hammermesh (1992). "Taxes, Fringe Benefits, and Faculty." *Review of Economics and Statistics* 287–296.

The NBER now offers subscriptions to its
Working Papers in Public Economics

These working papers represent new research of over 60 economists associated with the NBER's program in public economics. By subscribing to these working papers, you have the opportunity to see this work long before it appears in books or scholarly journals. This kind of fast communication of research findings is very important for active researchers.

During the last twelve months, the NBER issued 42 papers in public economics. There will be about as many papers during the coming year. A list of the NBER researchers who wrote those papers indicates why the series is valuable to anyone working in this field.

The NBER offers a special price of $135 to faculty members, academic institutions, and government agencies in the U.S. The standard price for other subscribers is $270. A subscription to the full Working Paper Series, including about 300 titles annually, is available for $650 for academic subscribers and $1300 for others.

To receive these papers, please send a check or money order to: Working Papers, NBER, 1050 Massachusetts Avenue, Cambridge, MA 02138-5398. For information, call (617) 868-3900

NBER Research Associates in Public Economics

Richard Arnott	Jerry Hausman	Michael Rothschild
Alan Auerbach	Patric Hendershott	Myron Scholes
Robert Barro	J. Vernon Henderson	Andrei Shleifer
Douglas Bernheim	Glenn Hubbard	John Shoven
Michael Boskin	Robert Inman	Hans-Werner Sinn
David Bradford	Kenneth Judd	Jonathan Skinner
Jeremy Bulow	Mervyn King	Joel Slemrod
Charles Clotfelter	Laurence Kotlikoff	Joseph Stiglitz
Angus Deaton	Alan Krueger	Lawrence Summers
Douglas Holtz-Eakin	Charles McLure	John Whalley
Daniel Feenberg	Robert Moffitt	Ann Dryden Witte
Martin Feldstein	James Poterba	Mark Wolfson
Don Fullerton	Harvey Rosen	Richard Zeckhauser
Roger Gordon		